$29.95

Room to manoeuvre

Room to manoeuvre

political aspects of full employment

Paul Boreham
Geoff Dow
Martin Leet

MELBOURNE UNIVERSITY PRESS

MELBOURNE UNIVERSITY PRESS
PO Box 278, Carlton South, Victoria 3053, Australia
info@mup.unimelb.edu.au
www.mup.com.au

First published 1999

Text © Paul Boreham and Geoff Dow 1999
Design and typography © Melbourne University Press 1999

This book is copyright. Apart from any use permitted under the *Copyright Act* 1968 and subsequent amendments, no part may be reproduced, stored in a retrieval system or transmitted by any means whatsoever without the prior written permission of the publisher.

Designed by Sandra Nobes
Typeset by Designpoint in 11½ point Bembo
Printed in Australia by Brown Prior Anderson

National Library of Australia Cataloguing-in-Publication entry

Boreham, Paul, 1947– .
   Room to manoeuvre: political aspects of full employment.
   Bibliography.
   Includes index.
   ISBN 0 522 84862 1.
   1. Full employment policies. 2. Employment (Economic theory).
   I. Dow, Geoff, 1948– . II. Leet, Martin. III. Title.
339.5

Contents

Preface   xi

1 Political aspects of unemployment: the great debate   1

2 The politics and economics of unemployment in
   Australia: the comparative context   22

3 Economic limits   59

4 Policy options   111

5 Political possibilities   152

6 The political path to full employment in Australia   185

Bibliography   226
Index   244

Tables and figures

Tables

2.1	Manufacturing Performance in 12 OECD Countries, 1970	*32*
2.2	Women's Marginal Attachment to the Workforce, Australia, 1996	*42*
3.1	Unemployment, Employment and Growth, 1974–1997	*66*
3.2	Economic Growth and Unemployment in 16 OECD Countries, since 1974	*68*
3.3	Inflation and Unemployment in 16 OECD Countries, since 1974	*77*
3.4	Openness of the Economy and Unemployment in 16 OECD Countries, since 1974	*84*
3.5	Size of the Industrial Labour Force and Unemployment in 16 OECD Countries, since 1974	*92*
3.6	Size of Labour Force and Unemployment in 16 OECD Countries, 1974–1988	*94*
3.7	Income Inequality, 1980s	*105*
4.1	Taxation and Unemployment in 16 OECD Countries, since 1974	*121*
4.2	Government Expenditure and Unemployment in 16 OECD Countries, since 1974	*122*
4.3	Social Security Transfers and Unemployment in 16 OECD Countries, since 1974	*125*
4.4	Unemployment and Social Security Transfers in 16 OECD Countries	*126*
4.5	Duration of Unemployment Benefits and Replacement Ratios in 16 OECD Countries, 1980s	*127*

4.6	Active and Passive Labour Market Programmes and Unemployment in 16 OECD Countries, 1985–1992	*133*
4.7	Government Capital Expenditure and Unemployment in 16 OECD Countries, since 1974	*137*
4.8	Private Capital Expenditure and Unemployment in 16 OECD Countries, since 1974	*137*
4.9	Public and Private Capital Investment in 16 OECD Countries, 1970s–1980s	*139*
4.10	Public Sector Capital Investment as Percentage of GDP in 15 OECD Countries, 1974–1992	*141*
4.11	New Political Institutions for Expanded State Capacity: Policy Implications of Post-Keynesian Political Economy	*151*
5.1	Unemployment Model in 16 OECD Countries, 1974–1988	*177*
5.2	Trade Union Confederation Participation in Economic Policy (LABEC), 1970–1992	*182*
5.3	Trade Union Confederation Participation in Wage Bargaining (WAGE), 1970–1992	*183*

Figures

2.1	Social Expenditure as Percentage of GDP, 1970	*23*
2.2	Pensions as Percentage of GDP, 1970	*24*
2.3	Total Taxes as Percentage of GDP, 1968–1973	*26*
2.4	Public Investment as Percentage of GDP, 1968	*27*
2.5	Unemployment as Percentage of Total Labour Force in OECD and 7 Countries, 1970–1997	*31*
2.6	Industry Protection and Employment	*34*
2.7	Gross Fixed Capital Formation as Percentage of GDP, 1973–1997	*35*
2.8	Index of Employment by Industry, 1972–1994	*36*
2.9	Manufacturing Employment as Percentage of Total Employment, 1970–1996	*37*

2.10	Manufacturing as Percentage of GDP, 1970–1996	37
2.11	Index of Employment by Occupation, 1972–1994	38
2.12	Employment in Industry Sectors for Men and Women, 1996	38
2.13	Part-time Employment as Percentage of Total Employment, 1972–1996	39
2.14	Male and Female Participation Rates, 1966–1997	41
2.15	Employment for Men and Women, 1997	41
2.16	Percentage Unemployment in the 1990s	47
2.17	Percentage Unemployment in OECD Countries, 1991–1996	48
2.18	Percentage Inflation in OECD Countries, 1991–1996	50
2.19	Wages and On-costs, 1992	51
2.20	Social Welfare Expenditure as Percentage of GDP in OECD Countries, 1985	52
2.21	Social Security Transfers as Percentage of GDP in OECD Countries, 1994	52
2.22	Government Receipts as Percentage of GDP, 1991–1996	54
2.23	Gross Public Debt as Percentage of GDP in OECD Countries, 1991–1996	54
2.24	Government Outlays as Percentage of GDP in OECD Countries, 1991–1996	55
2.25	Labour Market Programmes as Percentage of GDP in OECD Countries, 1995–1996	56
2.26	Research and Development Expenditure as Percentage of GDP in OECD Countries, 1988	56
2.27	Value Added in Manufacturing as Percentage of GDP in OECD Countries, 1960–1994	57
2.28	Manufacturing Employment as Percentage of Labour Force in OECD Countries, 1974–1994	57

3.1	Unemployment and Inflation in OECD Countries, 1974–1990	72
3.2	Postulated Increasing Institutional Intractability of Recessions	109
4.1	Private Consumption Expenditure as Percentage of GDP in OECD and 10 Countries, 1960–1995	123
4.2	Relation between Investment and Unemployment: Private and Public Sectors in 15 OECD Countries, 1970s and 1980s	138
4.3	Gross Public Debt in 9 OECD Countries, 1980–1993	143
5.1	From Markets to Politics: Changing Modes of Regulation	160–1
5.2	Political Divergence and Modes of Regulation	166
6.1	Alternative Micro-level (Enterprise) Strategies	217

Preface

Writing in 1986, Göran Therborn commenced his comparative study of the OECD countries with the observation that 'unemployment has become the plague of advanced capitalism in the 1980s'. At the end of the 1990s, after more than a decade of economic analysis and policy development, the veracity of Therborn's assertion is very little changed. What has changed is the degree of complacency with which governments of all persuasions, the media and many in the general public view unemployment. Major political and economic institutions in Australia now accept the notion of a 'natural rate of unemployment', thus diminishing the obligation of policy-makers to aim for full employment. The most important outcome of this process has been the tolerance of rates of unemployment in the 1980s and 1990s four times higher than those that prevailed in the postwar decades.

The conventional focus on exclusively national data leads to an almost metaphysical claim that governments and policy-makers have little room to manoeuvre in developing programmes for the unemployed. The comparative approach adopted in this book questions that claim. It provides answers to the questions: How have some countries been able to maintain low rates of unemployment while others with similar economic and social structures have performed badly? Which policies and strategies for full employment have worked and which have failed? Why have some governments surrendered to the view that they have lost sovereignty and the national ability to develop unorthodox policies while others have not? Is is reasonable or possible for governments to assert political capacities in the face of increasing global pressure to conform to an international policy orthodoxy? Who gains from the present policy impasse?

Our concern with unemployment stems from two bases: first, from a firm moral conviction that there is unconscionable damage done to individuals to communities and to nations by the political failure to aim for a full employment economy; second, from decades of social science analysis of comparative data from the OECD countries demonstrating the economic and political feasibility of policies to reduce unemployment.

Most of the analysis presented in this book is based on a major comparative time-series database covering sixteen countries for the period 1969–94. The variables include all major economic aggregates, detailed employment and unemployment data, and constructed variables reflecting the major institutional configurations for the formulation of economic and employment policy for each country for each year. The sources of this data are too extensive to be detailed here, but they are outlined in many of the publications listed in the bibliography.

The data set was constructed by the Labour & Industry Research Unit at the University of Queensland with the financial support of several Australian Research Council grants. The authors also owe a debt of gratitude to Hugh Compston, Rachel Parker, Gillian Whitehouse and Richard Hall without whose help the database would not have come into existence and whose ideas generated much of the argument in this volume. Many others also contributed to the development of our analysis, not least those who responded to our arguments in numerous conference presentations in the United Kingdom, Sweden, Austria, Canada and Australia. We also received generous institutional assistance from Arbetslivsinstitutet in Stockholm. We know that the force of our argument has been sharpened by these encounters. We trust that those who have helped along the way are gratified by the outcome of the reflections and revisions presented in this volume.

Chapter 1
Political aspects of unemployment: the great debate

1   The state alone . . . can prevent there being at one and the same time in a community unsatisfied needs, and idle men and machinery by whose employment those needs could be met.

William Beveridge, *Full Employment in a Free Society*, 1944

Most of the keys to full employment are problems of courage, either political or intellectual courage.

Michel Rocard, cited in *A Program for Full Employment in the 1990s*, 1989

2   Full employment is a fundamental aim of the Commonwealth Government.

Parliament of the Commonwealth of Australia, *Full Employment in Australia*, 1945

The Government is determined to reduce unemployment.

Commonwealth of Australia, *Working Nation: Policies and Programs*, 1994

As Keynes noted in the 1930s, a worm is eating at the heart of contemporary civilization.

The two sets of citations above, in each case containing pronouncements made a half century apart, exemplify what have become defining features of, and probably the most intractable problems of, wealthy capitalist societies. The first is the awareness among thoughtful architects of public policy and thoughtful politicians devoted to implementing ameliorative policies that the political process has quite substantial responsibilities that are dependent on 'political and intellectual courage'. The second illustrates the shift in governments' sense of their responsibilities during the postwar period—from the assertion of full employment as a 'fundamental aim' to the much more open-ended promise to reduce unemployment. These two themes constitute our concern in this book: we examine the capacity of politics to manage national economies in times of significant structural transformation, and the all-too-common retreat from past commitments.

The first two citations were penned almost fifty years apart by authors grappling seriously with the devastation caused by high levels of unemployment. Both featured in official reports which were aimed directly at the policy process of government. Both argued that unemployment was neither inevitable nor morally acceptable. Both voiced an awareness that problems which could be solved were not. The latter report, by the Kriesky Commission, castigated 1980s governments for lacking the political determination to make employment a central policy priority. The fact that some countries have maintained low unemployment in the quarter-century since 1974 indicates that there is a great deal that can be done to significantly reduce unemployment. Unemployment is far from natural and clearly not beyond our power to control. Our purpose is to add to the weight of evidence demonstrating to reluctant or recalcitrant governments that the well-being of society depends on their ability to exploit the always-present capacity to pursue political solutions to the crisis of unemployment, a polity's room to manoeuvre. At stake is the very claim of modern society to be civilized.

Politics can be defined as the efforts of a community to control its destiny by arranging collectively for the solution to problems which are unamenable to individual solution. At the heart of political processes are the difficulties of implementing decisions made to advance the public good, and resistance to them. We intend in this study to cast some light on both these matters. The first is addressed in terms of the public institutions required to achieve the goal of balanced economic development in the rich societies; the second, possibly more important, in our criticism of the common assertion that technological, economic, financial, ideological and practical impediments to political will have made some significant public policy goals of the past anachronistic. Though we do not confront directly the claims made in discussions of globalization, we do accept a principled commitment to the idea that nations, through their polities, ought to engage whatever struggles are necessary to preserve social and political autonomy. As John Kenneth Galbraith has said: 'there can be no case for the narrow commitment to the nation-state. But neither can there be one to a mindless course which sacrifices the social gains of the century just past and those for which there is still need' (1997: 8).

The Labor government in Australia (1983–96) embodied both the promises and failures that we wish to discuss. It renewed public discussion of the policy aspects of unemployment, through its Green Paper process, published as *Restoring Full Employment* in 1993, and subsequently in its White Paper, *Working Nation*, in 1994. Since then, there has been considerable disquiet with the policy process, concerning unemployment in particular, economic management generally and possibly the capacities of politics as a whole. Even to the extent that governments are tempted, by public unease concerning unemployment and insecurity, to rekindle commitments to full employment or balanced societal development, actual efforts seem insincere—readily diluted into programmes that can be accommodated within the prevailing unchallenging and modestly visioned policy consensus. Since the change of government in 1996 there has been very little official enthusiasm for any direct approach to the ongoing problem of unemployment and this has become a phenomenon that, to our shame, characterizes contemporary politics. What are the dimensions of the problems we now face? What has gone wrong? Must we succumb to the pressures of those who maintain that the high-minded goals of 1945 are now unreasonable? How might we reconstitute, against the temper of global economic imperatives, the right of our polity to impose its own criteria on our patterns of development and problem resolution? Why have we, rather gracelessly and in defiance of popular sentiment, accepted defeat? Is the impotence of politics inevitable?

A series of contributions expressing various degrees of alarm over how the government has handled unemployment, and the pressures to which the policy process is subjected, appeared in the 1990s. Increasingly, commentators have been suggesting that policy mistakes have been responsible for continuing high unemployment. Others conclude that both government and policy advisers have so frequently been surprised by the failure of their own policy expectations that both public faith and internal confidence have been lost. It is sometimes suspected that bureaucratic policy-makers have become cynical, advising politicians to pursue policies of doubtful credibility just to maintain their own independent agendas. A pragmatic conventional wisdom has endorsed the pronouncements of many economists that full employment is unachievable without compromising more important policy goals such as price stability or 'external balance'; others have argued that full employment is still possible if only 'economic reforms' are pursued more assiduously, despite the likely further disruption to community values and expectations.

Even before the loss of office by Labor governments across Australia, a common thread in the disquiet about economic reform was that political aspects of unemployment warranted at least as much scrutiny as the economic forces themselves (see, for example, Emy 1993; Walter 1996). Put more forcefully, something has happened to politics that demands investigation— in short, government seems to be less willing than it once was to challenge the resistances to full employment. The policy process or the state or the institutions of government or the broader trends in relations between the public and private sectors are being reconstructed in so far as they contribute, negatively or otherwise, to economic outcomes including, most crucially, unemployment.

Furthermore, occupying an increasingly visible place in the shadow of political responsibility for policy failure is the policy advice—from economists—that governments and potential governments have been accepting. Much of the present policy debacle is the result of attempts to subject people's behaviour to theoretical solutions whose elegance was established but whose relevance to society was severely questionable. Brian Toohey, for example, in *Tumbling dice: the story of modern economic policy*, followed earlier critiques of the economic rationalism of Canberra's economists by pointing to the continuing influence of the 'official family' of policy advisers, now a policy player in its own right with a political agenda and a distinct set of intellectually fashionable but politically constraining approaches to reform (Toohey 1994: 145–6, 242–3). As a result, the scope for, the preoccupations of and eventually the nature of politics itself has been transformed. It can be argued, therefore, that too little policy attention has been directed towards the creation of new industries, that too much emphasis has been placed upon labour-shedding cost reductions and that some indefensible economic policies have been pushed too far. Prominent bureaucratic economists have even admitted urging politicians to implement policies based on conceptual arguments that the advisers knew to be false, as a way of disrupting legitimate political claims (1994: 161–2).

Laura Tingle's discussion of the politics of economic policy debates in the 1990s is a coherent reconstruction of the conventional government view of its policy intentions. It shares much with Paul Kelly's more notorious *The end of certainty: the story of the 1980s* (1992), but it also amounts to speculation that the recession has been largely 'policy-induced', or rather that, by pursuing the advice offered by economists, politicians made the Australian economy more vulnerable to recession than it needed to be. This is a syndrome that infects policy-making across regimes and across epochs in Australia. In *Chasing the future: recession, recovery and the new politics in Australia*, Tingle suggests that 'reform fatigue' has created a new policy milieu where economists' credibility is reduced; the influence of policy elites has also suffered as Treasury's confidence and morale has slumped because its policy advice has become 'too pure' (1994: 14, 16, 329, 339).

'The smug sense of control over economic change that had existed in Australia since the post-war rise of Keynesian thought disappeared' (1994: 13). Tingle's account highlights some of the unexpected consequences of policy advice from the dominant institutions, but it differs from ours in that she accepts the basic legitimacy of the economic reforms since 1983.

We do not accept that the 1890s settlement (Kelly 1992) has been reversed only in the 1990s; we conclude that Australia has steadily departed from its image of itself (as a country of social experiments and egalitarianism) ever since the end of World War I. The post-1945 model of economic and social development was never really consolidated in Australia in that appropriate institutions for Keynesian economic management were never developed here and the welfare state has always been residual, so the retreats or reforms of recent years should be seen more as continuities than as ruptures with the past. In the chapters that follow, we adopt a different approach to the common belief that something profound has happened in politics as a result of the past decade's concern with economic reforms and the recession. Neither do we sympathize with the suggestions that Australia was faced, sometime after 1974, with a need to become more flexible, less cosseted, more competitive, less protected, more internationalized, less autonomous in its economic and social profile. Such pressures have been accepted by a political system which could have done more than it has to resist them. The efforts to harmonize Australia with the global environment remain a domestic political choice which has forever harmed our standards of living. They were not and still are not incorrigible facts of life. As Keynes argued in the 1930s and 1940s, the existence of a global sphere of economic activity does not imply that all nations ought to surrender the political entitlements they each have to develop innovative and nationally specific solutions to internationally transmitted problems.

Consequently, we argue against the journalistic convention that recessions ought to be reckoned by reference to rates of growth (and in quarters of a year); like the OECD economies as a whole, Australia has been in recession for twenty-five years and despite high economic growth by international standards (with unemployment still above 8 per cent) has not yet entered a post-recession phase. Furthermore, in view of 'competition policy reforms' that will empty Australia's public sectors of their public capacities, there is commensurately little reason to accept that a new, more pragmatic, 'post-recession politics' has arrived, still less, given the dramatic increases in inequality, a robust or sophisticated social democracy. Deficit reduction strategies will continue to define and to plague the country's politics for a little longer yet.

In their critique of the policy orthodoxy of the moment, *Work for all: full employment in the nineties*, John Langmore and John Quiggin note that the political will to maintain full employment that characterized the 1945–70 period has been lost, replaced by less defensible goals. Consequently, both misjudged policies and economic theories 'have led to the current disaster', including the loss of civic amenity. Langmore and Quiggin conclude that much of the fault lies with those incumbents of political office who developed 'a narrow view of what can be achieved through politics' (1994: 235). They assert that the political process ought to be expected to take on new responsibilities, shedding much of the drive for efficiency and the inappropriate use of private criteria in the public sector. Their agenda for the regeneration of the Australian economy, especially their call for increased public outlays on capital investment and infrastructure, financed through higher direct taxes, is one we share. Nonetheless, there remain important areas for public debate, for example whether the policy focus should be on employment growth or unemployment reduction, whether conceptions of work ought to change, how to generate new industrial activity, and the real origins and nature of the 'persistent fundamentalism' of the government's advisers. At least one contributor to the current debates, Heinz Arndt in *Full employment in historical perspective* (1994), has claimed that the current recession is not a case of secular stagnation and that public sector induced expansion through public infrastructure would not be appropriate.

From a different perspective, Helen Hughes, in *Achieving full employment* (1994), also criticizes the conventional wisdom that tolerates high unemployment, arguing that more diligent attention to microeconomic, public savings and labour market reforms can deliver genuine full employment. By insisting that full employment is still possible but that the current line of policy needs to be extended, Hughes' conclusions are the direct opposite of those reached by, for example, Tingle.

Our aim is to contribute yet another line of reasoning to the great debate on contemporary unemployment. Our approach derives both from a conceptual appreciation of the difficulties of macroeconomic management in the advanced economies as they become more complex and from detailed empirical studies of the OECD countries during the period of recession. As the following chapters indicate, we are not surprised that policy errors have played such a large part in bringing Australia to its current widespread disillusionment; after all, this is what happened in the 1930s too. The lesson to be learned is that unemployment persists because there is insufficient political will to do what can be done to eliminate it. Our book is oriented to a regenerated knowledge of how politics and markets, the state and the economy, the public and the private sectors, the regulated and the unregulated spheres interact to produce our material standards of living.

For at least the last decade, few would have been able to avoid the sometimes frenetic attempts within the Australian economic policy milieu to rewrite the terms of the 'postwar development model'. The efforts made within the political process, perhaps by a finite number of politicians, their advisers and economic policy bureaucrats, have been notable for their strident willingness to confront and dismantle what they see as many of the shibboleths of the past. The inherited aspects of labour's traditions that have been sacrificed include, most importantly, the capacity in the political system to forge and maintain a nationally distinct route to national economic and social development. A former Treasurer, Ralph Willis, expressed this rationale for the then government's policy profile in a speech to the International Banks and Securities Association in Sydney in August 1995:

> Thirteen years ago, the Australian economy reflected the end product of the postwar economic development model, in which Australia had sought to become an industrialized country through high protection, extensive regulation of industries, overwhelming reliance on commodities for exports and a highly regulated labour market . . . Since then, the Labor government has replaced the clapped-out Liberal/National Party postwar economic development model with one which is more relevant to Australia's economic future.

The process of political transformation in Australia since 1983 has even been regarded as a modernization of the Australian Labor Party (Beilharz 1994) which its architects accepted as vital and necessary and overdue. We argue that the grand experiment in neo-liberalism, the concerted campaign by government to reconstitute 'a market mode of economic regulation', has been mistaken; it has amounted to a sustained endeavour, neither originating in nor limited to Australia, to absolve the political process of responsibility for economic outcomes. The postwar experience should be seen not as a now anachronistic and aberrant experiment but as a period in which populations attempted to do what they have always attempted to do—to gain some control over their political and economic destinies through deliberated social and political processes. Admittedly the pressures on governments everywhere to conform to new competitive standards, especially those determined by the context of globalization of national economies, have been significant. We nonetheless want to claim that acquiescence of national political possibilities to international demands is neither necessary nor inevitable. It is the responsibility of politicians, and the political process they are supposed to nurture, to overcome obstacles to behaving politically. Instead they have grasped every opportunity to depoliticize economic decision-making by importing criteria developed in the market sphere, where different (non-democratic) imperatives often rightly apply, into the sphere of public policy, where they don't.

The economic and social outcomes of this experiment—continuing unemployment, with its implied gap between potential and actual living standards, and steadily increasing insecurity, as lower quality and less reliable employment becomes more common—have been entirely predictable. They were anticipated by critical or maverick traditions of economic analysis such as post-Keynesian theory, and they have been criticized from both conservative and social democratic perspectives. The nature of the problems we have faced—not just since the 1980s but continuously since about 1974—is such that we are compelled to realize that the economic system in which we operate does not behave or respond in the way that conventional policy-makers have imagined. The unorthodox conceptions of contemporary capitalist economies do not accept that economies are or should be wholly market phenomena; they do not accept that interventionist procedures are impotent in dealing with the sectoral and structural and secular changes that produce unemployment. They have argued, and we produce evidence to support the conceptual argument, that the long-term trend in market economies is for them to become more managed, not more deregulated. Therefore it is not necessary, though it is common, for governments to orient their policies towards market conformity. If the thrust of policy is to defy clearly observable and wholly understandable trends, the consequences will continue to be perverse; and that is what has been happening.

Hence it seems to us that politics has lost its way. Each government seems to bequeath to its successor a more diminished conception of what is possible. This is not entirely a recent phenomenon. Politicians and political parties have never allowed themselves to develop the capacities they really need to control unemployment. More recently, they have discarded instruments they had previously created to deal effectively with economic conditions, and settled for others known to be ineffective. Political operators devote considerable effort to, and risk the loss of public support in, dismantling the accomplishments of the past. The tenor of contemporary politics and public administration is that politics ought not even try to accomplish the tasks it was formerly able to embrace. As a result economic conditions have steadily worsened for a quarter of a century. Public expectations have been thwarted, if not abused, in a number of ways. Insecurity and inequality have increased and the political process has disclaimed responsibility: as inequalities have widened, the political response has been to assert that they are necessary; as the quality of employment has deteriorated, the official view has insisted that public guarantees of civility belong to an era or to a worldview that has been lost forever; as security has been lost governments have insisted that we need to be more flexible.

In an important sense, then, unemployment is not a function of economic mismanagement, but of diligent application of inappropriate policies in an environment where the institutional capacity to create and to maintain full employment has never fully existed. This is more so in countries like Australia, with liberal institutional biases, than in others, like Japan or Sweden, where anti-liberal forces (statist or social democratic) were developed in the postwar period, or earlier, to guide capitalist development in more politically determined directions. Therefore, full employment is as much a political as an economic phenomenon. We require not better economic management but different economic management with more appropriate techniques than exist at the moment; these need to be created by and through the political process. The discrepancy in Australia between calculations of per capita wealth and per capita income give some indication of the extent to which our potential is unrealized or squandered.

In Australia, four times as many people are out of work now as in the 1960s. Though there has been continual employment growth throughout the recession (in fact, since 1788), in recent years it has been low-quality employment. The new jobs that have appeared have been predominantly part-time or casual (an increase of 73.3 per cent between 1983 and 1994) favouring mainly female employees in service sector jobs (41.6 per cent of all new jobs between 1983 and 1993). A high proportion of these jobs have poor working conditions directly attributable to the climate of labour market deregulation that has been fostered as part of an ideological drive to assert market discipline. An increasing proportion of the workforce is in precarious jobs lacking employment or income security or decent future prospects and isolated from even the most basic employment rights.

Unemployment is a major indicator of the erosion of national capacities. It afflicts not only those directly affected but also the employed, whose careers and prospects are limited in an economy operating below full capacity. Given the erosion of Australia's relative affluence since the 1970s, it seems that real incomes, even of those in full-time employment, are lower due to mass unemployment than they might otherwise be. Ultimately unemployment affects the economic and social fabric of society as a whole, as market regulation tends to reinforce and reproduce social inequalities. Unemployment not only means a loss of economic security but an increase in poverty and social dislocation as the consolations of civil society are severed—evidenced, for example, in crime or violence or the anti-social responses to them. In most democratic societies advances such as the granting of social rights of citizenship and concern for equity have been, for the past century, at the heart of politics. But politics is now itself subject to utilitarian forces which produce a radical disjuncture between society's private and public personae. Public forms of knowledge, values and morality have been subsumed by individualized needs, privatized calculation and rational technique. So, as James Walter's *Tunnel vision: the failure of political imagination* has argued, 'once we abandon politics for economics, we abandon the capacity to imagine new solutions' (1996: 52).

During the 1980s these forces have encouraged what ought be termed an unreasonable depoliticization of the problem of unemployment. Despite the experience and lessons of the 1930s, governments have demonstrated an increasing reluctance to intervene directly to achieve full employment. Throughout the

1980s a high degree of consensus emerged among professional economists in the finance sector, in the media, in academia, in the public sector and in the political realm that the task of government was to improve the functioning of markets. This was apparently expected to bring about the most efficient allocation of resources in accord with the preferences of individual market actors, which was expected, in turn, to lead to zero, low or optimum levels of unemployment. This argument was propounded with the full ideological force of those who placed a high value on individualism, freedom and the expression of self-interest and who thereby undervalued notions of social responsibility, community and public interest. Margaret Thatcher encapsulated such views in her now infamous assertion that 'there is no such thing as society'. The outcomes of this policy milieu have been, to a very great extent, self-fulfilling. That is, as regulatory institutions have been eliminated or have had their realm of activity greatly circumscribed (for example, in industrial relations and wage fixation in Australia) and as other regulatory practices have been removed or diminished (for example, in the labour market and international financial transactions), government action has been increasingly and overwhelmingly subject to the evaluation of the market.

The long recession, or 'leaden age' (Pollin 1998: 433), in Australia and elsewhere has its origins in government reactions to the structural crises that began to beset most of the major industrial economies in the 1970s. Restrictive macroeconomic policies and repressive industrial relations approaches both allegedly designed to 'fight inflation first' had the imprimatur of 'the market' as interpreted by financial institutions and currency traders, even though the consequences were manufacturing decline, profitability crises, reduced per capita growth and dramatically increased unemployment. The converse of this distinctive policy configuration has now become part of the contemporary policy wisdom which for more than two decades has asserted that expansionary economic policies lead only to higher budget deficits and inflation, not to lower unemployment. Yet, in restricting growth (and activity) as the only prophylactic against inflation, productive capital and organizational resources are depleted and human capacity is diminished. A predictable implication of this approach is that in some major areas of macroeconomic policy the government's capacity to act has been significantly lessened.

There is an intrinsic conflict between, on the one hand, the domestic industrial sector which generates economic capacity and employment and therefore requires a certain level of macroeconomic and institutional stability and, on the other, financial markets which emphasize price stability and freedom of speculative capital movements without regard to macroeconomic or national outcomes. The power exercised by the international private financial sector, operating in and preferring largely deregulated national environments, substantially erodes national autonomy to develop policies, especially unorthodox or experimental policies, to fight unemployment. Even non-repressive mechanisms for the control of inflation, such as incomes policies, are opposed by the financial sector. Governments which endeavour to pursue reflationary policies to counter unemployment, for example by increasing domestic capital investment expenditure, may be faced with, and intimidated by, a potentially damaging deficit on the capital account in the short term because of the exchange rate effects of substantially speculative financial outflows. The inappropriate policy response to these circumstances is to retreat from expansionary measures and to accept global market perceptions and forces as immutable constraints on domestic action. Globally conceived rules for the conduct of national economic policy—such as free trade and the free flow of capital, which are central to the prescriptions of GATT, the WTO, the IMF and the OECD—have rarely respected national commitments to full employment or even to national development. Globalization of markets has created a discursive environment which has unnecessarily constrained national policy goals in Australia in contrast with the more active policy interventions practised elsewhere. The attempts in the late 1990s to effect the multilateral agreement on investment (MAI) is the most absurd and potentially most damaging of these globally conceived constraints on domestic policy autonomy.

Until quite recently, the domestic economy was an explicit object of policy designed to support nationally coherent development strategies and social stability. However, the multitude of deregulatory initiatives since the 1980s has led to control of economic policy shifting from principles developed by governments to those favoured by financial markets. The credibility accorded by federal governments to market reactions, whose immediacy is often only marginally connected to economic reality, has critically undermined their political capacity to set a socially responsible economic policy agenda.

The irony of this situation is that what is celebrated as the 'free market' by Australian policy-makers is no more than a particular form of economic organization. Markets are not formed naturally; they are socially constructed and depend upon a range of supporting institutions and regulations for their effective operation. The form of these structures reflects the political power of particular segments of society. The institutions (such as the federal Treasury and the Reserve Bank) which dominate policy advice and implementation in Australia have always been committed to keeping government small, impotent and market-oriented; they are not primarily concerned with national prosperity. They differ in structure, function and degree of enthusiasm for market prerogatives from the institutions that have managed economic development and economic success in the low-unemployment countries. To imagine that a 'return' to free markets is the best policy is really no more than to sanction a shift in the sectors of the economy which are most favoured by (deregulatory) policy. The sectors which benefit from the current arrangements in Australia are those which profit from fluidity of activity. Previous modes of development required different regulatory conditions and extreme flexibility was a characteristic or precondition of neither early national development nor later manufacturing maturity. The altered requirements tend to be the characteristics of the financial services sector, in particular those segments which are globally focused.

On the other hand, those sectors which require some stability in their operating environment in order to undertake and profit from longer-term productive investment tend to be significantly disadvantaged by volatile market conditions. Manufacturing industry is the key sector affected by these arrangements. Having lost the battle for a regulated national economic environment, industry, if it is to be profitable, must assume the characteristics of the successful sectors. This produces manufacturing's contemporary focus on short-term profits and elimination of long-term commitments—results which manifest themselves in management initiatives such as contracting out support services, encouragement to decentralize industrial relations and labour market interventions which limit tenure and increase the proportion of work which can be undertaken by casual employees, subcontractors or outworkers. Employees are the clear losers in this process. They suffer not only from a deterioration in their security and conditions of employment but also from repressive legislation which weakens the ability of trade unions and industrial institutions to support the working arrangements that minimize risk, insecurity, competition, uncertainty and the possibilities of political displacement of market forces.

There is no doubt that one way for a nation's industrial structure to adapt to changing technological or global conditions is for losers to be usurped by winners in a process of ceaseless (global) competition—the so-called 'race to the bottom'—but this is obviously an undemocratic and undesirable way to decide which industries a country should retain and which should be surrendered. Ultimately, what is at stake in these struggles over whether to control or unleash the market is the issue of who will exercise power in the economy and society and who will be favoured in the changes to our governing rules and regulations. The lines are drawn between those who can use financial resources to benefit individually from their market capacity and those who seek through democratic political processes to provide resources more equitably to the entire society through public social and economic policies. The long-standing claim of the proponents of intervention has been that the former situation is essentially undemocratic; the long-standing retort from the advocates of the market mode of regulation is that political democracy is sufficient compensation for the lack of democratic access to economic resources and the exclusion of economic decisions from the forums of notionally democratic politics.

Despite the resistance to economic democracy, a range of regulatory institutions has been developed in capitalist economies to guide economic development and to support and regulate the market. These have significantly altered and even defined the character of the various capitalist nations. National development, international competitiveness, social equity and full employment are all outcomes of these structures and the political processes and social conflicts which sustain them. Quite different institutional arrangements have proved to be compatible with economic and social development. However, it is clear that the pursuit of private profit in an unfettered 'free market' places a great deal of pressure on collective responsibility for the well-being of the entire community. Our message, elaborated in the chapters that follow, is that governments have much more room to manoeuvre to achieve socially desirable employment goals than the ideologues of the free market and the practitioners of globalization would have us believe. Our objective is to expose the misunderstandings perpetrated by those powerful voices which venerate the 'judgement of the market' and oppose the rule of democratic politics. Our approach is comparative, drawing on the experiences of the other major industrial democracies of the OECD to show that there are still, at the turn of the millennium, socially responsible pathways to economic prosperity with low unemployment.

The method we adopt demonstrates the relationship between policy measures, and the political institutions through which they are implemented, and various economic outcomes, primarily unemployment, in the OECD countries. Our aim is not to suggest that Australia ought to adopt any particular foreign model but to argue that successful policies can be distilled from comparative examination of broadly similar cases (the advanced market economies) in similar situations (the economic downturn since 1974). Successful policies, wherever or whenever put into practice, need to be considered as alternatives to what has become a narrow and sterile and derivative policy environment in Australia. We use a pooled time-series model to investigate unemployment policy performance in the major OECD countries since 1974 and to provide policy and political options for beyond the 1990s. Such a model allows us to consider not only why some nations have more successfully maintained low unemployment and the quality of jobs but also why historical changes to policies and institutions within nations have been associated with particular employment outcomes. The model shows the interaction of country effects and time effects in a way that enhances our understanding of the contemporary crisis of unemployment. This analytical process illuminates much that is omitted from contemporary economic debates which have focused on changes over time within countries and neglected the longer-term structural or institutional phenomena which characterize different countries. It is always important to ensure that empirical studies of particular policy problems are informed by comprehensive analysis of how advanced economies actually operate, and to use empirical research to inform the equally important task of contributing to broad cross-national understandings of capitalist economies. Ultimately, the importance of our model is that it illustrates the manner in which policies interact with social structure and political institutions to influence economic outcomes. For example, policies encouraging just-in-time manufacturing processes will be relatively ineffective in countries which lack Japan's high degree of vertical integration; that is, particular manufacturing processes may be appropriate to particular manufacturing industry structures but not to others. Policies supporting long-term capital investment in industry may be easier to organize in countries with a high degree of horizontal integration of manufacturing and finance sectors, as in Germany. Active labour market policies and industry policies encouraging a transfer of resources from unsuccessful to successful industries are unlikely to realize their aims without substantial non-discriminatory welfare entitlements such as those in Sweden.

The range of variables that can be included in many studies of unemployment is restricted by the limitations of reliable data. Models in political economy based on changes over time in each country allow for only about thirty-five years for which reasonably accurate data exist. Studies in political science have focused on fewer than twenty of the twenty-nine OECD countries for which reliable comparative data are available. In this study we have assembled data on a large number of OECD countries for nineteen years since the 1970s. Many studies in the field of comparative political economy since the early 1980s have drawn attention to the realization that 'politics matters', that is, that institutions can successfully override market forces and that market outcomes need not be respected. Our study does not replicate these but adds to the critical evidence concerning policy stances that have improved and those that have worsened economic outcomes since 1974.

Most of our pooled data apply to the 1974–92 period. Normally, we have included data for sixteen countries, resulting in 304 readings. Some countries have been omitted because of their atypical prior experience of authoritarian government and resemblance to developing rather than developed economies, though this is changing rapidly. Others were omitted because of size, still others because they have become OECD countries only recently or were in the socialist bloc until the 1990s. The countries normally included are the United States, Canada, Japan, the United Kingdom, Germany, France, Italy, the Netherlands, Belgium, Austria, Switzerland, Australia, Sweden, Norway, Denmark and Finland. These countries account for 752 million people, or almost 80 per cent of the OECD total population.

In the period studied, the recession and the policy positions we identify as damaging have been invoked and consolidated. Our objective is to demonstrate that the political responses to the recession after 1974 actually produced many of the outcomes that we have been living with since, most notably structural unemployment. They also led directly to the erosion of some crucial state capacities that would still, if regenerated, be capable of allowing nationally specific paths out of recession. Because 'policy mistakes' are not capricious, but are systematic biases introduced to economic policy through the forms of economic policy-making a country allows itself to develop, documentation and analysis of the policy distinctiveness that constitutes policy error ought to provide a basis for a political task—the reconstruction of a policy regime more in keeping with the requirements of the actual economy. Even though the structure of state–economy relations, and the resulting economic outcomes, has changed in most OECD countries during the 1990s, it is the policy routes embarked upon after 1974 that must be examined to define the political project we advocate for the rest of the 1990s and beyond. The empirical relationships observed during the 1970s and 1980s do not hold for the late 1990s, but the legacy of economic damage and the lessons for policy do. We believe we can therefore offer more robust support for the critique of policy failure during recession than has been the case in many previous studies.

The next chapter provides the context for the long recession. It indicates the broad patterns of development which have characterized the Australian economy over the past twenty-five years and which distinguish it from similar democratic capitalist polities. The key feature to which we draw attention is the derogation of nation-building responsibilities by successive Australian postwar governments. Chapter 3 commences our analysis of the comparative data focusing on what might be considered the economic dimensions of the unemployment crisis. Our concern is to demonstrate that the policy process needs to be informed by a clear understanding of the extent to which different aspects of recession necessarily or independently result in unemployment. Our analysis focuses on the specific links between unemployment and economic growth, inflation, international trade, the level of manufacturing industry and labour costs. Chapter 4 turns from the economics to the politics of unemployment. We consider that full employment has always been a matter of political contention concerning the direction of society; thus we examine the policy options available to governments prepared to contemplate alternative political directions. This examination of policy possibilities and policy mistakes focuses on the implications for unemployment of taxation and government expenditure, the welfare state, labour market policies, public and private investment, and various regulatory institutions. Chapters 5 and 6 return to the larger themes underwritten by our analyses—those concerning the political aspects of full employment and the possibility of developing political resistance to the neo-liberal destruction of national competences (Gills 1997). Despite high and persistent levels of unemployment, increasing social inequality and a declining sense of community, the political agenda has become increasingly insensitive to arguments supporting national development, societal integration, public morality and political principle. Unemployment is a political problem because politics has left itself only a very limited role. The task of reconstructing a political capacity equal to the task of reinstituting a respect for civility and for the political project itself is one which ought to be the concern of all those who have been distressed by the unhelpful political responses to economic circumstances of the past quarter-century. Our endeavour is to show that, however difficult the development of political capacities is, governments have a much greater range of options and much more room to manoeuvre than their current preoccupations and current intellectual fashions suggest. We have much to learn not only about how to manage the economy but also about the possibilities of politics.

Chapter 2

The politics and economics of unemployment in Australia: the comparative context

For more than a quarter-century following World War II almost all of the advanced industrial democracies including Australia experienced a period of near full employment, low inflation and sustained economic growth. This was the era that is referred to as the 'long boom'. It was a period during which living standards improved as economic prosperity was distributed according to more or less agreed-upon political and industrial conventions established by the major political actors in society including employers, investors, labour movements, political parties and public officials.

These developments took place in a climate of innovation and economic expansion that characterized the aftermath of World War II. The war had spurred a new wave of military research and development which provided the impetus for civilian applications of new technologies and the associated growth of manufacturing industry. Reconstruction of both the economic infrastructure and social fabric of nations which had been engaged in the war opened the way for economic and social policy initiatives as well as a great deal of public investment that served as a catalyst for further economic development.

In most of the capitalist societies this period also witnessed the growth of government, not in the negative sense of bureaucracy and red tape, but in the positive interpretation of a democratic political will for social development. As a consequence, this was the period of the expanding welfare state, encompassing the evolution of public pensions and unemployment benefits and the flowering of public health, education and housing. However, these developments did not occur evenly and some countries, of which Australia was the prime example, remained laggards in their provision of societal resources and services during the postwar period.

This chapter briefly reviews some of the historical and comparative evidence relating to Australia's development since the early 1970s. By surveying various indicators of social and economic welfare, it is possible to trace the broad contours of the trajectory of the last few decades. It is a trajectory which singles out Australia from both its historical past and its contemporary economic competitors.

The derogation of nation-building responsibilities

As Figure 2.1 demonstrates, Australia was conspicuously last among advanced democracies in its social welfare spending in 1970. The figures represent total government expenditure on

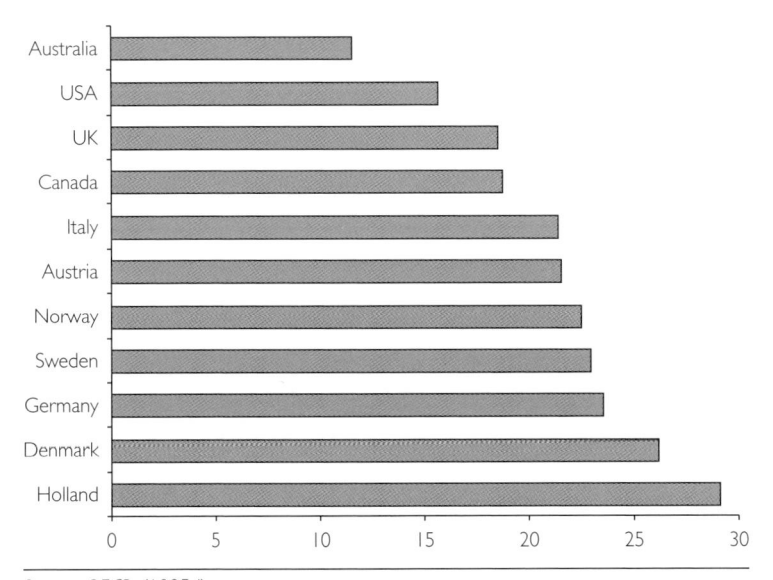

Figure 2.1: Social Expenditure as Percentage of GDP, 1970

Australia	~11
USA	~15
UK	~18
Canada	~19
Italy	~21
Austria	~21
Norway	~22
Sweden	~23
Germany	~23
Denmark	~26
Holland	~29

Source: OECD (1985d)

education, health, old age and disability pensions, family and child allowances, and unemployment assistance. They show that Australia spent only half as much on these items as did many similar countries. When disaggregated, the data show that Australia fell well behind most other countries on each item of expenditure. Figure 2.2 shows the extent to which spending on old age and disability pensions lagged well behind most other countries.

It was not only in the realm of welfare expenditure that significant changes were taking place in the growth of public spending. Aided by the emergence of Keynesian economic policy and the accompanying philosophical justification for greater political intervention in the economy, governments in most of the advanced capitalist economies devoted increasing attention to the regulation of industrial and economic development. These policies and associated expenditure took a number of forms. First, many governments sought to foster a climate in which private investment—the engine of economic development—could be sustained and directed to nationally desirable outcomes. This often involved strategic government expenditure on public infrastructure—such as railways, roads, communications,

Figure 2.2: Pensions as Percentage of GDP, 1970

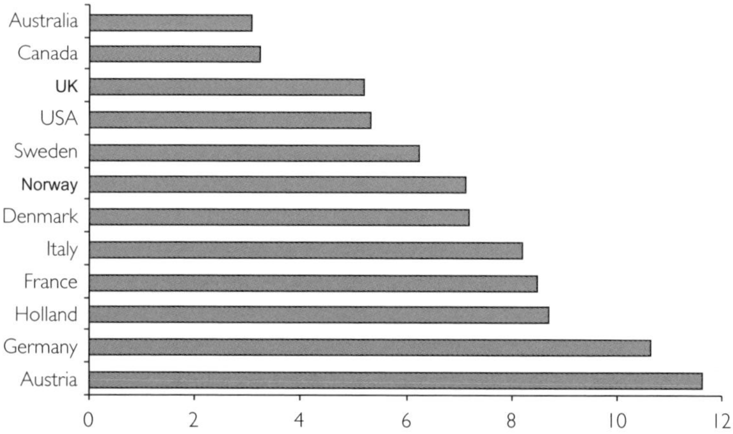

Source: OECD (1985c)

electricity and water supply, port facilities, and some areas of research and development—to encourage private sector investment in what were established as appropriate regional locations and areas of economic activity for national development.

A second, emergent form of government intervention was in the realm of industry policy. Policies affecting the structure of industry have taken a number of forms, with varying degrees of economic success, ranging from nationalization (usually an attempt by governments to maintain ailing industries when private commercial criteria could no longer be applied without state support) through industry protection (often in the form of tariffs and quotas but also through subsidies and forms of public purchase) to various regulatory measures concerning, for example, support for local investment, access to venture capital, support for research and development and alternative investment funds. The evidence would suggest that the latter approaches have much greater chances of success than the first two because public criteria can be more explicitly and selectively applied. Again, there was a great deal of variation in both the form of policy and the resources that governments were prepared to devote to its implementation. Again, Australia tended be a laggard in both respects, relying heavily on protection through tariffs.

Australia emerged from the boom conditions of the 1950s and 1960s in a precarious economic state. Whereas, for many capitalist societies, the past quarter-century had been an era of social and economic consolidation, Australia had celebrated a period of policy abstention. This is amply illustrated by Figure 2.3, which shows the extent to which governments have established the fiscal capacity to sustain public expenditure for national developmental purposes. Most of the major democracies, except Australia, extended their abilities to undertake various policy initiatives in the postwar decades by increasing their taxation revenue as a percentage of GDP. Australia, however, had taxes well below the average of the OECD countries. Many of the other OECD countries devoted substantial political effort and economic resources to establishing a foundation for

Figure 2.3: Total Taxes as Percentage of GDP, 1968–1973

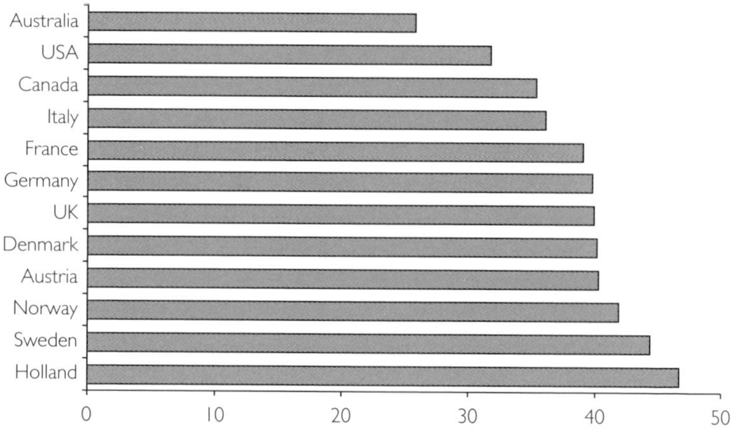

Country	%
Australia	~26
USA	~31
Canada	~34
Italy	~35
France	~38
Germany	~39
UK	~39
Denmark	~40
Austria	~40
Norway	~42
Sweden	~44
Holland	~46

Source: OECD (1985d)

economic renewal. In particular, much policy detail aimed at combining existing human, material and organizational resources in a manner that would facilitate the extension and application of industrial innovation.

In short, there was a strong positive assessment of the value of manufacturing industry as a key element of economic success. This was not a nostalgic longing for a past era of spectacular engineering accomplishments and mass production factories but the combination of technology and productive capacity to meet the needs of an increasingly complex society. Manufacturing provided the milieu in which research and development could be cultivated, scientific and technical skills could be developed, and society's ability to innovate could be fostered. The application of these techniques in production was the source of significant employment growth, multiplier effects in support industries, export capacity, and economic growth supporting a higher standard of living.

There was also a strong view that it was the responsibility of government to give social direction to the development of manufacturing. This meant paying attention not only to the defensive capacity provided by industry but also to broader economic and social capacities. The governments of the advanced industrial nations differed greatly not only in the strategies adopted but in the degree of political willingness to deal with the issues.

In many industrial nations attention was focused on matters such as the facilitation of access to venture capital; regulation of the financial sector to provide long-term access to capital for the manufacturing sector; provision of appropriate infrastructural development for the growth of private industry through public capital expenditure; labour market policies directed at retraining and relocation as industries waned or evolved; welfare policies to provide a safety net for workers caught in rapidly changing employment conditions; industrial relations policies designed to give formal accord to the views of the key economic actors of labour and capital in the future direction of economic activity; and protection of developing industries from international predators. These were the elements of successful industry policy. They were rarely matters that occupied the attention of Australian legislators in the postwar period.

The derogation of nation-building responsibilities which characterized successive Australian governments in the 1950s and 1960s is evident in the manner in which public investment in national infrastructure was inhibited. As Figure 2.4 indicates, by

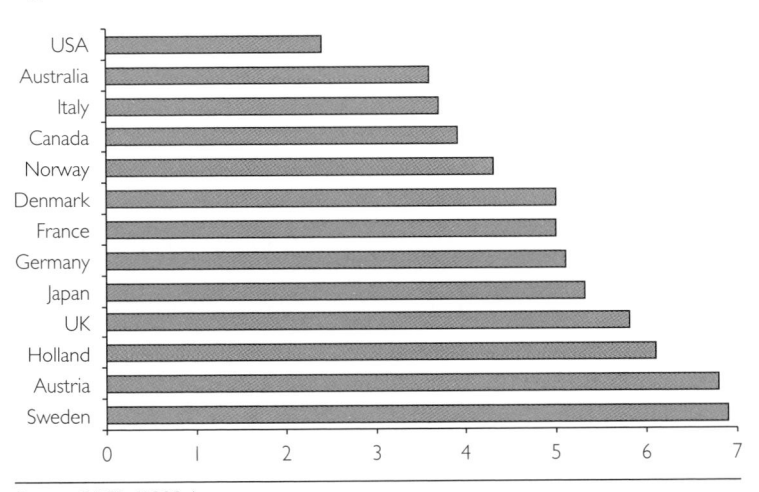

Figure 2.4: Public Investment as Percentage of GDP, 1968

Source: OECD (1990a)

1968 Australia was devoting less attention to government capital expenditure than virtually all other countries and spent less than half the amount spent by many of the successful economies.

With the exception of its tariff system, Australia conspicuously ignored the types of economic regulatory policies and those concerned with industry development which were taking place in other advanced capitalist countries. The extent to which government planning had been consciously rejected by a series of conservative governments in Australia is evident in Liberal Prime Minister Menzies' comments on the 1965 Vernon Committee, which had recommended the establishment of an economic advisory council along the lines of the Economic Council for Canada. After intense lobbying from the Treasury, which was opposed to another economic advisory group vying for the government's attention, the recommendation was vetoed by Menzies. Such a proposal, according to Menzies, 'predicated a degree of planning and direction in the economy which . . . would not be either appropriate or acceptable in Australia'. Similar issues were raised and similar responses were evident in the reception of the report of the (Jackson) Committee to Advise on Policies for Manufacturing Industry, commissioned in the mid-1970s. The task force stressed the problems caused by the lack of machinery with which to develop a framework of economic policy goals and objectives, but its substantive recommendations were largely ignored by the incoming government.

Protectionist policies, manifested in high tariffs levied on imported products, constituted an economic policy automatic-pilot for successive Australian governments. A combination of liberal aversion to the process of government itself and a sanguine view of the relative fortunes of Australia in a prosperous international community of capitalist nations camouflaged the predicament toward which the economy was headed.

Commencing in the early 1970s, various elements in the equation which we have been describing began to alter. More importantly, the complacent view that we were witnessing a convergence in the economic fortunes of all the advanced capitalist nations was shattered.

The onset of national economic decline

There was no one factor that precipitated the economic malaise that has continued unabated since the mid-1970s. The OPEC oil price rises in 1974 merely exacerbated trends that had already become evident (and were predictable) in the preceding years. Certainly, investment in new products, materials technologies and methods of production had slowed somewhat as the impetus from wartime research had waned. Multinational enterprises turned their attention to reducing production costs by employing cheaper labour in the developing world rather than investing in new methods of production. Finance capital became more internationally mobile and deployed in areas of speculative activity which brought greater returns than national manufacturing sources could provide. Accounting conventions and stock market valuations placed a high priority on short-term profitability, often at the expense of investment in longer-term product and process development. All these developments were facilitated in a political environment that was increasingly characterized by market liberalization as governments abandoned or were reluctant to use regulatory measures that might have allowed them to influence the direction and pace of change.

Associated with these factors was a marked falling-off in the performance of the western economies. A variety of economic indicators warned of the growing crisis. Capacity utilization in industry showed a progressive downward trend (OECD 1985a). Investment in maintaining and renewing plant and equipment showed a similar decline. This is graphically captured in the data showing that the growth of gross private non-residential fixed capital formation in the OECD countries declined from 11.6 per cent in 1969 to 1.4 per cent per annum for the decade 1974–83 (OECD 1989).

Employment was the main victim of these economic failures. During the decade 1961–70, unemployment rates in the OECD countries averaged 3.1 per cent. The decade 1975–84 saw the average rates more than double, to 6.6 per cent (OECD 1986b). For the first time, there was a tendency for unemployment and inflation rates to rise simultaneously. Consumer prices in the OECD which had exhibited an average annual increase of 3.7 per cent in the five years from 1965 to 1969 increased by an average of 9.6 per cent annually through the decade 1974–83 (OECD 1989).

It was hardly surprising that the rate of economic growth would slow, when fixed capital investment—the cause of accumulation—was scarcely enough to replace obsolete and depleted plant and equipment and the proportion of the productive workforce that was unemployed had doubled. The OECD countries consequently witnessed growth rates declining from an annual average of 5.0 per cent during 1965–69 to 2.1 per cent from 1974 to 1983 (OECD 1985b).

So, commencing in the early to mid-1970s, all OECD countries exhibited economic decline. All suffered from unemployment rates far in excess of anything experienced in the two previous decades. Without a comparative perspective, it was easy for voters in each country to turn to national political explanations for the decline and to eject incumbent governments for their inability to manage the economy. Governments as disparate as the Conservatives led by Heath in the United Kingdom, the Labor Party under Whitlam in Australia, and the Gaullists under Pompidou in France were victims of these perceptions.

However, it is not our intention to conclude that economic downturn and escalating unemployment in particular were international economic phenomena outside the control of national governments. Clearly, from the evidence in Figure 2.5, the policy approach of governments does matter. Thus, unemployment rates increased dramatically between 1973 and 1983 from 2.2 per cent to 11.2 per cent in the United Kingdom, from 2.3 per cent to 9.8 per cent in Australia and from 4.8 per cent to 9.5 per cent in the United States. However, some of the other advanced capitalist countries managed to achieve significantly better results during the same period—increases from 1.3 per cent to 2.6 per cent in Japan, from 2.5 per cent to 3.5 per cent in Sweden and from 1.0 per cent to 3.8 per cent in

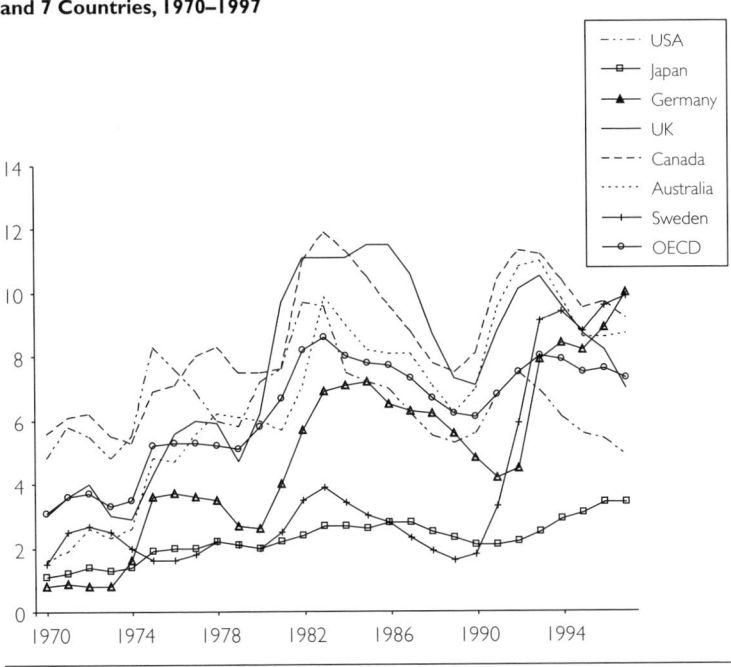

Figure 2.5: Unemployment as Percentage of Total Labour Force in OECD and 7 Countries, 1970–1997

Source: OECD Economic Outlook *(various issues)*

Austria. Some countries were obviously in a better position than others to deal with the changing circumstances that had precipitated an economic malaise. The reasons for this divergence provide the major focus of the chapters which follow. First, however, we turn to a closer examination of Australia's anomalous performance.

As the preceding material has emphasized, the most perspicacious depiction of Australian public policy in the postwar era is that of policy abstention. This resulted in a national economy characterized by some of the OECD's lowest levels of government activity: taxes; government expenditure on industry development; social welfare expenditure on health, education, housing and pensions; public expenditure on national infrastructure; and expenditure on economic policy institutions. There were many victims of Australian policy neglect at both personal and institutional levels. Outstanding among these was one that was destined to play a major role in Australia's unemployment crisis—manufacturing. As we have already argued, manufacturing lies at the core of national economic achievement. It exemplifies the technological capacity of nations, their ability to innovate through applying knowledge and skill to production, and their facility to create jobs and develop employment conditions maximizing the benefits of experience and training. In 1970, Australian manufacturing industry was in a parlous state, with Australian industry among the least successful four countries on every measure shown in Table 2.1.

It is extremely ironical that Australian governments in the 1970s and 1980s, in looking at international analyses of national economic decline, adopted a model which targeted excessive government expenditure and regulation as the key contributors to declining economic performance. This analysis derived from a trenchant critique of the prevalent Keynesian view of demand realization, which portrayed the facilitation and regulation of investment as the key to overall levels of economic performance.

Table 2.1: Manufacturing Performance in 12 OECD Countries, 1970

	Manufacturing Employment [a]	Manufacturing in GDP [b]	Value Added	Export Share (%) [c]
Australia	26.4	24.3	22.5	1.6
Canada	22.3	19.8	20.2	7.3
USA	26.4	25.2	24.9	20.3
Norway	26.7	21.6	21.7	1.3
Japan	27.0	36.0	35.2	11.0
France	27.5	29.9	28.3	9.3
Sweden	27.6	21.6	24.1	3.7
Netherlands	28.6	25.8	28.5	5.8
UK	34.7	28.7	28.5	10.4
Denmark	37.8	18.5	17.9	1.7
Germany	39.4	38.4	36.3	18.9
Italy	39.5	27.1	30.0	7.3

a Percentage of total civilian employment.
b Manufacturing's contribution to GDP.
c Export market shares as a proportion of exports to the world.
Source: OECD (1994d)

In the neo-Keynesian view, investment performs the dual function of creating the potential for enhanced profitability and establishing extra productive capacity, for whose output new sources of demand must be found. Governments need to manage this process in three important respects. The first involves demand management intervention through increased public expenditure, through the maintenance of welfare benefits or through incomes policies designed to transfer resources from increased profits to households. The second intervention involves influencing the direction of investment through government industry policy. Most importantly, this might involve using public capital expenditure to provide the infrastructural support for private investment. It might also focus on subsidies or taxation incentives for particular forms of investment. Investment regulation might also be effected through institutions involving employers and unions in decisions concerning industrial restructuring, labour market strategies and training policies. The third level of government involvement involves establishing some form of centralized incomes policy for capital and labour. This is to promote the conditions in which both sides are assured of influence over the distribution of profits and wages, thus mitigating uncontrolled industrial conflict and inflationary pressures.

The neo-liberal critique of this analysis suggested that government intervention, particularly the welfare state, imposed a burden of taxation and regulation upon capital which amounted to a disincentive to invest. There was no suggestion of any disjunction between what was privately profitable and what was socially desirable. Nor was there any implication that governments had a role to play in guiding the otherwise capricious nature of private investment which produced major fluctuations in employment, social inequality and living standards. The solution, proposed most vigorously by the Thatcher government in the United Kingdom, was dismantling the institutional infrastructure of the Keynesian welfare state and withdrawing government spending and regulation. The strategy of 'supply side' economics which flows directly from this approach was the precursor of the 'economic rationalist' approach to government which, to varying degrees, overtook the policy institutions of governments throughout the OECD countries.

This is the path which Australia has enthusiastically followed for more than two decades. With the exception of a brief detour between 1983 and 1987, it has set the pace and direction of Australia's economic demise.

The Australian policy regime affected the economy with heightened intensity from the mid-1970s, particularly the manufacturing sector. One of the first pillars to be undermined was industry protection. Figure 2.6 shows that tariff reductions have precipitated a decline in employment in industry, as is amply illustrated by the patterns of employment in the textile, clothing and footwear industry group (TCF). The 25 per cent across-the-board tariff cuts instituted by the Whitlam government in 1973 was followed by a decline of employment in the TCF manufacturing sector by almost 25 per cent (34 000 jobs) between March 1974 and March 1975 (Capling & Galligan 1992).

Successive governments were placed under considerable pressure by the Industries Assistance Commission (IAC) (later renamed the Industry Commission and subsequently included

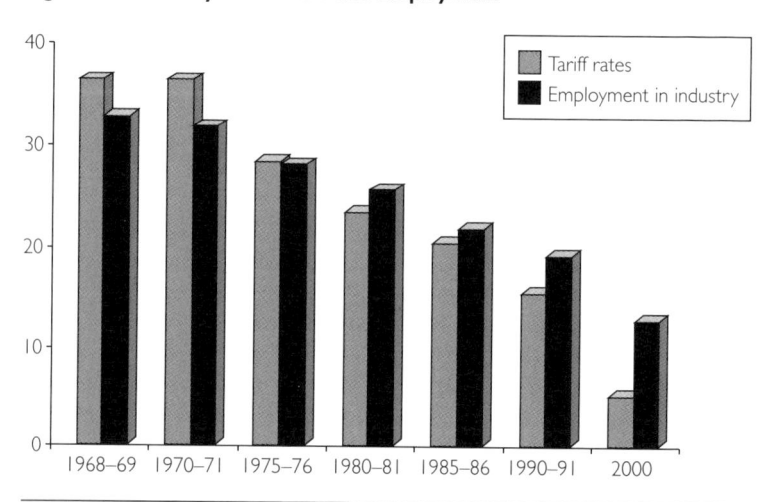

Figure 2.6: Industry Protection[a] and Employment

a Average effective rate of assistance to manufacturing industry from tariffs.
Source: Industry Commission (1990)

in the Howard government's Productivity Commission) to further reduce assistance and phase out quotas. The IAC specifically rejected employment as a trade-off for the costs of industry protection (IAC 1977). The Labor government again succumbed to pressure in 1988 and announced a faster scaling-down of protection for the TCF industries. It was anticipated that the industry would contract as a result of these measures and that many jobs would be lost—a projection that proved accurate as a further 27 000 jobs were lost between 1988 and 1992. While most other countries use some form of import quotas or volume restriction, Australia has led the OECD in embracing deregulation. The result has been the once and for all substitution of a viable national industry by imports, accompanied by a great deal of social and economic dislocation.

A second major example of the negative impact of the distinctive economic policy regime in Australia is the decline in public capital expenditure. From its position of second-lowest on the table of government infrastructural investment, public gross fixed capital formation in Australia has continually declined. Moreover, as Figure 2.7 shows, the anticipated increase in private investment, said to have been crowded out by public expenditure, has not eventuated. The data show that, contrary to government

Figure 2.7: Gross Fixed Capital Formation as Percentage of GDP, 1973–1997

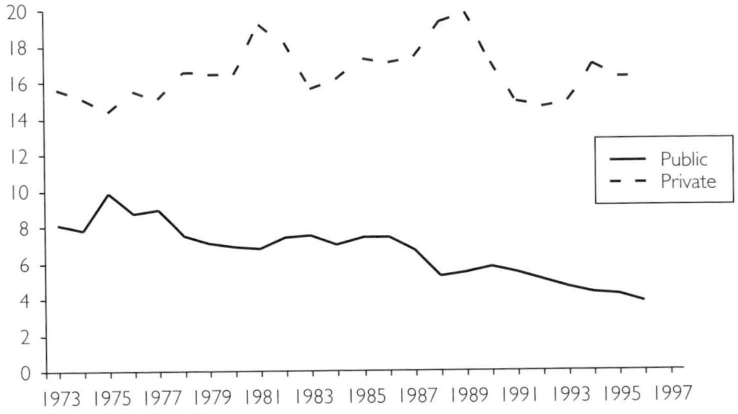

Source: OECD (1998b)

expectations, much private activity depends on a foundation of public investment.

The two policy measures outlined above are key indicators of Australian government approaches to economic policy—approaches which directly affect the structure of Australian industry. Employment patterns are crucially contingent upon the longer-term changes in the pattern of Australian industry set in train by these political decisions. Figure 2.8 indexes the relative growth and decline of employment in the various industry sectors. In particular, it shows that, despite the substantial population and employment growth between 1972 and 1994, manufacturing now supports considerably fewer jobs than it did two decades ago. On the other hand, the proportion of employment in the three service sector groups has increased dramatically. Figure 2.9 focuses on the effects of this redistribution on the manufacturing sector. It shows that manufacturing has continually declined as a source of employment from 24.5 per cent of all jobs in 1970 to 14.3 per cent in 1994. Figure 2.10 shows that the contribution of manufacturing to

Figure 2.8: Index of Employment by Industry (1972 = 100), 1972–1994

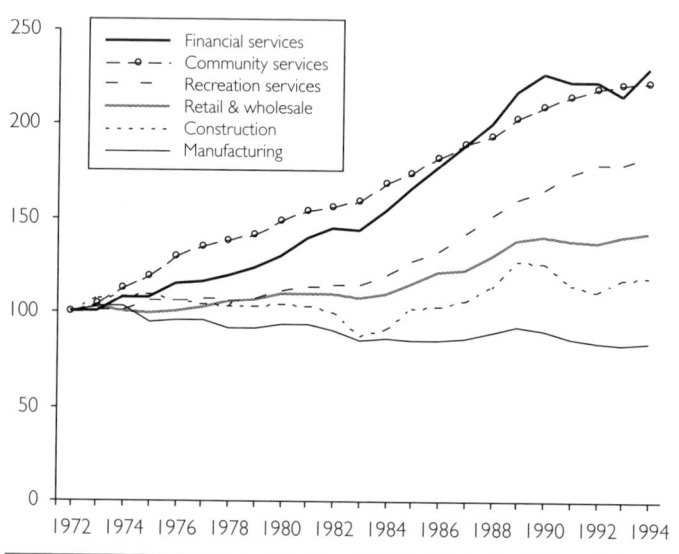

Source: ABS, The Labour Force

Figure 2.9: Manufacturing Employment as Percentage of Total Employment, 1970–1996

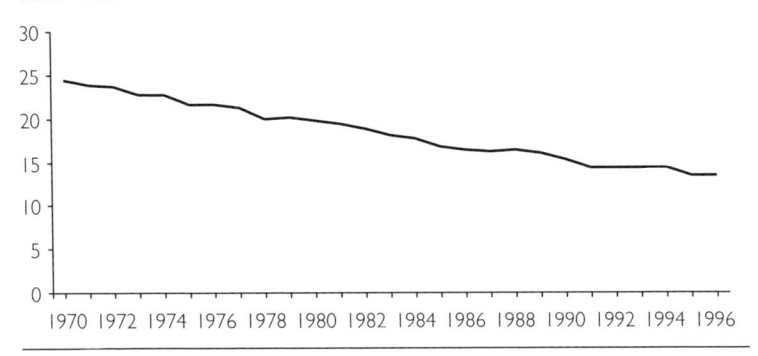

Source: ABS, Labour Statistics Australia

Figure 2.10: Manufacturing as Percentage of GDP, 1970–1996

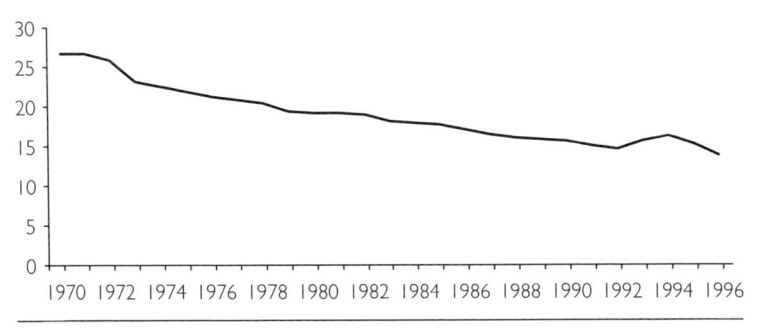

Source: ABS (1997)

GDP has been subject to a similar downward slide, from 27 per cent to 14 per cent.

Of course the spectacular loss of jobs in manufacturing is only part of the equation that describes Australia's contemporary employment crisis. Figure 2.8 also shows the substantial growth of the services sector as a source of employment during the same period. This process is captured in Figure 2.11, which demonstrates the decline of trades and blue-collar jobs and the parallel growth of white-collar jobs. Underlying these figures is a process of industrial and occupational reorganization which has seen the destruction of the major area of male full-time employment. At the same time there is a large increase in (often part-time) service sector jobs in which the growing number of women in

Figure 2.11: Index of Employment by Occupation (1972 = 100), 1972–1994

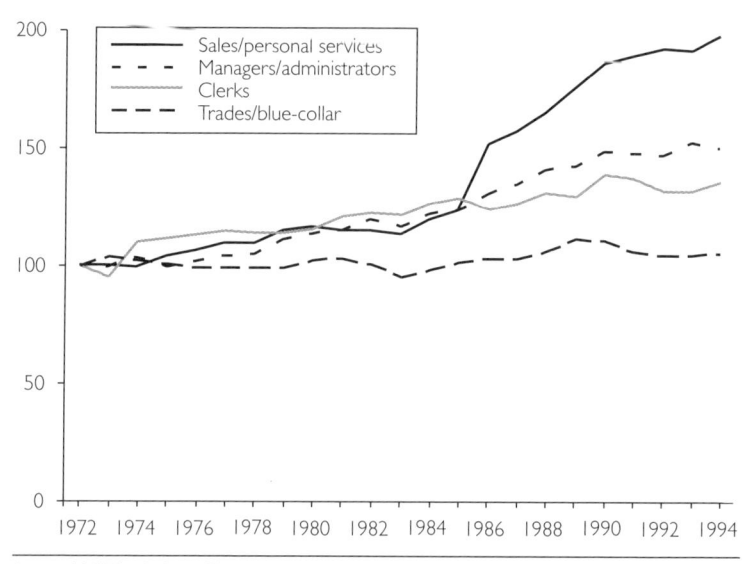

- Sales/personal services
- Managers/administrators
- Clerks
- Trades/blue-collar

Source: ABS, The Labour Force

Figure 2.12: Employment in Industry Sectors for Men and Women (Per Cent), 1996

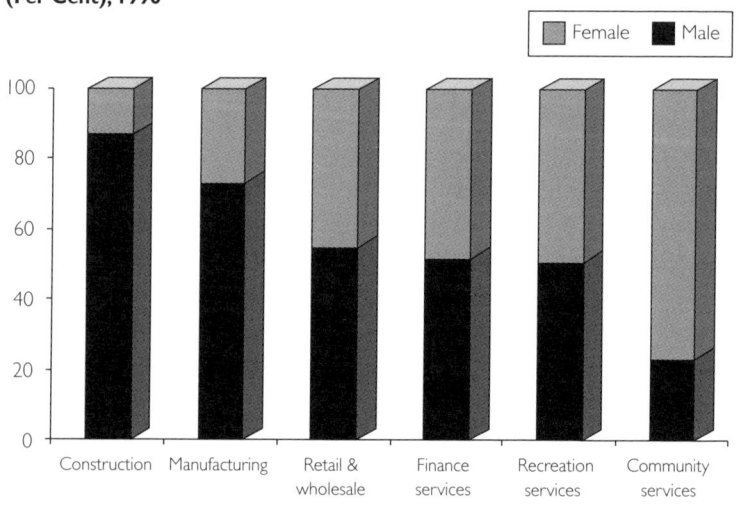

Female / Male

Construction, Manufacturing, Retail & wholesale, Finance services, Recreation services, Community services

Source: ABS, Labour Statistics

the workforce have found employment. Figure 2.12 illustrates the gendered pattern of industrial segregation which characterizes the Australian workforce in the 1990s. The growth and decline of particular sectors which have traditionally provided the majority of employment for women and men is clearly depicted, as the basis for understanding some of the structural forms of unemployment. In essence, the jobs that are being created are not those likely to provide employment for displaced male (or female) blue-collar workers—at least, not without active labour market policies such as retraining and relocation support which focus on the employment consequences of industrial restructuring.

One of the most important aspects of Australia's employment crisis revealed by these data is that the employment growth experienced over the past decade should not leave us sanguine about the future prospects for unemployment. The changes we have described have led to an increase, within a quarter-century, of about 150 per cent in the percentage of the workforce who are employed part-time (see Figure 2.13). While it is possible to think of these changes as responses to the preference of particular categories of workers for part-time employment and the

Figure 2.13: Part-time Employment as Percentage of Total Employment, 1972–1996

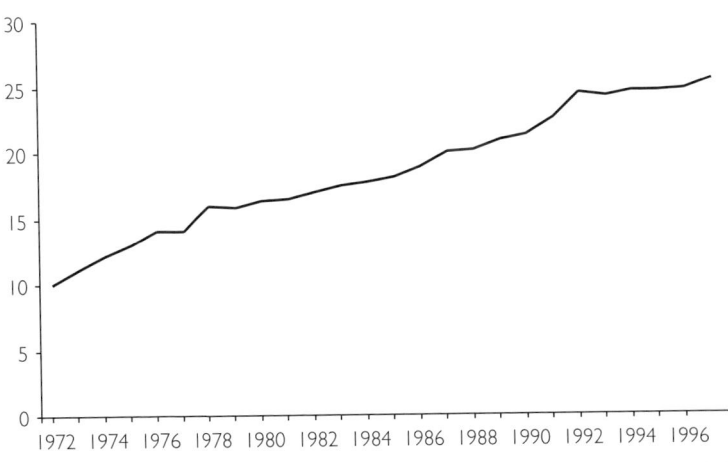

Source: ABS, The Labour Force

transformation of the workplace to accommodate more flexible working arrangements, the reality is that most of the new jobs involve a deterioration in working conditions. A common example is cleaning and maintenance services, formerly undertaken by employees of large enterprises but now being contracted out to individuals who must work without the security, social environment or working conditions previously found in most forms of permanent employment. Another example is where tasks previously undertaken at the workplace are now performed by outworkers employed without the benefit of occupational and health and safety regulations in unsatisfactory domestic working conditions. Tens of thousands of such jobs characterize the new employment environment in the clothing industry alone. A third major growth area is casual work for students as check-out operators and floor staff in retailing outlets or kitchen or table staff in fast-food operations or restaurants. Training, the acquisition of skills and experience, and the development of careers are far removed from the requirements of most of these positions. The chances that they might meet the needs or aspirations of displaced manufacturing employees are almost negligible. The jobs also seem unlikely to confer the human capital—greater skills and credentials—which provide a wider choice of employment, which is the conventional view expounded by labour economists.

Some important consequences of the expansion of part-time jobs in services and retailing is illustrated in Figure 2.14. From 1966 to 1994 participation rates of particular groups altered markedly. The participation rate for males dropped from 83.5 per cent to 74.0 per cent while that for females increased from 37.2 per cent to 52.6 per cent. While the proportion of males employed part-time increased from 4 per cent in 1967 to 10.1 per cent in 1994, the proportion of females in part-time work increased from 24.5 per cent to 41.1 per cent. Currently, 59.3 per cent of female employees compared with 90.8 per cent of male employees are engaged in full-time work, while women make up 76.1 per cent of the part-time workforce. Some significant relationships between age and gender may also be discerned.

Workers aged 15-19 years are much more likely to be employed part-time. However, whereas over 90 per cent of male employees (under sixty years of age) work full-time, female employees, especially those older than thirty-five, tend to remain in part-time employment (see Figure 2.15).

Figure 2.14: Male and Female Participation Rates (Per Cent), 1966–1996

Source: ABS, Labour Statistics

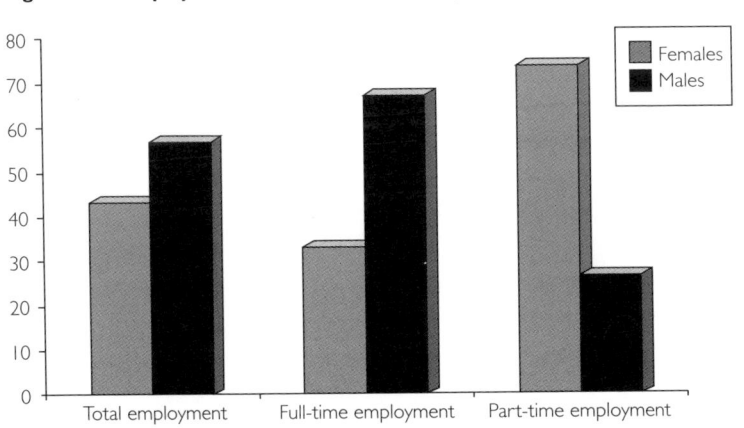

Figure 2.15: Employment for Men and Women (Per Cent), 1997

Source: ABS, The Labour Force

There are several additional considerations. First, among those with marginal attachments to the labour force there is a strong gender-based profile. Table 2.2 indicates that women predominate among what are termed the 'hidden unemployed'—persons who currently want and are available for work together with those people who are actively seeking work but are not available to start within the next four weeks. Within this category, women also make up the great majority of 'discouraged jobseekers' who want work but do not actively seek employment because they believe that they lack necessary training, skills or experience or because jobs are not available in their locality or type of work.

Another issue affects the employment opportunities afforded new entrants to the labour market. Young people have always experienced significantly higher levels of unemployment than the general population. This was particularly evident during the 1991–92 period when the rate of unemployment among 15–19-year-olds rose to 34 per cent in seasonally adjusted terms. However, these data need to be interpreted in the light of increases in the school retention rate from 33 per cent in 1974 to 60 per cent in 1989 (DEET 1991: 54). Thus, the absolute numbers of unemployed in this age category have, in fact,

Table 2.2: Women's Marginal Attachment to the Workforce, Australia, 1996 (000s)

	Males	Females	Female (%)
Persons not in the workforce	1202.5	2412.9	67
With marginal attachment	262.0	617.6	70
Wanting work, actively looking	354.4	833.6	70
Wanting work, not actively looking	233.3	588.2	72
Discouraged jobseekers	29.8	89.4	75
Without marginal attachment	928.1	2025.8	69

Note: Approximately 25 per cent of those in the 'not actively looking' category cited 'childcare' as the main reason.
Source: ABS (1996)

declined. Finally, it should be noted that the figures tend to obscure very high levels of localized unemployment in particular country towns and regions, where youth unemployment rates of up to 60 per cent have been recorded.

In summary, these trends suggest significant long-term changes in the way work is organized. The decline in full-time career opportunities has been only partly compensated for by an increase in part-time work. There has also been a 'feminization' of the workforce, with the rate of employment increasing four times faster than that of male employment. These changes have allowed for much greater flexibility in the manner in which work is deployed. Part-time and casual employment at lower rates of pay, and the absence of the training costs normally associated with full-time career development, have provided employment for a large number of young workers, especially females, but at considerable cost to the quality of employment available more generally in the economy.

The costs of unemployment

Costs associated with the rates of unemployment in Australia in the 1990s may be measured in a number of ways. The first measure captures the cost to the nation and, therefore, the entire community, of production forgone. One recent study estimated the loss associated with one percentage point of unemployment to be between $3 billion and $6 billion per year. This must be combined with the loss of revenue to governments and the additional spending required to meet various forms of welfare assistance, estimated at around $2 billion per year (Junankar & Kapuscinski 1992).

The second mechanism through which unemployment creates a major cost to individuals and the community is the strong correlation between employment status and physical and mental illness and crime. Much of the literature concentrates on the effect of the lack of security associated with regular employment in increasing the potential for criminal behaviour

(Hensen 1990). The unemployed are significantly over-represented among people who appear before the courts, and a study by Devery (1991) demonstrated a strong association between high crime rates and socioeconomic disadvantage. More than 50 per cent of Queensland prisoners were unemployed at the time of their arrest. Unemployment has also been strongly linked to high suicide rates for males, with one study finding that, even in the 1970s, the rate of attempted suicide for unemployed persons was twelve times the average rate (Krudinski 1977). In general, unemployment severs an important set of social relationships without which many people have little support or security in dealing with often profound economic hardship. Self-esteem, stress and dietary inadequacy have been shown to be significantly associated with mental and physical illness (Windschuttle 1980).

A further measure focuses on the direct financial cost to individuals. The most direct measure indicates that the unemployment benefit rate in 1991 was about 34 per cent of average weekly earnings (net of tax) for females and 28 per cent for males. In only exceptional instances (fewer than 1 per cent of cases) could the unemployed earn more from unemployment benefits than from full-time wages (EPAC 1992). On the contrary, as Saunders concluded from a study of employment and poverty in Australia in the 1980s, the rise in unemployment 'left its mark in terms of a "new poor" comprising working age families, many with children, whose unemployment condemned them to a situation of joblessness and poverty' (1990: 41). Similar results were reported by Cass (1988) who showed that the unemployed fell within the poorest 10 per cent of income units. These social and economic costs heavily affect the long-term unemployed.

Unemployment has rapidly transformed the prevailing patterns of social inequality in Australian society. In the financial year 1989/90, the top 30 per cent of income units earned 60.4 per cent of total gross income while the bottom 30 per cent earned only 8.3 per cent. After taking personal taxes and social welfare transfers into account, the amounts were 56.1 per cent and 10.1 per cent respectively. Most importantly, however, data presented by Saunders (1993) indicates that in the eight years between 1981/82 and 1989/90, the tide of inequality increased by 10.7 per cent (gross income) and 8.6 per cent (net income). In essence, in a very short period in the 1980s, the pattern of increasing equality that had characterized the decades until the mid-1970s was significantly reversed. These changes are not directly attributable to different unemployment rates at the beginning and end of the 1980s. As Figure 2.16 shows, both years exhibited similar levels of unemployment of about 6 per cent. Rather, the explanation lies in the shift in the labour market to part-time work together with a relatively lower increase in wages for lower-paid workers in full-time employment (Raskall 1993: 42–3).

One of the key developments in the labour market, revealed by research undertaken by Gregory (1993), has been that almost all of the net growth in men's employment between 1970 and 1990 occurred in the lowest income quintile. The attendant marked decline of middle-paying jobs in both the public and private sectors will probably lead to experienced, displaced workers occupying lower-level positions that would otherwise have been available for unskilled workers, thus exacerbating the problems of unemployed low-skilled workers. Paralleling these changes is evidence of rapidly rising real incomes for those in the highest income bracket during the 1980s (Saunders 1994b). The resultant extension of the distributional ranking which allows the highest income earners to increase their advantage over those below them is a natural consequence of the market-oriented policies pursued in Australia over that decade.

Research on poverty in Australia using the measurement framework developed by the Commission of Inquiry into Poverty in 1975 has been reported by Saunders (1993, 1994a). The results show an increase in poverty between 1981/82 and 1989/90 for every income unit type. The poverty rate among all income units increased dramatically from 10.8 per cent to 16.7 per cent over this relatively short period. Saunders concludes that 'the increased incidence of long-term unemployment has . . . expos(ed) the inadequacy of the levels of income support for the unemployed generally'. The use of savings and debt to meet financial commitments allows unemployed people to defer a fall in living standards temporarily, but the outcome is the decline into poverty demonstrated by the data.

The strong employment growth that has recently characterized the Australian economy has not led to the reduction of unemployment. The new jobs that have been created have provided part-time and casual work that has in many respects failed to meet the aspirations of those seeking employment or those who have been displaced from existing jobs. Continuing high levels of unemployment, underemployment and employment in low-paid jobs has been the result. These outcomes contributed strongly to the significant increase in poverty and social inequality which occurred during the 1980s (Saunders 1993, 1994a). The momentum of orthodox economic prescriptions concerning the efficacy of unfettered markets has produced a policy agenda dominated by a vocabulary of labour market flexibility. It needs to be clearly understood that this means low wages, insecure jobs and declining employment conditions. The same policy orthodoxy led to the dismantling of the two key elements of social protection in Australia—the tariff barrier and the centralized system of wage determination. The ability of the social security system to provide adequate levels of social protection has been severely compromised by these developments. The tensions placed on the social fabric have affected the lives of most Australians. Yet these results have not occurred as a result of capricious forces that lie outside our understanding or our control. On the contrary, as we will show in the chapters which follow, they are outcomes of deliberate political choices and, more recently, a lack of political will to redress the mistakes of the past decades.

Australia in the 1990s: a comparative perspective

Australia entered the 1970s with comparatively underdeveloped policy machinery. The problems posed by this policy-making inertia were exacerbated in the uncertain political climate, in which a range of economic indicators all pointed to the potential for crisis if the precarious balance of industrial structure and social protection were subject to an exogenous dislocation. When this dislocation became apparent, in the mid-1970s, Australian policy-makers adopted a set of policy prescriptions that had been popularized by economic advisers to right-wing regimes in the United Kingdom and the United States. This led to a deterioration in the Australian economy, which now shows in unemployment levels substantially in excess of those in most comparable OECD countries (see Figures 2.16 and 2.17). More importantly, it accelerated the retreat from political intercession in the economy, leaving present Australian governments with neither the theoretical rationale nor the fiscal capacity to undertake the public responsibilities of modern economic management.

The macroeconomic and microeconomic policies that have been set in train in Australia have set the parameters of industry, labour market, industrial relations and welfare policies and have been pursued with increasing vigour during the past decade.

Figure 2.16: Percentage Unemployment in the 1990s

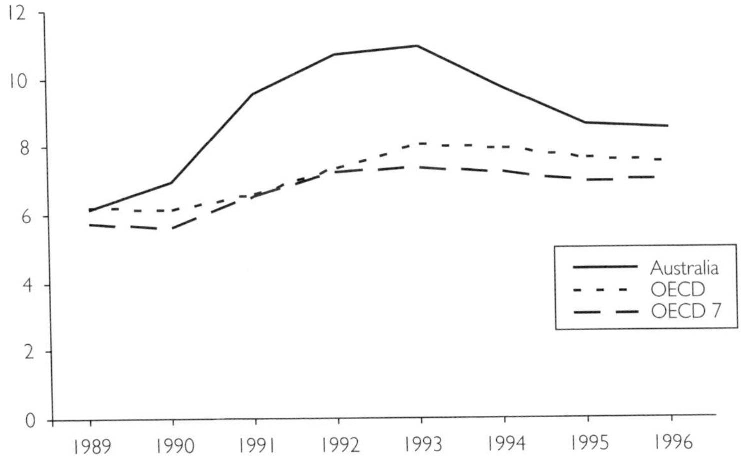

Source: OECD (1997a)

Figure 2.17: Percentage Unemployment in OECD Countries, 1991–1996 Average

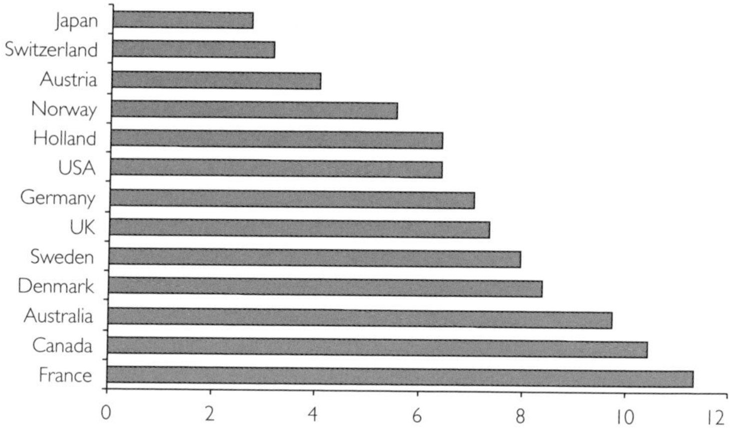

Country	Unemployment (%)
Japan	~3
Switzerland	~3
Austria	~4
Norway	~5.5
Holland	~6.5
USA	~6.5
Germany	~7
UK	~7.5
Sweden	~8
Denmark	~8.5
Australia	~9.5
Canada	~10.5
France	~11.5

Source: OECD (1997a)

The changes wrought by these policies have been described above. But let us clarify the present elements of the policy agenda. In this last section, some of the evidence for and against aspects of this policy agenda are previewed, to set the stage for a more detailed analysis in the chapters which follow.

Policy settings have been dominated by the view that fighting inflation must take precedence over combating unemployment. The Reserve Bank of Australia, which is the key economic agency espousing this view, often demonstrates a singlemindedness amounting to an indifference to the unemployed. In its submission to the Committee on Employment Opportunities it asserted that 'increases in the pool of potential workers in times of high unemployment should, by exerting some discipline on wage settings, help to reduce inflation and set the scene for recovery' (Reserve Bank of Australia 1993: 18).

Notwithstanding the disciplining effects of a pool of one million unemployed, there remain structural factors preventing lower wages from being passed on. Australian governments have therefore sought to sever the links between pay rates and conditions of work, established in federal and state awards, to allow the potentially reduced wages that might be accepted by despairing unemployed jobseekers to be registered in the system. The rubric under which these changes have been promulgated is one of flexibility and the machinery is enterprise bargaining. Reserve Bank economists argue that these considerations apply equally to wages, on-costs and conditions of employment.

> A key factor in stabilising structural employment [is] the restoration of lower levels of real unit labour costs (1993: 5).

> Structural unemployment is increased by industrial relations arrangements which make it more difficult for the unemployed to offer their services at a realistic wage rate (1993: 6).

> Structural unemployment is increased by rises in labour on-costs such as workers compensation premia, payroll tax, training and other levies indexed to the payroll, which also add to the unit cost of employing labour (1993: 6).

> Labour market rigidities such as restrictions on how employers may hire and dismiss workers (e.g. minimum notice and severance pay requirements) artificially raise the cost of labour and amplify unemployment (1993: 15).

> A large part of the focus of the current microeconomic reform agenda will lift efficiency by varying award conditions and reducing non-wage costs and working conditions (1993: 22).

These assertions are part of the current agenda which seeks fundamental change to the prevailing institutional arrangements for establishing equitable wages and working conditions in Australian workplaces. That the comparative data (and associated analysis which we present in the following chapters) suggest they are seriously flawed has not been a serious deterrent to their implementation.

The comparative evidence which we first consider concerns the 'fight inflation first' strategy. As Figure 2.18 shows, Australia has one of the better inflation performances among the major

Figure 2.18: Percentage Inflation in OECD Countries, 1991–1996 Average

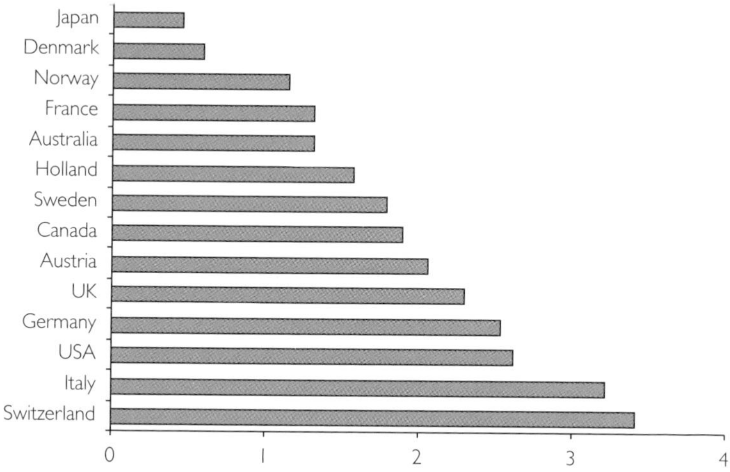

Japan	~0.5
Denmark	~0.7
Norway	~1.2
France	~1.4
Australia	~1.4
Holland	~1.6
Sweden	~1.8
Canada	~1.9
Austria	~2.1
UK	~2.3
Germany	~2.5
USA	~2.6
Italy	~3.2
Switzerland	~3.4

Source: OECD (1997a)

fourteen OECD countries through the 1990s. To the extent that reducing inflation is seen as the key to recovery, the criterion seems to have been met—but without any significant evidence of the anticipated reduction in unemployment.

The other major element of the argument concerns the impediment to employment created by excessive wages and on-costs. This is an argument which becomes increasingly difficult to sustain in light of the comparative evidence prepared by the United States Bureau of Labor Statistics about wages and on-costs for production workers in manufacturing in 1992, shown in Figure 2.19. These data clearly place Australia in the lowest category of total labour costs and the second-lowest of on-costs among the countries studied. The obsessive concern with working conditions and non-wage labour costs represented in the Reserve Bank's and the government's assertions is certainly little justified by the international data. The current enterprise bargaining agenda in Australia has undoubtedly focused on labour market flexibility and allowed the removal of some conditions associated with working hours and employment security. However, justification for these changes must come in the form

Figure 2.19: Wages and On-costs ($US'000s), 1992

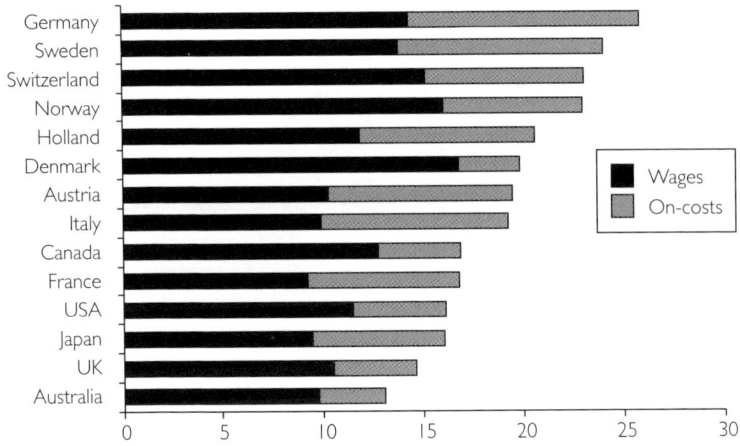

Source: DIR (1993a)

of enlarging the share of production accruing in the form of returns to capital and not in spurious claims about barriers to employment.

An ongoing feature of the unemployment policy debate in Australia and elsewhere is the argument that unemployment benefits in particular and social welfare payments in general create a disincentive to work. This is said to be because generous unemployment benefits make unemployment less undesirable, thus interfering with market incentives. The Reserve Bank submission put the argument this way: 'structural unemployment is increased by increased generosity of, or access to, unemployment benefits which may reduce the incentive to search for, and then hold on to, employment' (1993: 6); and 'there is a reduced incentive for some workers, particularly those with low skills and dependants, to be employed, if they can obtain welfare assistance instead' (1993: 20).

Again, these arguments do not stand up to scrutiny in the face of the international data. As Figures 2.20 and 2.21 show, far from providing extensive welfare provision, Australia has some of the least generous social security arrangements of all the

Figure 2.20: Social Welfare Expenditure as Percentage of GDP in OECD Countries, 1985

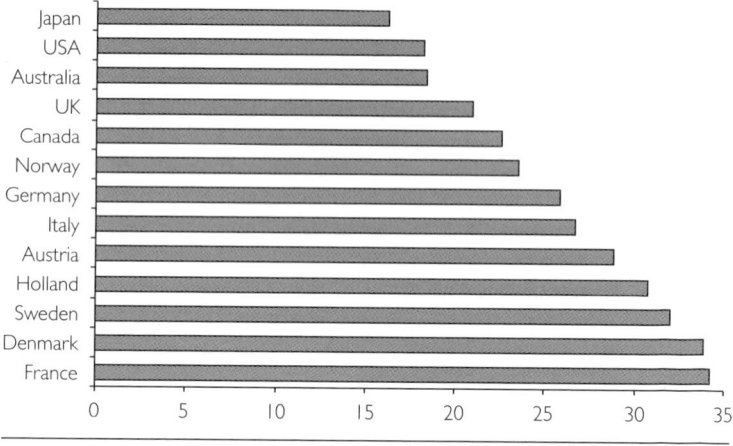

Source: OECD (1988)

Figure 2.21: Social Security Transfers as Percentage of GDP in OECD Countries, 1994

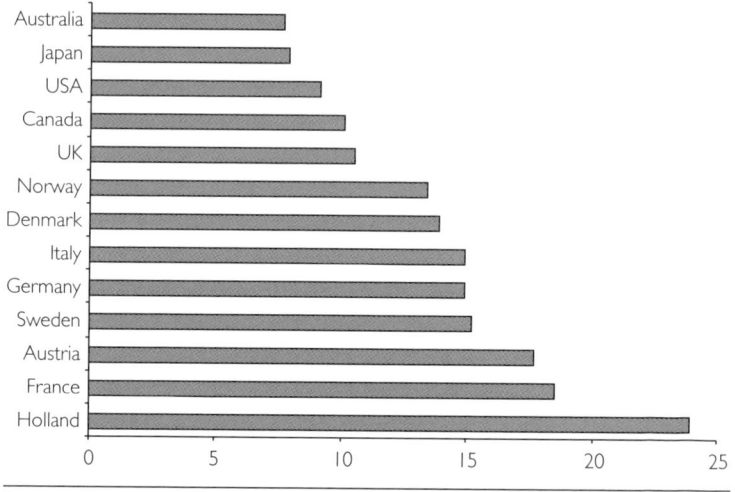

Source: OECD (1996b)

advanced countries. Australian spending on social security transfers involving pensions, unemployment benefits and other disability allowances is lower than that of any of the other countries in our study. A comparative view of total expenditure on the 'welfare state'—social security, health, education and housing—also locates Australia among the countries least supportive of the welfare needs of their citizens. If the burden of the welfare state is a factor in unemployment, it is a very limited burden indeed in the Australian context.

Two final aspects of the contemporary employment policy regime are the neoclassical approach to fiscal policy, which essentially focuses on restraining government expenditure, and taxation. The thesis being asserted is that expansionary demand management will, in the long run, produce only accelerating inflation. Management of the economy requires government abstention (apart from microeconomic intervention on the supply side, especially with respect to labour costs) and strong faith in the efficacy of the mechanisms of the unfettered market. The Reserve Bank position embodies these propositions:'higher taxes on business may impede capital accumulation (profits) and employment growth' (1993: 21) and 'the federal budget deficit is already large and is proving difficult to reduce. Further fiscal expansion (government expenditure) must therefore be constrained' (1993: 25).

The extent to which these articles of faith were absorbed by the former Labor government was manifested in the 1989 budget speech by then Treasurer Keating: 'Real government spending is cut for the fourth year in succession, to its lowest share in sixteen years . . . three years from now Labor will have succeeded in reducing Commonwealth Government spending to the levels of the 1950s' (Keating, cited in INDECS 1990: 197).

The outcome of these fixations is clearly demonstrated in the comparative data presented in Figures 2.22, 2.23 and 2.24. All show average data for the six years to 1996 and represent government receipts, public debt and government expenditure as a percentage of GDP. The broad picture is one of a government, beholden to the propositions of neo-liberal supply side economics, faced with a dramatic incapacity to pursue alternative economic strategies. Australia has the lowest levels of government receipts through taxation, commercial activity or asset sales of any of the major OECD countries other than

Figure 2.22: Government Receipts as Percentage of GDP, 1991–1996 Average

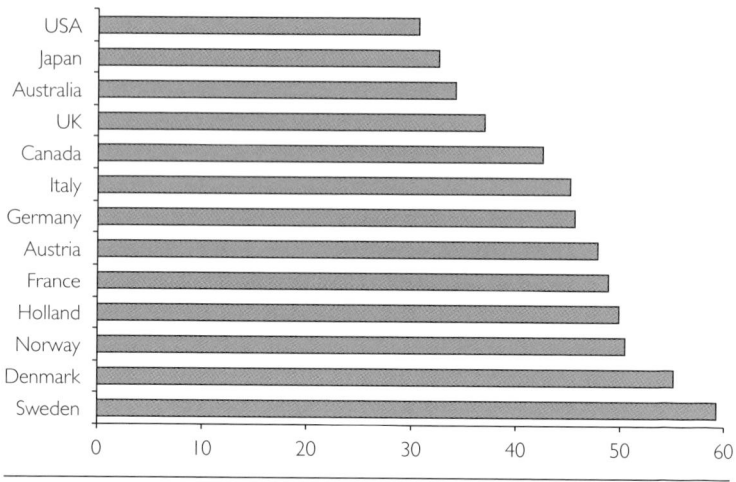

Country	%
USA	~30
Japan	~32
Australia	~34
UK	~37
Canada	~42
Italy	~45
Germany	~46
Austria	~48
France	~49
Holland	~50
Norway	~51
Denmark	~55
Sweden	~59

Source: OECD (1997a)

Figure 2.23: Gross Public Debt as Percentage of GDP in OECD Countries, 1991–1996 Average

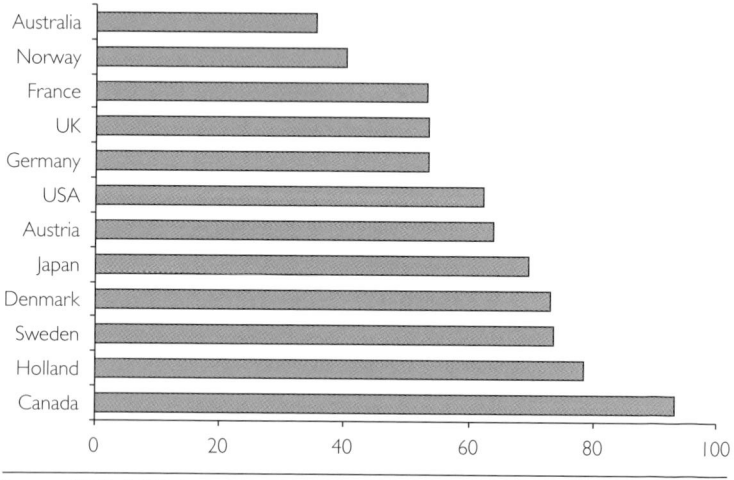

Country	%
Australia	~35
Norway	~42
France	~50
UK	~53
Germany	~54
USA	~62
Austria	~64
Japan	~68
Denmark	~72
Sweden	~73
Holland	~78
Canada	~92

Source: OECD (1997a)

the United States. Government spending could still be effected through budget deficits but neither has this been the chosen course of action. Indeed, Australia's gross public debt is

Figure 2.24: Government Outlays as Percentage of GDP in OECD Countries, 1991–1996 Average

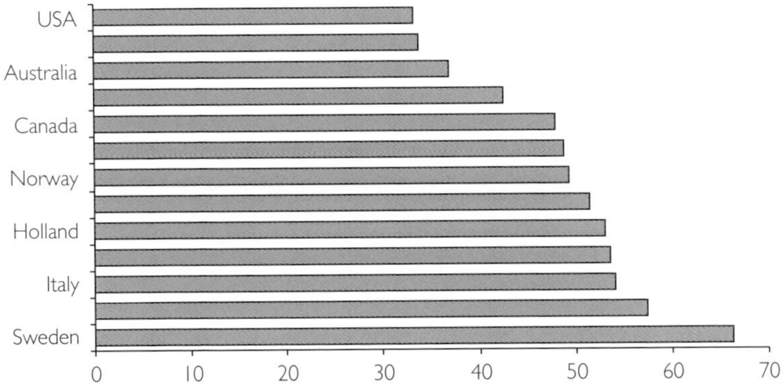

Source: OECD (1997a)

significantly below every other country studied (if net public debt is considered, only Japan falls below Australia). Australia's almost obsessive focus on deficits is highlighted by the comparative perspective. The dilemma faced by future, more activist governments in Australia concerns the electorally unpalatable requirement to substantially raise taxes in order to bring the public sector up to OECD standards.

A more interventionist approach to policy became even less likely when the political momentum shifted away from Labor. However, as we have illustrated, the contemporary policy settings have been established without regard to Australia's comparative standing among the advanced nations. A combination of historical abstentionism and contemporary economic rationalism has placed Australia's future as an advanced industrial economy in some jeopardy. In almost all areas of public activity that might indicate a degree of political will to influence the direction of the nation's social and economic future, there is inaction and underperformance. Expenditure by the nation on training and on active labour market programmes designed to assist the unemployed into new employment, as evidenced in Figure 2.25, scarcely provides grounds for optimism about the future of skilled employment (while passive expenditure on unemployment benefits stands at comparatively high levels). Total expenditure on research and development, shown in Figure 2.26, adds to the evidence that notions of the 'clever country' are seriously misplaced. All this is reflected in the collapse of manufacturing as a

Figure 2.25: Labour Market Programmes as Percentage of GDP in OECD Countries, 1995–1996

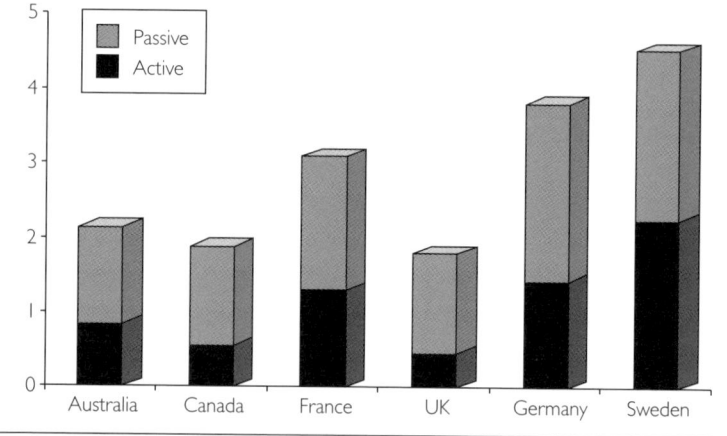

Source: OECD (1997c)

Figure 2.26: Research and Development Expenditure as Percentage of GDP in OECD Countries, 1988

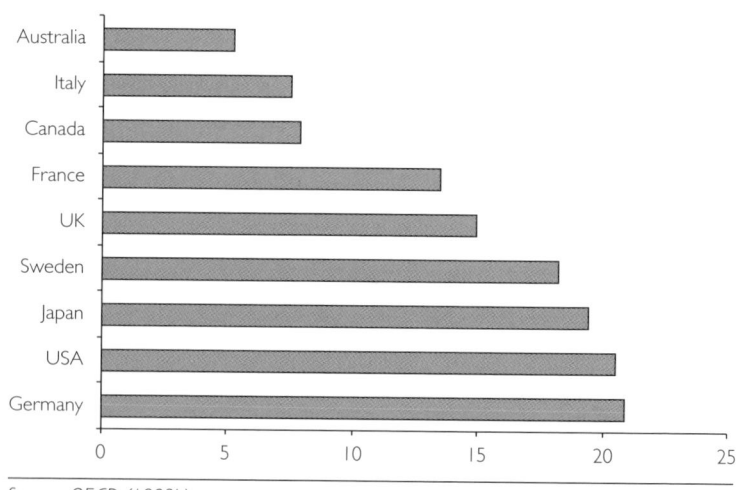

Source: OECD (1993b)

source of economic sustenance and export income (Figure 2.27) or of employment prospects (Figure 2.28) for those unprepared to place their faith in economic recovery through tourism and recreation development.

Figure 2.27: Value Added in Manufacturing as Percentage of GDP in OECD Countries, 1960–1994 Average

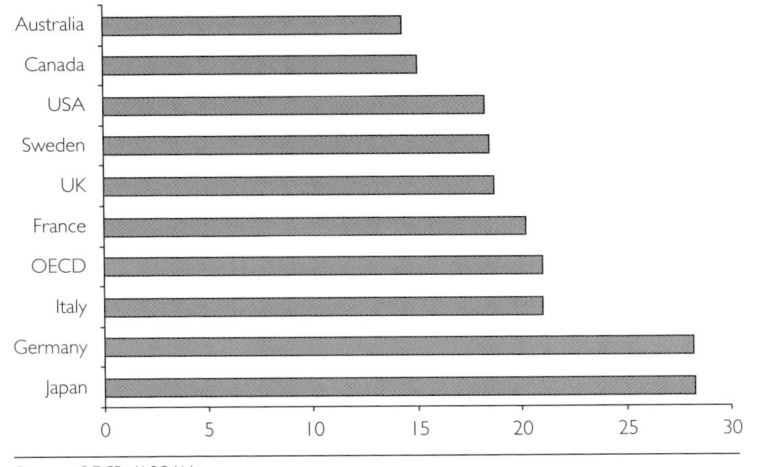

Country	%
Australia	~14
Canada	~15
USA	~18
Sweden	~18
UK	~18.5
France	~20
OECD	~21
Italy	~21
Germany	~28
Japan	~28

Source: OECD (1996b)

Figure 2.28: Manufacturing Employment as Percentage of Labour Force in OECD Countries, 1974–1994 Average

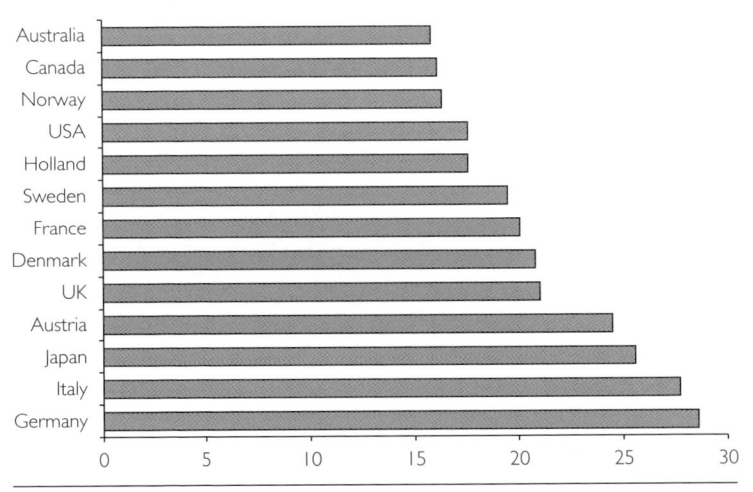

Country	%
Australia	~16
Canada	~16
Norway	~16
USA	~17
Holland	~17
Sweden	~19
France	~20
Denmark	~21
UK	~21
Austria	~24
Japan	~25
Italy	~27
Germany	~28

Source: OECD (1996c)

The general picture painted in this chapter is of a series of economic policy approaches to unemployment that have patently failed to pay heed to the comparatively underdeveloped state of Australia's machinery of public policy and the limited economic and social infrastructure that it has produced. That the current policy regime is likely to exacerbate these problems is clear from the comparative perspective we have portrayed. But our examination of the perfidiousness of current policies and the analyses on which they are based does not end with these claims. In the material which follows we will demonstrate that much of the analysis that underlies Australia's present policies is not supported by a careful study of the factors associated with unemployment in the major industrial economies. However, the same analysis reveals that there are strategic options that illuminate the path to full employment. These are the issues which provide the focus for the remainder of this book.

Chapter 3
Economic limits

The current recession began in 1974. The last chapter demonstrated this primarily with respect to Australia, but the economic downturn has affected all the OECD countries. In 1974 industrial production slumped and unemployment began to increase in all these advanced capitalist nations. Figure 2.5 shows unemployment rates in the OECD and seven specific countries since the 1970s. Although unemployment has increased significantly on two further occasions in the past quarter-century, the confluence of circumstances from 1974 marks that year as the end of the long boom and the beginning of recession. Since then, unemployment in the OECD countries has averaged 6.7 per cent, and the figure is still increasing with a projected average of about 8 per cent for the rest of the century. National rates have ranged widely, from below 1 per cent (Switzerland) to over 10 per cent (Belgium) for the 1974–97 period, with higher rates in the 1990s remaining widespread, particularly in Europe. Unemployment above 10 per cent is projected for Germany, Italy, France, Belgium, Finland, Greece and Spain; with many other wealthy countries (the United Kingdom, Canada, Sweden, Australia and New Zealand) experiencing unemployment close to that level in the 1990s. In addition, most of the formerly low-unemployment countries (Austria, Norway and Switzerland) have experienced or are expected to experience mass unemployment (above 4 per cent) before the turn of the century (OECD 1996a: A24, 1997a: A24). The widespread unemployment over the past quarter-century illustrates the international nature of the phenomenon, but divergences between countries illustrate, equally emphatically, that nationally specific conditions, including political responses to economic downturn, influence outcomes, sometimes favourably, sometimes for the worse. Figure 2.5 illustrates the rise and divergence of unemployment in the major economies during this long recession.

No economy is an economic phenomenon alone. Market conditions are not the sole determinants of economic outcomes. Understanding the economy, whether in its normal or abnormal mode, therefore depends upon understanding the non-economic aspects of economic activity. Economic activity has always been constituted by non-economic forces as well as by decisions made according to a purely market logic. Social, political, legal and institutional conditions always underwrite individual and corporate economic behaviour and hence nations' economic outcomes. Historically, the very structure of capitalist economies has depended on the prior implantation, through essentially political processes, of what are often referred to as market relations of production, the defining features of capitalism. Political processes have always been required to allow market principles to govern the conduct of economic activity. But these market modes of regulation have never governed all, or even an unchanging proportion of, economic decisions (Jessop 1997). Further, in times of economic dislocation, the extent to which non-economic considerations, including political responses to recession and societal conditions intended to overrule economic imperatives, infringe upon market prerogatives has tended to increase. Extrapolated, such changes would be expected to eventually transform what previously appeared to be established relations between the political system and the market, between the state and the economy.

The discipline of the market is neither natural, nor timeless, nor inevitable. The significance of such non-economic conditions of economic activity has been recognized in most intellectual traditions, from Adam Smith through the contributions of Marx, Keynes, Schumpeter and Polanyi to contemporary post-Keynesian, institutionalist, radical and neo-Marxist scholarship. In various ways, analysis of the economy derived from these perspectives on the long-term developmental tendencies of capitalist economies suggests, in advance of significant empirical substantiation, that economic maturity is likely to be accompanied by social, legal or political changes that significantly alter the decision-making environment. In other words, well-developed capitalist economies increasingly require an institutional framework that subverts the integrity of the market mode of regulation. A corollary of such suggestions is that economic performance will tend to be less volatile (that is, its capacity to reproduce itself is more 'regularized') if effective institutional mechanisms for deliberated, rather than atomated, economic decisions are constructed. Poor economic performance will tend to result, to the extent that principled decision-making has not been institutionalized. Extra-market criteria tend to become more necessary and less illegitimate. Symptoms of economic recession, such as unemployment, can therefore be seen to be as much the effect of political and policy failure as the inevitable consequence of uncontrolled economic conditions, particularly where the state capacities to control unemployment remain underdeveloped. Before discussing the propensity of state capacity through policy and politics to influence economic outcomes (chapters 4 and 5), however, it is necessary to examine further the purely economic dimensions of economic crisis.

Unemployment as an indicator of recession

Though unemployment is never a purely economic phenomenon, the effects of broad economic conditions on unemployment need to be understood both generally and on a nation-by-nation basis. The recession since 1974 was initially defined in terms of the unusual and unexpected concurrence of unemployment and inflation in about half the OECD countries, disrupting a series of presumptions concerning an irremediable trade-off between the two. But throughout the OECD area, the rate of growth of GDP was lower after 1974 than had been experienced in the post-1945 period—2.8 per cent for 1974– 99) compared with 5 per cent for 1950–73 (Maddison 1991:

50; OECD 1992b: 175, 1997a: A4). In addition, manufacturing production contributed less to both the economy and total employment. Perhaps commensurately, the openness of national economies to international movements of commodities (including partly manufactured commodities) and capital has also increased.

Consequently, the long recession can be characterized as:

- the secular end of the age of growth;
- the outcome of an altered balance of institutional power (between labour and capital) that allowed trade unions to claim and receive wage rises despite increasing unemployment;
- the period of sectoral change (away from manufacturing industry) in advanced capitalist economies;
- a new era of globalized economic activity which adversely affects some of the less flexible or innovative centres of activity;
- the inevitable indicator that forces of competition and 'creative destruction' are once again revolutionizing the location, structure and productive content of market economies, as they always have;
- a manifestation of policy failure or institutional failure, that is, the lack of competency that develops when institutional capacities lag behind the altered requirements of the economic conditions they are meant to facilitate and regulate; or
- the more or less deliberate and voluntary breakdown of national and international 'settlements' in the postwar era which had committed both governments and multinational organizations to 'managed' development, high standards of living and employment and social cohesion despite their costs and inflexibilities.

Unemployment then becomes the primary, the most visible and the most politically sensitive (if academically contested) indicator of recession. Unemployment is both a manifestation and a non-arbitrary indicator of recession because no other possible national indicator—industrial production, the rate of growth, inflation, manufacturing employment, competitiveness, or productivity—so unambiguously delineates a macroeconomic failure and a policy problem. This delineation does not, of course, represent a full specification of the phenomenon—recession—with which we are concerned.

Recession is always the result of structural change in industry, of a shift from one pattern of productive activity to another, in so far as new employment-generating activities do not emerge immediately or sufficiently or in the required locations for full employment. The extent of the structural shifts during the recession is indicated by the collapse in manufacturing's contribution to the total economy from 27 per cent of value added to 20 per cent (OECD 1996b: 67), the decline in industrial employment in the OECD countries from 36 per cent to under 30 per cent of the total, and the associated increase from 53 per cent to 65 per cent in service employment's share of total employment (OECD 1994b) in the two decades after 1974. Endogenously produced fluctuations in capitalist development constitute the process championed by such theorists of capitalism as Adam Smith and Joseph Schumpeter, and are acknowledged as the basis of capitalism's dynamism even by critics such as Karl Marx. John Maynard Keynes' most important contributions to the understanding of capitalism accept, too, that it is the absence of automatic mechanisms of industrial regeneration, the chronic tendency in the market system for periods of boom to be followed by periods of underinvestment, which causes and prolongs recession.

Economic downturn is, in other respects, an effective means of economic rationalization, but we have not yet developed the institutional or policy-implementation acumen to eliminate its unfortunate effects. In some places we have not tried. In the more liberal polities, notably the English-speaking countries, an anti-interventionist policy process has evolved with sedulously developed public incapacity to moderate the market determination of economic, structural or industrial change. Hence, the economic determinants of unemployment derive from the founding rationale for market economies; recession has been regarded as a normal process of economic adjustment. Furthermore, because industries neither emerge nor disappear quickly, it is a process which must be reckoned at least in years, more probably decades. Advocates and critics of capitalism agree that structural change is achieved through crisis-riven development, a process that rewards competitive success but which denies to the policy process any legitimate countervailing capacity to maintain useful, though non-competitive, economic activity.

What less orthodox theorists have added to the Smithian and Schumpeterian formulations is a series of suggestions that sustained good economic performance in capitalist economies is possible, provided some of the specifically capitalist elements are subordinated to more substantive consideration.

To some extent, reduced economic growth, the relocation of economic activity, the rise and decline of industries and even altered power and institutional conditions are constituent elements of the same phenomenon. Consequently, what needs to be examined is the extent to which these different aspects of recession necessarily or independently result in unemployment. Because the policy process is normally ill-adapted to a democratic or politicized deliberation of how to generate new economic activity to replace the old, it remains possible to base policy processes on mistaken understandings of the links between the various factors. That is, before investigating whether policy is able to control such economic outcomes as unemployment within a nation, it is necessary to establish as precisely as possible the relationship between unemployment and the economics of the recession. This is the concern of this chapter.

Does economic growth reduce unemployment?

Both mainstream and maverick traditions of political economy recognize the role of economic growth in national economic development. Expanding output implies increasing standards of living, although cognizance ought to be taken of levels of inequality, changes in the quality of employment, income security and continuity, the extent to which services are provided independently of the cash nexus and the general physical and social environment. Yet growth has not stopped during the recession. After 1974, annual economic growth slowed in the OECD countries from around 4 per cent (in the late 1960s and early 1970s) to about 2.5 per cent (for the twenty years after 1974). In the 1990s, the rate has fallen still further, to 2.2 per cent. Throughout the recession, therefore, despite the steadily increasing numbers of people unable to find employment, nations have been becoming wealthier, not poorer. This is the case even if per capita GDP growth is used as the basis of calculation. Per capita GDP increased on average throughout the OECD from the mid-1970s to early 1990s by 1.9 per cent per year. If we revise our understanding of growth, it must include an evaluation of the relationship between growth, employment and unemployment.

Table 3.1 indicates that economic growth has not been necessary for either employment growth or low levels of unemployment in the OECD nations. Not only is jobless growth possible, but so, too, is full employment without growth. The conjunction of economic growth and rising mass unemployment has been one of the central paradoxes of the recession (Therborn 1986). We can recognize, too, a paradox of equal importance: some countries have achieved low rates of unemployment without high levels of GDP growth. Even for countries with successful growth records additional factors seem to be involved in converting growth into good overall economic performance.

Expansion of industrial production, employment levels and GDP in the OECD has been below the level necessary to secure full employment for the entire period. Activity has slumped at three distinct points in the past twenty years—1974–75, 1980–82 and 1990–91—thus exacerbating an existing problem or wiping out previous improvements. However, understanding the nature of the recession requires an understanding of the level of economic activity, not just its rate of change from one

Table 3.1: Unemployment, Employment and Growth, 1974–1997

	Unemployment annual average (%) (1974–1997)	Employment increase (1974–1993)	Growth[a] annual average (%) (1974–1992)
Switzerland	1.4	1.04	1.3
Japan	2.4	1.23	3.8
Norway	3.3	1.19	3.8
Sweden	3.5	1.02	1.5
Austria	3.8	1.12	2.5
Germany	6.5	1.06	2.2
USA	6.7	1.36	2.2
Netherlands	7.1	1.39	2.2
Australia	7.4	1.30	2.7
Finland	7.7	0.91	2.2
UK	8.0	1.05	1.6
Denmark	8.6	1.08	1.8
France	8.6	1.03	2.3
Canada	8.7	1.34	2.9
Italy	8.9	1.02	2.7
Belgium	10.3	1.00	2.2
OECD average	6.7	1.20	2.5

a   For the 1990s, OECD growth projections were lower for all countries except Germany and the United Kingdom. The (averaged annual) percentages are as follows: Switzerland 0.7, Norway 2.5, Japan 2.1, Sweden -0.2, Austria 2, Finland -1.8, Germany 2.3, Australia 1.9, the United States 2, France 1.3, Denmark 1.6, the Netherlands 1.6, the United Kingdom 2, Italy 1.4, Canada 1.5, Belgium 1.7. The OECD average is 1.8 per cent (OECD 1993a: 126).

On a per capita basis, GDP growth rates (averaged percentages for 1974–91) were: Japan 3.6, Norway 2.8, Austria 2.3, Luxembourg 2.3, Germany 2.2, Italy 2, Belgium 2, Finland 2, France 1.9, Denmark 1.9, the United Kingdom 1.7, Canada 1.5, the United States 1.4, the Netherlands 1.3, Sweden 1.3, Australia 1.2, Switzerland 0.9. The OECD average for the period was 1.9 per cent. In the 1990s (1990–94), per capita growth has averaged 1 per cent (per year) in the OECD as a whole and in the 16 countries (OECD 1996b: 50).
Sources: OECD (1996a: A24, A25, Tables A1, A21 & A22; 1995: 26–7, Table 4.0)

period to the next. Small variations in the level of economic activity, whether upwards or downwards, matter much less when the level of development (or income) is high than when it is low. Countries with already high levels of economic activity do not need high rates of economic growth to maintain low levels of unemployment. Nations such as Australia, with comparatively low levels of resource utilization, may not dent unemployment even with high rates of growth. In other words, periodic increases in the level of activity and income are an inadequate indicator of whether the existing level is sufficient. The point to be made is not that growth is unnecessary, just that its presence does not signify an absence of economic problems.

It is little remarked, but not at all extraordinary, that Australia is one of a number of OECD countries where high rates of economic growth for a long period have not mitigated the recession. High levels of both economic growth and employment growth are compatible with high unemployment. Canada is another high-growth nation with bad performance; Switzerland is the country with the lowest economic growth of all over the past twenty years, but also the highest per capita GDP and the lowest unemployment in the OECD. Indeed, Switzerland recorded the single lowest growth rate, of –6.7 per cent in 1975.

Table 3.1 shows that all nations actually averaged positive GDP growth after 1974. Australia is in a group which averaged better than the OECD mean of 2.5 per cent, the others being Japan, Norway, Finland, Italy, the United States and Canada. Of these, only Japan and Norway have recorded consistently low levels of unemployment; Canada and Italy have been among the worst three performers within the rich nations.

A more detailed analysis of the relationship between economic growth and unemployment is presented in Table 3.2. This allows greater precision when examining what kinds of interaction exist between the two variables. The cross-tabulation is compiled by 'pooling' the unemployment and economic growth data for sixteen OECD countries over (normally) nineteen years (1974–92), producing (normally) 304 readings, or cases, to be categorized for analysis. A similar technique is deployed in many of the tables in this chapter and chapter 4.

For Table 3.2, the readings for each variable (yearly data on growth rates and unemployment rates for each country) have been clustered and categorized as low, medium or high. Using this method of analysis, individual country effects that could

Table 3.2: Economic Growth and Unemployment in 16 OECD Countries, since 1974

	Economic Growth			
	Low (%)	Medium (%)	High (%)	Total (%)
Low unemployment	27.1	22.7	30.8	27.3
Medium unemployment	35.4	33.6	35.6	34.9
High unemployment	37.5	43.7	33.6	37.8
Number of cases	48	110	146	304

skew the results (if, for example, conclusions were reached solely by recourse to the averaged data presented in Table 3.1) are avoided. All cases are treated equally and indiscriminately. Negative to zero growth has been characterized as 'low' growth, zero to 2.5 per cent (the OECD average) as 'medium' growth, and above 2.5 per cent as 'high' growth. According to this scheme, Australia experienced 'high' growth for eight of the fifteen years under consideration. The unemployment readings here, and throughout, have been sorted into the following categories: 'low' 0–3 per cent; 'medium' is 3.1–7 per cent, and 'high' is 7.1–10 per cent (see Table 3.1).

The results reported in Table 3.2 reinforce the conclusions noted above. Of all the cases of low economic growth, 27.1 per cent also recorded low unemployment while a somewhat higher proportion (37.5 per cent) had high unemployment. The inference to be drawn from this observation is that low economic growth is only slightly less likely to be associated with low as with high rates of unemployment. In other words, there is no strong relationship between economic growth and unemployment. To support this generalization it is necessary to refer to the other columns. Only within the category of medium economic growth is there a significant difference between the proportion of cases in the different unemployment categories. But from one growth category to the next, no clear relationship emerges: the specific categories of unemployment have been associated with all levels of economic growth. The conventional expectation would have been that most readings should fall along the low–high and medium–medium diagonal. Low growth could have been expected to produce high unemployment, and high growth to have produced low unemployment, much more often than has in fact been observed. The important conclusion is that there is now no reason to expect that economic growth will necessarily solve our problems, nor to think that the absence of economic growth necessarily constitutes a problem. There has been no stable, predictable or causal relationship between unemployment and economic growth.

The lesson for public policy is that higher economic growth, on its own, is insufficient to guarantee lower unemployment. Full employment ought not to be displaced as an explicit policy goal by other, less direct indicators of economic performance and living standards. The crucial considerations for policy must therefore be the type of economic activity, not just its rate of increase. Instead of framing policy discussion in terms of the 'level of economic growth needed to reduce unemployment', which occurred during deliberation over the Australian government's 1994 employment White Paper, it would be more useful to directly address the problem of how to increase employment at a rate sufficient to lower unemployment. Moreover, because much recent job growth has resulted from increases in part-time work exceeding aggregate declines in the amount of full-time employment, it is necessary to enquire into the quality of jobs that are being created.

From this analysis, it is possible to derive a broader appreciation of the nature of the economy. Investment is more important than either economic growth or employment growth because it produces new (or renewed) activity. The urgency of such lessons is amplified by the recent official assessments that if the economy were to grow at somewhat more than 4 per cent over the next few years, unemployment could be brought under control. But even if these growth ambitions were achieved, remembering that average GDP growth rates for the past quarter-century have been only 3.8 per cent (Japan), 2.7 per cent (Australia) and 2.5 per cent (OECD), there is no basis for optimism about unemployment unless other measures are adopted as well. High growth, even if sustained, would not be tantamount to economic 'recovery'. Given the irremediably structural nature of recession noted earlier, expansion of productive capacities would be a more hopeful, if institutionally more difficult, strategy to adopt than waiting for growth/recovery. It is always necessary to ensure that the generation of new industrial and economic activity matches the displacement of older activity and therefore to ensure that competitiveness is not the sole criterion for the dismantling of existing activities.

The Australian government's 1994 White Paper *Working Nation: policies and programs* made some unwarranted assertions about the effects of growth on employment by ostentatiously proclaiming: 'The government is determined to reduce unemployment . . . Economic growth is the best way . . . to make inroads into unemployment' (1994: 1). 'The ambition to create a dynamic social democracy' was always, however, a rhetorical flourish wholly incompatible with the government's abandonment of the full employment goal and with the empirical relationships we have detected.

To summarize, macroeconomic growth does not guarantee good economic outcomes. Growth rates themselves are an outcome of policies which affect the level of economic activity sometimes favourably, sometimes detrimentally. The current emphasis on economic growth and its relationship with unemployment needs to be more nuanced. The level (and therefore the content) of economic activity is more important than its annual augmentation. In any period of economic downturn, it is necessary to discover both new economic activities and the means by which they may be developed. No solutions to the problems of industrial restructuring are likely to be unproblematic or conflict-free. This is partly because of failures or weaknesses in the policy processes and partly because of intellectual and analytical failures: we simply do not understand all that needs to be known about recession or appropriate anti-recessionary strategies. Popular rhetoric concerning the need for wealth creation is not being matched by policies which will ensure it; instead, economic growth is proceeding, as it always has, with a permanent residue of unused capacity, notably unemployment. Employment growth remains too low, as it always is in recession, to reduce unemployment. And the political system seems content to accept mass unemployment (5 per cent) as its most achievable ambition. This is neither the epitome of economic efficiency nor the match of other countries' achievements (Sweden, Norway, Austria, Luxembourg, Japan and Switzerland) in the past quarter-century. Although unemployment cannot be eliminated directly or immediately by political or administrative fiat, the strategies being envisaged at the moment depart greatly from what would be required for economic and social strength. They are also an explicit violation of the policies that would be required for cohesion in communities or a dynamic social democracy.

Does inflation affect unemployment?

As noted earlier, the current recession has been characterized, until the 1990s at least, not only by structurally induced unemployment but also by the seemingly paradoxical phenomenon of simultaneous unemployment and inflation.

Figure 3.1 groups seventeen OECD countries according to their combination of unemployment and inflation for the period 1974–90. All possible combinations of high and low unemployment and inflation have been experienced during the recession. As indicated, the largest group of countries experienced unemployment and inflation together after 1974. Some experienced little of either; there are two groups of countries where it may be claimed that the policy process prioritized control of one rather than the other, thus providing some reason to argue for the existence of a trade-off between them. Inflation rates ranged from 3.5 per cent (in Germany) to 12.8 per cent (Italy) for the 1974–90 period (unweighted average of yearly

Figure 3.1: Unemployment and Inflation in OECD Countries, 1974–1990

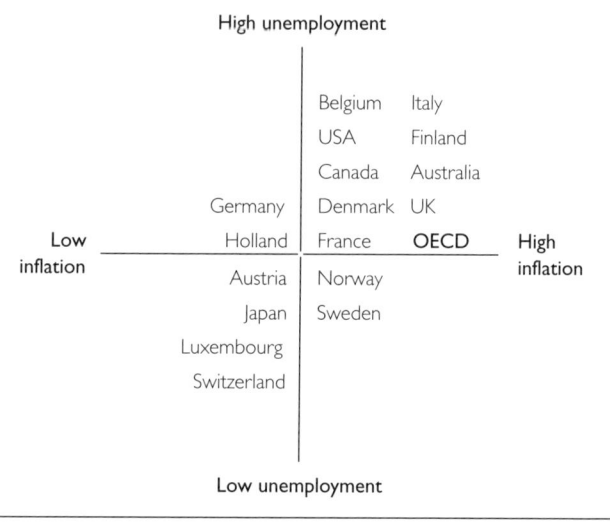

```
                        High unemployment
                              │
                        Belgium    Italy
                        USA        Finland
                        Canada     Australia
              Germany   Denmark    UK
   Low        Holland   France     OECD        High
 inflation ───────────────────────────────── inflation
              Austria   Norway
              Japan     Sweden
              Luxembourg
              Switzerland
                              │
                        Low unemployment
```

Source: Calculations from OECD (1993a: 140, Table A15)

rates). The OECD average has ranged from 3 per cent to 13.7 per cent with individual yearly figures from zero to over 20 per cent in particular countries. The unweighted average percentage rate of increase in consumer prices for the period 1974–90 for each country was: Germany 3.5; Switzerland 3.7; Netherlands 4.4; Austria 4.7; Japan 5.2; Luxembourg 5.6; Belgium 6.0; United States 6.6; Canada 7.4; Denmark 8; Norway 8.2; France 8.3; Sweden 8.7; Finland 9.2; Australia 9.7; United Kingdom 10.5; Italy 12.8. The OECD average was 7.8 per cent.

There are two broad views of the cause of inflation. The first, associated mainly with monetarist doctrine, considers inflation to be a monetary phenomenon—the principal reason for rising prices is an excess of money, creating tendencies for prices to rise faster than the productive capacity of the economy. The general policy lesson from this account is that the growth of the money supply ought to be constrained by the rate of growth of output, assumed to be fixed in the short term. The second view, associated with Keynesian and post-Keynesian analyses, has pointed to institutional and historical factors leading to the rise of inflation after 1974. The first view affirms the liberal biases in economic management, while the second develops post-liberal capacities; the orthodox strand favours deflation of the economy, while the policy response considered appropriate by the post-Keynesians is incomes policy, to institutionally control the conflicts over income distribution that underlie the wage–price spiral.

The first concept produced a policy milieu, the monetarist experiment, which was such a complete and explicit renunciation of the intellectual and policy presumptions of economic management in the postwar mixed economy, that it itself has helped to characterize the post-1974 recession. In monetarist theory, inflation of the currency derives not from wage and price increases but from too much money chasing too few goods. If the supply of money exceeds that warranted by the level of output, the rate of increase in, or perhaps even the total amount of, the money supply needs to be reduced. With this doctrine, the predominant focus of attention devolves fairly readily to the contribution of government spending to the total, although logically any spending would be equally culpable. Hence monetarist responses to inflation led to austerity policies and the exacerbation of recession, and attempts to cut back government spending had downward multiplier effects throughout the economy. Perversely, policy often favours deflation of the economy rather than expansion of production.

The alternative institutional and sociological explanation of the coincidence of inflation in recession, elements that had previously been thought to be mutually incompatible, is based on post-Keynesian economic analysis and its derivatives. Unfortunately, the unorthodox nature of these diagnoses prevented their conclusions from systematically permeating either the received wisdom or the policy process. Powerful explanations of the concurrence of unemployment and inflation since the mid-1970s derive from observations that the institutional power of the participants in wage bargaining had increased beyond that which obtained in the 1930s. This allowed trade unions to bargain successfully for wage increases despite widespread unemployment and for corporations to increase prices commensurately despite falling sales and revenues. Such accounts are supported by parallel observations of the efficacy of macro-level incomes policies in countries where they emerged as pragmatic or ad hoc responses to inflation in recession, but they have been inadequately incorporated into consolidated understandings of the recession. As a result, many governments in the 1970s and 1980s coerced bargaining restraint and other concessions from union movements, despite scepticism from the latter concerning the ability of governments, even labour or social democratic governments, to deliver the quid pro quo required to compensate for reduced money wages.

The monetarist response to inflation presumed that it was an economic phenomenon alone. It justified alternative policies to the integration of economic and social policies, a difficult task for both technical and ideological reasons. But there was another orthodox response, derived from 'bastard Keynesian' rather than monetarist theories, which produced very similar policy priorities to those of monetarism. In this view of the distinctiveness of the recession after 1974, a trade-off between unemployment and inflation was reinvoked. Prognoses about the relationship between unemployment and inflation based on the Phillips Curve, originally drawn as a descriptive representation of the relationship for one country in one particular period (the United Kingdom, 1861–1957) but later extrapolated as a timeless and contextless general inverse relationship, were, of course, incompatible with the observation that, in about half the OECD countries, unemployment and inflation had been increasing together. Despite the evidence, dogmatic adherence to the inevitability of a trade-off was retained by postulating that the inverse relationship did in fact still exist—but at higher levels of both variables. This reinterpretation absolved policy-makers from any obligation to see that unemployment and inflation were separate phenomena with separate causes and separate (policy) solutions. As long as unemployment could be seen as self-correcting (provided other distortions were first removed), it did not need to be addressed directly. Inflation could then be prioritized as the policy problem. We now know that the effect of the 'fight inflation first' strategy was to discount the political and social importance of increases in unemployment, while crude and contradictory austerity measures were adopted in the attempt to reduce inflation.

The theoretical and empirical case against monetarist doctrine, from post-Keynesian and institutionalist perspectives, seems never to have been acknowledged in mainstream economics. The subsequent insouciance of the policy process to the extra-economic dimensions of inflation is something that must now be reckoned as integral to the problems of economic management in liberal polities. The monetarists and the political practitioners who followed their advice erred first in assuming that inflation could only be of one type, a monetary phenomenon alone. All inflation was ascribed to 'demand–pull' or boom conditions. The Keynesian view, on the other hand, recognized the sociological and organizational underpinnings of 'cost–push' inflation. The latter—inflation in recession—was acknowledged as a product of conflict over the distribution of a declining income, to be countered by a combination of anti-recessionary policy and incomes policy. A return to periods of expanding output would reduce the bitterness of the distributive conflicts which, in the context of stagnating growth and no institutional management of income distribution, could take only inflationary form. Because the recession was accompanied by falling output, excess capacity, unemployment, widening inequalities and an apparently increasing gap between actual and potential standards of living, it is not reasonable to ascribe inflation after 1974 to 'too much money'. This would be a boom phenomenon. Monetarists, by recognizing only the inflation typical of a situation where production cannot be increased, fundamentally misunderstood the nature of contemporary inflation and thus the most appropriate policy responses. Instead of developing policies to expand the level of economic activity and to nurture democratic input into the determination of economic activity, monetarist policy had the opposite effect.

The explicit focus of monetarist policy on monetary aggregates like the money supply and, hence, on monetary policy (the use of interest rate changes) as a regulator of economic activity weakened the impact of public criteria and economic capacities generally. National economic and industrial restructuring seems to be an implicit intention of monetarist doctrine, and it is a restructuring which accords as little role as possible to consideration of which industries ought to replace those that are in decline. Market-induced transformation of the industrial and economic patterns of the past leaves national economies without viable or sustainable economic activity, but this is not regarded as a problem for policy.

Formal application of the monetarist experiment ended in the Anglo-Saxon countries fairly quickly in the 1980s as it became apparent that monetary targets were both ineffective and damaging. Although inflation was reduced in the United Kingdom from an average of 14.7 per cent (from 1974 to 1982) to 5.5 per cent (for the 1983–92 period), unemployment remained high throughout the 1980s and into the 1990s. In Australia, the equivalent reduction was from 11.4 per cent for the decade after 1974 to 5.5 per cent for the decade after 1983, when wage fixation procedures changed dramatically. Reductions in government spending in the United Kingdom (from well above to somewhat below the OECD average) in the first Thatcher decade were not accompanied by reductions in unemployment, disproving the central monetarist hypothesis. In Australia, inflation was high (almost 10 per cent) throughout the recession until the 1990s despite the low levels of government spending and an increasing gap between government outlays in Australia and the OECD total. The simultaneity of unemployment and inflation in the 1970s and 1980s refutes the hypothesis of a necessary trade-off between unemployment and inflation, even in its 'expectations augmented' form. Although institutionalized bargaining and institutionalized responses to past cost and price increases certainly did reflect 'expectations' of continuing inflation, this did not confirm the proposition that high levels of unemployment would constrain (inflationary) wage demands nor that low unemployment would facilitate wage demands. Low unemployment leads to high inflation only if there is no ancillary incomes policy to institutionally control the conflict over income distribution; high unemployment constrains wage increases only if the bargaining power of trade unions has been significantly weakened. Inflation during recession has causes unrelated to the level of unemployment. Unemployment is also an independent phenomenon. For example, as shown in Figure 3.1, two low-unemployment countries, Sweden and Norway, had inflation rates above the OECD average; the Netherlands, which has had comparatively high unemployment, achieved the third-lowest inflation rate (1974–90); in Japan and Switzerland both unemployment and inflation have been controlled.

Table 3.3 presents the relationship between inflation and unemployment data for sixteen OECD countries for the 1974–92 period. As before, there are 304 readings to be analysed. The country data on inflation has been divided into three categories: 'low' (less than 3 per cent), 'medium' (3–7 per cent) and 'high' (above 7 per cent).

The table indicates that there is no systematic relationship between unemployment and inflation. Among the low-inflation cases, almost 32 per cent experienced low unemployment, but a further 43 per cent experienced high unemployment. Hence, low inflation does not necessarily lead to improved economic performance. It is true that when medium (that is, high enough

Table 3.3: Inflation and Unemployment in 16 OECD Countries, since 1974

	Inflation			
	Low (%)	Medium (%)	High (%)	Total (%)
Low unemployment	31.5	22.9	29.7	27.3
Medium unemployment	25.9	32.0	41.4	34.9
High unemployment	42.6	45.1	28.9	37.8
Number of cases	54	122	128	304

to be annoying) levels of inflation were experienced, unemployment was more likely to be high than low. However, examination of the high-inflation category shows that low levels of unemployment are just as likely (almost 30 per cent) as high. Inflation and unemployment therefore have independent causes and different policy solutions. In other words, increased unemployment is not a means of reducing inflation and low inflation is not necessary to achieve lower rates of unemployment.

Nonetheless, many components of the orthodox prescriptions of policy abrogation have remained. Although continuing unemployment and industrial decline indicate that there is unutilized capacity, claims persist that 'overheating' occurs in most economies. It is now claimed that supply bottlenecks and skill shortages in certain industries occur at higher levels of unemployment than in the 1930s, thereby excusing persistent unemployment and diverting the policy process from what was once universally accepted as its responsibility to ensure full employment. Clearly, whenever production is unable to keep up with demand, the sensible policy solution would be to expand production rather than to reduce demand through deflationary or austerity policies, especially when the latter are implemented indiscriminately through monetary policy. Keynesian and institutionalist commentators have protested through the past twenty years that monetary policy almost always damages productive capacities because, as a policy tool, it works in only one direction—to depress activity. It worsens the conditions it is ostensibly committed to alleviate, as John Kenneth Galbraith has observed:

> Monetary policy can pull economic activity down; it cannot so assuredly shove it up . . . The financial community finds explicit satisfaction in an active central-bank policy. It sets high store by preventing inflation, and in the larger culture of contentment inflation is more to be feared, on balance, than unemployment. It has an especially strong commitment to interest rates that more than compensate for the rate of inflation, and it also seeks to have the central bank move strongly against

inflation—more strongly than against recession . . . Central-bank policy . . . strongly favours the rentier class, a group that is both affluent and vocal (1992: 91–2).

Other commentators have also made the point that despite the excess capacity of the 1980s, manufacturing now suffers from underinvestment: 'The problem today is that depressing demand is more effective in reducing capacity than expanding demand is in increasing it' (Grieve Smith 1996: 15).

Whereas the monetarist experiment had failed in its own terms, because low inflation has been accompanied by continuing unemployment, the conventional bastard Keynesian view has contorted itself to accommodate its preferred policy response (deflation) to the reality of inflation in recession. Orthodoxy still insists that too much activity is the cause of continuing (or potential) inflation. That is, there remains pressure for wage increases despite high levels of unemployment. The moderating effect that low levels of unemployment could have been expected to exert on workers' wage claims no longer operates. Overheating exists in a depressed economy, so the argument runs, because of 'hysteresis'—a substantial proportion of the unemployed become permanent outsiders, unable to accept available jobs because they have lost the necessary work and communicative skills, partly because welfare and compensation systems reduce the urgency of employment for unemployed people.

Perhaps the most insidious of all the conventional explanations of contemporary unemployment, one which exonerates the policy process from effective responses to unemployment, is the version of the trade-off argument which insists that some level of unemployment is inevitable. The so-called natural rate of unemployment purported to depict a level of unemployment at which inflation could be contained, as if there were a connection between the two that was inaccessible to policy. Currently this rate is referred to as the non-accelerating inflation rate of unemployment (NAIRU, also known as the NAWRU, see OECD 1994c: 31–2)—the rate of unemployment below which skill shortages and wage pressures threaten inflation.

In an even more obscene twist, it is claimed that the NAIRU, like the expectations-augmented unemployment-inflation tradeoff curve, is constantly increasing (Arndt 1994: 13–16). By invoking a NAIRU, policy-makers are admitting they have no desire to devote resources to training and retraining, to active labour market programmes, or even to incomes policies. In fact there is no logical basis to a 'natural rate' that changes so dramatically from economy to economy or from time to time in the same economy, particularly as it is virtually identical to the actual unemployment rate. The natural rate of unemployment and the NAIRU are nothing more than the rate of unemployment that governments and economists want to ignore because they wrongly imagine that the policy process is powerless to affect it. There has emerged an unreasonable unwillingness to activate institutional mechanisms which are known to reduce unemployment. This policy acquiescence amounts to official acceptance of unnecessarily high unemployment. Hence, it can be said that the rate of unemployment regarded as unimportant by economists and governments is steadily increasing. Use of the term 'hysteresis' reflects this because there is now said, with doubtful empirical support, to be a pool of unemployed people that could not readily be accepted by employers even if labour shortages began to appear. If we spent as much effort ensuring jobs were created and people were retrained as we have spent shifting the employment service out of the policy area, perhaps there would be no long-term pool of damaged jobless. But there is now a rate of unemployment governments want to ignore, a rate of unemployment below which policy-makers wrongly assume inflationary pressure cannot be contained by incomes policy. Supply blockages emerge only if no other policy remedies are initiated.

The level of unemployment which governments want to ignore is increasing. With such cynical and meretricious abrogation of responsibility, iatrogenic policies can be reembraced. Recession and unemployment become policy tools; growth can be stymied because it impedes growth; there can be too much activity at unusually low levels of activity; the elimination of industries becomes part of the regeneration of industry; and we can be made poorer as part of the process of making ourselves richer.

Inflation in recession is a product of distributive conflict between labour and capital, asserting its effects through increases in wages and prices (Burdekin & Burkett 1996). This type of conflict and the inflation it causes can be solved only through a combination of anti-recessionary policy and incomes policy. Inflation is exacerbated to the extent that deflationary policy responses make the national economic cake smaller and the distributive conflicts more bitter than need be. Permanent institutional solutions to the problem are available, although they require no small amount of strategic gumption and political will.

Liberal polities for most of the postwar era have so protected their anti-interventionist proclivities that they have only underdeveloped institutional mechanisms for recognizing the dimensions and effects of recession. In some situations, not only do flawed understandings of problems such as inflation in recession continue to give rise to inappropriate policies, but institutions which have the capacity to subject parts of the economy to political control tend to be bypassed or, as with centralized wage fixation, dismantled.

The control of inflation as much as the elimination of unemployment requires significant institutional change and consolidation. Without firmer recognition of the nature of recession, the structural changes in the economy it leads to tend to eliminate what are considered inefficient or redundant industries without developing any alternative bases for wealth generation. Without ongoing institutional development, policies designed to eliminate inflation have the effect of reducing the economic activity whose preservation would remove the basis of the conflicts that take inflationary form. As the recession and the restructuring are global, new economic activities tend to be located elsewhere, with decreasing national voice or autonomy. Consequently, both administrative and productive capacities in countries like Australia have been severely weakened as a direct result of the economics of recession. This outcome is neither desirable nor inevitable. To resist existing trends, it is necessary to engage in institution-building, not to destroy existing managerial capacities. This suggests not only that increasing exposure to the international economy, through domestic liberalization, has become the cause of domestic problems, but that alternatives to such public strategies can be imagined. We now turn to this issue.

Does exposure to the international economy affect unemployment?

No country is an island, it might be said, not even Australia. If so, trading capacity and trade strategy will always largely determine national economic affluence.

In Australia, for much of this century, public discussion of national economic development has been dominated by the protection versus free trade debate, a key locus of economic policy debate since Renaissance times (Reinert 1997). The nation's economic prosperity has supposedly depended on the trade policy adopted. Until the early 1970s, protectionist policies were developed, although this rarely became a responsible basis for industry development as the policy process was not ceded the capacity to determine the content, technological quality, location or overall structural role of each protected industry. So, although industry development was largely shielded from international competitive conditions, little public capacity for a robust industry policy—to foster linkages with other parts of the productive economy, to integrate financial and manufacturing sectors, to ensure long-term rationality or viability, to prevent under-dimensioning of production, to temper foreign ownership with national priorities, to subject corporate strategies to public audit—was contemplated. As commentators on the crisis in manufacturing later pointed out: 'Australian governments took little or no interest in the pattern of industrial development behind the tariff wall, and in particular, they never made protection conditional upon manufacturers' undertaking modernization or expansion, or meeting efficiency targets' (Ewer, Higgins & Stevens 1987: 11).

Furthermore, because other (export-oriented) sectors applied for compensation for the higher prices implied by tariff protection, a policy of 'protection all round' emerged. Though there is no reason why all economic activity ought to be judged by the criterion of competitiveness, Australia's non-participation in the expansion of international trade during the 1960s, 1970s and 1980s, along with a somewhat complacent acceptance of the continuing reliability of the agricultural and mining sectors to fund import requirements and the underdevelopment of a principled commitment to manufacturing, helped to produce an economic order that has been described by the critics of protection as cosseted and inward-looking. 'Fortress Australia', it is claimed, undermined flexible adaptation to changing patterns of demand, nurtured non-innovative management styles and discouraged the more selective approaches to industrial development that a less immature involvement of government (and trade unions, too) could have been expected to produce. Whether the low level of trade (exports and imports as a proportion of GDP) in Australia was responsible for the comparative decline in living standards and per capita incomes by the 1980s is, sotto voce, another question.

From the onset of the recession, the policy milieu shifted from relative insulation from, to more active engagement with, the rest of the world. Consciously or otherwise, wisely or otherwise, liberalization began in 1973 with an indiscriminate 25 per cent tariff cut, apparently in response to a sudden and unexpected increase in consumer prices. Since then, Australia's economic 'reforms' have been based on the principles derived from international liberalization, basing its strategy for national economic development on wishful thinking and faith in spontaneous private sector led regeneration of industrial (or post-industrial) activity. What has been called the 'Keating–Garnaut agenda', since 1983, has extended the principle of tariff cuts to the virtual elimination of tariff protection by the end of the century. This policy shift dovetails with global initiatives to extend free trade through the GATT and other multilateral agreements, including the troubled Asia Pacific Economic Community (APEC) and the now-jettisoned Multilateral Agreement on Investment (MAI) proposals. Through many government-sponsored reports, the policy community has convinced Australian policy-makers of the need for a higher trade profile (more openness) in order to reduce unemployment (see, for example, Garnaut 1989; Industry Commission 1990; EAAU/DFAT 1992).

Australia, and probably many other countries with similar patterns of institutional underdevelopment, seems unable or unwilling to evaluate, after more than twenty years, its commitment to the 'rationalization through competition' strategy for economic recovery. Will the destruction of existing activity be matched by the creation of new industries of equivalent standard and development potential? What is the relation between trade dependence (openness of the economy) and unemployment?

Table 3.4 shows the effects of trade dependence or openness (defined as the total of exports and imports as a proportion of GDP) on unemployment. As previously, data for sixteen countries for years since 1974 has been pooled. A figure of 50 per cent is used to demarcate 'low' from 'high' levels of openness. The first observation is that relatively closed economies, where trade plays

Table 3.4: Openness of the Economy and Unemployment in 16 OECD Countries, since 1974

	Openness		
	Low (%)	High (%)	Total (%)
Low unemployment	19.5	31.9	27.3
Medium unemployment	37.2	33.5	34.9
High unemployment	43.3	34.6	37.8
Number of cases	113	191	304

a comparatively small role (low openness), have been associated more with higher than with lower levels of unemployment. Of the low-trade cases, about 80 per cent recorded medium or high unemployment. However, the reverse is not the case—high levels of openness do not correlate well with low (or any other level) of unemployment. In other words, while low openness is associated with high unemployment, the evidence does not suggest that increased trade dependence will necessarily result in better economic performance (low unemployment). Australia, in particular, ought to consider and specify more carefully the policy changes that would need to accompany any transition from a comparatively closed economy to a more open one, if the objective is improved economic performance rather than just improved trade.

Many countries have discovered during the recession that openness to the world economy does not prevent continuing national decline. Countries with low unemployment have generally had open economies (combined exports and imports exceeding 60 per cent) with the exceptions of Japan and the United States, the two most closed OECD economies. In those countries, trade constitutes only a minor part of the total economy. Belgium and the Netherlands are the most open economies but have been among those with the highest unemployment.

In line with international fashion, Australia has become more open in the past quarter-century, but was one of only six OECD countries to do so. In other words, most nations have not implemented the hegemonic OECD rhetoric, but have kept trade barriers, or at least the capacity for managed trade, in place. As global reorganization of production requires international competition in reorganized markets, there are inevitably losers as well as winners. Australia seems to have embraced the free trade rhetoric more enthusiastically than most countries, without considering that it is more likely to lose than to enhance the capacity to provide for its population: 'Over the next fifty years world trade is likely to be dominated by Japan, the European Union and the United States. The lesson Australia must learn is that they will write the rules in a self-interested way' (Teese 1994: 50).

The reduction of trade barriers is an example of the abstentionist policies discussed in chapter 2. Future economic security requires a range of policy interventions able to impose substantive industrial goals onto economic restructuring, even if the increasingly complex and conflictual world trade situation is accepted as part of the new environment in which nationally oriented policy must operate.

Australian public policy has ignored attempts in both the prewar and postwar eras to develop more explicit policies for manufacturing viability. Public reports by Brigden (1929), Vernon (1965), Jackson (1975) and Crawford (1979) all acknowledged that the structural weaknesses in the economy resulted from the manufacturing sector's inability to operate at efficient levels and that public economic management ought to facilitate an export capacity for some manufactured products and base structural adjustment on factors other than competitive pressures. Business-dominated reports in the 1990s reached the same conclusions, albeit more cautiously (Parker 1997). Australian industry policy could begin to dismantle the blanket protectionism of the past yet avoid the proliferation of ad hoc responses to industry assistance that characterized postwar industrial development. The 1990s reports affirmed the importance of manufacturing and considered that continuing dependence on the export of unprocessed mining and agricultural products was impractical. The implication is that an unselective policy of unmonitored industrial protection, reliance on market forces for structural adjustment and recourse to deflationary short-term policies which lowered living standards were all antithetical to industry policy (see Ewer, Higgins & Stevens 1987: 13–23). Hugh Stretton has also discussed some of the 'dreadful policy mistakes':

> Tariff protection was allowed to become excessive and indiscriminate. Industries got what they wanted by threatening breakdown, rather than by hard bargaining with unions and government for efficient investment and work practices. But

that shortcoming called for Button-style reforms, not a free-trading extinction of Australian manufacturing (1993: 52–3).

It is often claimed that Australia faces a perennial 'balance of payments constraint'. In fact this fear is invoked to short-circuit growth when it occurs spontaneously and to mobilize policy-makers against expansionary policies before they occur. Openness itself does not necessarily imply a tendency for imports to outpace exports, but that will be the consequence of policy abrogation, of doing nothing to increase local production. Economic 'recovery' is recurrently truncated because policy-makers wrongly assume that increased activity will lead immediately to increased imports and, eventually, to unsustainable current account deficits. This will occur only if the policy process completely eschews any expansion of productive activity, whether export-oriented or import-replacing. Elimination of tariffs before the creation of new industry has already aggravated this problem, particularly with respect to capital goods in the service sector (see ACTU 1993: 20). It has been easy to illustrate the consistent increases, since tariff cuts began in the early 1970s, in the absolute value of Australia's manufacturing sector's trade deficit (see Bell's reproduction of Derek Sicklen's comparison of the two aggregates, 1997: 270). In other words, opening up Australia's economy, without policies to regenerate new activity, has actually reduced productive capacities. It is always important to recognize that immediate problems are usually the result of long-term circumstances; short-term policy responses may, especially if repeated, consolidate the problems they were intended to redress. Reversing this situation might even require toleration of continuing trade deficits if it is necessary to maintain imports of capital equipment for the expansion of domestic capacities. In such circumstances, a 'resurgence of import growth will need to be accommodated rather than "choked off" by overly restrictive demand management policies' (ACTU 1993: 22).

The effect on unemployment of conventional economic management—fiscal and monetary policy, exchange rate policy and so-called competition policy—is well known. The willingness of the policy process to postulate a balance of payments constraint and then to reduce purchasing power, incomes, employment, growth or activity as a legitimate part of economic management is clearly an example of the liberal approach to national economic governance, where indirect and ineffective mechanisms are preferred to direct and selective interventions. It is self-defeating, counter-productive and perverse. It is a minimalist approach to trade and industry policy which defers responsibility for civilized outcomes such as full employment. It is an approach which prioritizes symbols rather than reality; money market evaluations of what is important (especially concerning inflation rates, exchange rates, budget deficits, foreign debt and systems of national regulation) are given more credit than production and living standards.

The current enthusiasm for free trade is derived from an acceptance of the comparative advantage argument which advised countries to specialize in the production of goods or services in which they had a natural comparative advantage. However, the philosophy of globalization has shifted to 'competitive advantage' which implies that nationally based industry policies can create competitive advantage where none existed. In this view it is industries and firms which compete, not nations. And economic success now derives as much from deliberate policy choices as from natural advantages. With deliberately created organizational competences, the opportunities associated with negotiated public or private sector economic conditions, or increasing returns to scale, many of the characteristics of the orthodox models cease to apply; synergies derived from policies, institutions and past successes become significant determinants of ongoing prosperity. Since 1945:

> a large and generally growing part of world trade has come to consist of exchanges that cannot be attributed so easily to underlying advantages of the countries that export particular goods. Instead, trade seems to reflect arbitrary or temporary advantages resulting from economies of scale or shifting leads in close technological races (Krugman 1986: 7).

This idea was put even more stridently in Michael Porter's influential contribution to industry policy debates:

> Competitive advantage is created and sustained through a highly localized process. Differences in national economic structures, values, cultures, institutions, and histories contribute profoundly to competitive success. The role of the home nation seems to be as strong as or stronger than ever. While globalization of competition might appear to make the nation less important, instead it seems to make it more so . . . We must explain the role of the nation in the innovation process. Since innovation requires sustained investment in research, physical capital and human resources, we must also explain why the rate of such investments is more vigorous in some nations and not others (Porter 1990: 19, 20).

As a matter of principle, multilateral free trade does not and cannot ensure that a nation will retain productive capacity or competitive advantage appropriate to either domestic survival or international success. As a matter of principle, a range of policy possibilities ought to be invoked to ensure that competitiveness does not become the sole criterion on which economic activity is judged. Nations ought to reserve the entitlement to decide how and where and when international competitiveness ought to apply to economic activity, because, as income increases, it is legitimate to allow an increasing proportion of it to be spent on comparatively unproductive activity. It is reasonable, perhaps even inevitable, that consideration be paid to the ability of a nation's industries to compete successfully in global markets, especially if it needs to pay for imports. But the balance between competitive and uncompetitive industries, between traded internationally oriented and non-traded nationally oriented production, is one that ought to be decided in the policy arena, where deliberate consideration of the country's domestic and international future can occur (Stokes 1992). The appropriate policy mechanisms are many, including negotiated, bilateral trade arrangements and selective and interventionist industry policy, but all require appropriate institutional developments. And all require a commitment to a permanent and viable manufacturing sector.

Does manufacturing matter?

The tripartite Australian Manufacturing Council commenced an influential report with this comment: 'No large modern economy has managed to stay healthy without substantial diversity and a strong manufacturing base' (AMC 1990: 16). By 1997, a series of industry and government-sponsored reports had repeated the general industry position concerning the importance of manufacturing. The Mortimer and Goldsworthy Reports of 1997, though criticized in the media and by some sections of industry such as the Australian Chamber of Commerce and Industry, called for selective industry interventions and even government investment funds to ensure that identifiable growth sectors (such as information transfer) would receive sufficient capital to ensure a long-term presence in Australia. Manufacturing is important for several reasons: to remain a high-income, high standard-of-living economy, it is necessary to ensure productivity improvement which occurs most notably in association with productive activity, whether agricultural or industrial; a productive manufacturing sector underpins a high wage services sector, indicating that the two are complementary rather than typical of different stages of economic development; and in so far as national goals depend on competitiveness in global trade, a reorganized manufacturing sector under domestic control can sponsor research and development activity and mollify the encroachment of low-quality service sector employment (see Cohen & Zysman 1987; Ewer, Higgins & Stevens 1987).

Mature modern economies are characterized by the declining importance of their manufacturing sectors as providers of total employment and as contributors to total economic activity, but this does not imply that the commitment to manufacturing activity can be relaxed. Many advanced economies now face a paradox: global excess capacity in almost all consumer industries at the same time as underinvestment in manufacturing activity, deindustrialization, insufficient domestic activity to secure full employment and strategies for the reorganization or reorientation of production which exacerbate rather than ameliorate current trends. Although manufacturing decline is a cause of many macroeconomic problems, it has been met with deflationary and austerity policies which, by reducing public sector investment, expenditure on training or the participation of trade unions in policy formation, for example, prevent a regeneration of industry. The emphasis on international competitiveness does further damage as it encourage 'off-shoring', promotes financial sector criteria ('short-termism') and discourages public sector activism as a modernizer of social infrastructure (Kitson & Michie 1996). There is much scope for the regeneration of manufacturing, though not an autonomous expansion of market demand; new activity could be triggered, for example, by public initiatives in public transportation, urban renewal, communications, health, education, infrastructure provision and construction.

In other words, even with considerable transformation of the structure of global production and world trade and even with the continuing importance of service sector activity and employment, maintaining living standards in the rich, formerly industrialized countries requires the maintenance of a strong manufacturing sector. The period when Australia's prosperity could depend on favourable terms of trade for unprocessed primary sector products has passed.

> We conclude that while services will make a growing contribution to exports, they and raw materials alone may not provide the basis for a strong trading economy because of the linkages involved, the highest value-added services and also the most highly differentiated resource-based products are likely to be competitive in Australia only if we also have a reasonably strong manufacturing economy (AMC 1990: 22).

The importance of manufacturing to employment and unemployment can be evaluated with the evidence presented here. Manufacturing's significance is indicated first by the level of employment in industry as a percentage of the civilian workforce. If manufacturing is a significant component of economic success, high levels of industrial employment should be associated with low levels of unemployment. 'Low' levels of industrial employment are defined as being below the OECD average of 34 per cent of the total workforce; 'high' levels are those at or above this level.

The pooled data in Table 3.5 reveal an unambiguous relationship. The higher the employment in industry, the lower the level of unemployment. Over half of all the cases with low rates of industrial employment experienced high unemployment and almost half of all high industrial labour force cases have been associated with low levels of unemployment. Clearly, a large manufacturing sector helps achieve lower levels of unemployment.

Although there was a universal decline in industrial employment in all the OECD countries from 36 per cent of total employment in 1974 to 27 per cent in 1995, making full employment a difficult policy problem everywhere, Australia has fared worse than most. In the 1974–95 period, Australia's industrial employment declined from 35.1 to 22.9 per cent of the workforce. Only the United Kingdom, the Netherlands and

Table 3.5: Size of the Industrial Labour Force and Unemployment in 16 OECD Countries, since 1974

	Industrial Labour Force		
	Low (%)	High (%)	Total (%)
Low unemployment	13.6	46.5	27.3
Medium unemployment	32.2	38.6	34.9
High unemployment	54.2	14.9	37.8
Number of cases	177	127	304

Belgium experienced more severe declines in their manufacturing sectors in the first two decades of recession. Australia's manufacturing decline was of course from an already low base in 1974. In Germany, Japan, Italy and Denmark, manufacturing employment was still over 80 per cent of the 1974 figure in 1995 (OECD 1997b: 42). Germany, Austria and Japan still, in the early 1990s, employed more than a third of their workforces in industry. In all these countries unemployment was below 5 per cent through the 1974–92 period. It seems clear that a lower unemployment threshold in Australia requires a stabilization or reversal of manufacturing decline. Loss of manufacturing is tantamount to loss of productive capacity. This is a common feature of recessions, but since the 1970s it has been accompanied by loss of administrative capacity and quite unaccompanied by generation of the new productive capacities required by the 'capital cleansing' properties of creative destruction. For all their activism on the trade liberalization and competition fronts, successive governments and their advisers seem wholly indifferent to the ongoing loss of manufacturing capacity. Acceptable economic outcomes cannot occur in such an uncreative environment.

We have suggested that the policy process ought to be expected to bear responsibility for unemployment. It is probably being asked to take on an increasingly complex task. A common reason for the apparent difficulty in discharging the commitment to full employment is the increasing size of the workforce. In 1994 there were about 20 per cent more people employed in the OECD than in 1974. There were also 26 per cent more people unemployed (34 million people in the OECD). This situation seems to have allowed some commentators (notably the *Australian* of 24 January 1994) to claim that unemployment is not as serious a problem as it might be:

> The reality is that the proportion of the working age population that is employed today is only fractionally less than the average for the 1950s . . . The increase in unemployment since the 1980s is thus almost entirely a reflection of the increase in the

proportion of the labour force that is actively seeking work—the so-called participation rate.

Conventional wisdom emphasizes the role of supply and demand for labour in determining unemployment, some proponents arguing that demographic and other sociocultural changes affecting the supply are determining factors in aggravating the problem. To suggest that unemployment is a sociocultural problem—a result of changed attitudes and behaviour (with respect to employment) rather than something to which the policy process ought to respond—is to suggest that unemployment does not constitute a real economic problem so much as a social dilemma. A postulated cause is women's entry to the workforce. Politics and economic policy supposedly have no obligation to interfere with these altered expectations. However, this presumes that there is a limited amount of employment in any particular economy.

In fact, the potential level of economic activity should not be seen as static; nations can create employment. The size of the labour force does not generally affect the level of unemployment, as the pooled OECD data demonstrates in Table 3.6.

Table 3.6 cross-tabulates unemployment with the size of the labour force in the sixteen OECD nations. It indicates that the influence of the size of the labour force on unemployment is

Table 3.6: Size of Labour Force and Unemployment in 16 OECD Countries, 1974–1988

	Labour Force Size		
	Low (%)	High (%)	Total (%)
Low unemployment	14.1	36.9	27.3
Medium unemployment	39.1	31.8	34.9
High unemployment	46.8	31.3	37.8
Number of cases	128	176	304

not as suggested by orthodox or intuitive opinion. 'Low' labour forces are characterized as those below the OECD average of 46 per cent of the population; 'high' labour forces are at or above this figure. As can be seen, small labour forces are clearly associated with medium and higher levels of unemployment (over 85 per cent) while a larger proportion of the cases with large labour forces have low levels of unemployment (37 per cent) than high levels of unemployment (31 per cent).

Governments and economic commentators often cite changes in labour force participation rates as the reason for periodic fluctuations in unemployment, or as the explanation of why unemployment rates do not always mirror changes in employment or other indicators of economic activity. It is true that increased employment can be accompanied by increased labour force participation and increased unemployment. Across the OECD, labour force participation increased 3 percentage points in the twenty years from 1974, while the unemployment rate increased by 4 percentage points (OECD 1996b: 40, 45). Nonetheless, the plain lesson from the evidence is that when a high proportion of a nation's population is engaged in work or is seeking work, unemployment levels tend to be lower rather than higher. An increased participation rate cannot reasonably explain an increase in unemployment even when both coincide. Governments can and ought to be criticized for not developing policies to create employment at a rate sufficient to reduce unemployment, even if this action increases the number of people seeking to re-enter the workforce. Increased participation in the labour force probably makes the policy responsibilities of government more difficult, but spurious explanations of failure ought not to pass unchallenged.

The overall message from the analysis of comparative evidence is that the current structure or level of employment cannot be accepted as given and unchangeable. Clearly, nations have created different forms and levels of economic activity that are unrelated to the fixed amount of their natural endowments. Many of the implications for contemporary policy-making are quite counterintuitive.

Do high or inflexible labour costs cause unemployment?

The role of the so-called labour market, particularly its treatment of wage levels and wage adjustments, has always been a controversial issue in economic policy discussion in Australia and elsewhere. Since the era of classical economics, economists have sought to interpret labour's need for employment and remuneration primarily in terms of market principles; labour has sought to resist the ascription of market motivation and incentives to what it sees as the human and societal right to an equitable standard of living. From the first concept derives a view of the economy which assigns blame for unemployment to the frustration of market mechanisms; from the second derives the assertion or defence of entitlements according to principles determined in the political rather than the market realm. Economists tend to suggest 'reforms' designed to reintroduce flexibility of wages, perhaps by dismantling the institutional achievements of the past; labour movements tend to struggle for money wages, a 'social wage' and employment conditions determined outside the market. Orthodox policy institutions prefer labour market flexibility as part of the liberal project of making wage and employment determination commensurate with other market phenomena; labour's institutions are designed to delegitimize the application of flexibility to incomes and employment. Labour and the social democratic tradition have always found the labour market—the commodification of labour—the most repugnant achievement of the liberal tradition and have therefore tried institutionally to usurp the 'market' elements of the labour market.

An extension of the market mentality is to imagine that lower wages are analogous to cost reductions and would therefore lead to an increase in the demand for labour by employers, thereby reducing unemployment. What the institutions of labour regard as protective mechanisms are seen by the liberal institutions (for example, those operated for, by or at the behest of employers, governments and economists) as rigidities to be eliminated. In some rather cynical and historically uninformed versions, some unemployment might remain even after 'reform' of industrial relations and wages systems because of the build-up of impediments to market adjustment processes. The Reserve Bank of Australia's 1993 submission to the government's Employment Opportunities Task Force, for example, considered that even if cyclical unemployment were eliminated and the economy reached full capacity, rigidities in the labour market might keep ('structural') unemployment at high levels (5–10 per cent). The wage structure has developed, it is said, in such a way that factors which would formerly have worked to reduce unemployment no longer can. Such a view requires policy-makers 'thinking twice about well-meaning but costly measures designed to improve further conditions for existing workers—in terms of training expenditure, severance payments and other "entitlements"—if these add to the cost of employing more staff' (RBA 1993: 26).

Even the government's Committee on Employment Opportunities conceded that cuts in real wages would be necessary to increase employment:

> The consensus is that for Australia a reduction of one per cent in the level of real wages would have a direct effect on employment over time of around three-quarters of one per cent. On this basis it might be presumed an increase in employment of 6 per cent could be achieved by cutting real wages by about 8 per cent (1993b: 54).

Whereas we have argued that there are no substantial economic grounds for this type of deflationary and contractionary response to unemployment, the official government view is that there is an economic rationale for wage reductions. We argue that there are economic as well as social reasons to maintain real wages, but it is orthodox dogma that has informed most of the important contributions to the debate on wages and their relationship to unemployment.

The theoretical rationale for the conventional policy position is well known or easily imagined. Because wages usually constitute a significant proportion of the costs of production, the wage level is considered a major determinant of the level of employment and unemployment. In this most contentious of all areas, the labour market, liberal reforms reassert the market mode of regulation, reducing unit labour costs rather than maintaining living standards or increasing production by more direct methods. Since labour costs can most easily be reduced when the laws and customs that protect employment and employment conditions are dismantled, the dominant policy discourse since the 1970s has centred on deregulation and decentralization. The move from centralized wage-setting procedures through arbitration to enterprise bargaining has been intended to treat wages as if they were properly considered the 'price' of labour, less subject to needs criteria, custom and equity and more open to the amoral forces of the market. The inevitable outcomes of such policies involve a depoliticization and deterioration of employment and economic conditions generally. In so far as contractionary possibilities of lowering wages are considered, the fall in unemployment is supposed to more than compensate. Supply and demand are granted sovereign legitimacy; in violation of radical and conservative traditions alike for over two hundred years, the liberal approach to economic management insists on the reasonableness of treating people in and out of employment as if they were commodities.

Similarly, the crucial determinant of the level and distribution of wages is the market mechanism rather than a calculation of societal capacity or political preference. Because the market metaphor presumes supply and demand will be matched at the optimal level of both, any non-optimal or non-market outcomes are regarded as distortions, the exogenous effects of policy (minimum wage legislation) or actors (trade unions exercising illegitimate extra-market power) or the residue of past imbalances (the long-term skill-denuded unemployed). Such distortions prevent the wage functioning like the price of commodities—wages can be too high or too inflexible or too egalitarian. And, because market theory is presumed to indicate how an economy would and should operate, societal impositions onto the market process are presumed to be unacceptable.

For non-economists, unemployment has been, for over two decades, a steadily worsening problem which the policy process has addressed only desultorily, leaving intact the basic non-interventionist principles of liberal economic governance. However, for economists, contemporary unemployment needs to be explained in terms which leave intact the integrity of the market mode of explanation. To effect this intellectual sleight of hand, the 'sellers' in the 'labour market' are reclassified as either 'insiders' or 'outsiders'. The prices demanded (wage claims) by the former are not as affected by the continuation of excess supply (unemployment) as the market model suggests they ought to be because there is no real competition within the group of employed or readily employable people for jobs which remain scarce. The outsiders, being no longer reasonably employable, are not operating in the same market. The only way to reproduce a market mode of adjustment is to increase unemployment further, use it as an even harsher policy tool and thereby induce competitive behaviour, which will help to lower wages among the presently employed (see RBA 1993: 18). Although this view shares some elements with a post-Keynesian and institutionalist account of the causes of inflation (that unemployment and a depressed economy are no longer sufficient counters to effective wage claims and price increases by institutionally strong organizations of labour and capital respectively), it amounts to a downgrading of unemployment as a public responsibility. The unemployed become 'mere pawns, whose number reconcile the claims to the national output' (Layard, Nickell & Jackman 1991: 34). The so-called Beveridge Curve—which purports to describe a relationship between job vacancies and unemployment—has 'moved outward' since the 1970s, producing the hysteresis discussed above.

Such reinterpretations of the unemployment problem deny the legitimacy of reasonable public responses: policy solutions are not available because the problem is seen as cyclical rather than structural. As the Reserve Bank of Australia claims, expansionary policy necessarily generates inflationary overheating:

All these influences combine to set a limit on how low the unemployment rate can fall in response to cyclical expansion before upward pressure on labour costs and inflation appear. Once this stage is reached, macroeconomic policies cannot successfully stimulate activity and reduce unemployment any further, unless structural impediments to lower unemployment can be removed at the same time (RBA 1993: 2).

Of course it is not a cyclical expansion that is being sought, but the long-term generation or regeneration of productive capacities whose erosion led to unemployment in the first place. In the Reserve Bank's view, structural impediments to lower unemployment are not the institutional conditions which prevent the expansion of productive activity, but the existing level of wages (including their rigidity) which would be reduced if there were more unemployment. Conventional economic institutions are loath to endorse economic expansion, to defend attained high levels of income and security or recognize the structural dimensions of unemployment. They insist, perversely, that to increase our standard of living we need to reduce it.

OECD evidence, however, contradicts the proposition that unemployment is wage- or cost-related. First, the evidence indicates that the levels of wages and unemployment are not related in the way usually imagined. In a study of sixteen OECD nations for the period 1974–84, Therborn found that 'the development of unemployment has become completely disassociated from changes in labour cost' (1986: 61). An analysis of eighteen OECD countries for the period 1960–86 by Korpi demonstrated that 'the central role accorded to the wage factor in discussions of unemployment in the OECD countries since 1973 cannot be supported by empirical data' (1991: 321). The 1993 Department of Industrial Relations submission to the Committee on Employment Opportunities, after reviewing an extensive range of evidence and opinions, concluded that wage levels contribute little or nothing to explaining rates of unemployment:

It is clear that promoting reduced wage levels is not likely to be a successful strategy in promoting international competitiveness. A number of countries which have achieved strong economic growth in the past decade, particularly Germany and Japan, have based their economic development around a highly skilled, productive and relatively high income labour force. Indeed, Germany and Japan have considerably higher wage levels than Australia . . . This economic development model offers far greater opportunities for Australia than a model based on low wages which focuses on labour intensive industries (DIR 1993a: 41).

Australia's comparatively low labour costs sit uneasily with assertions that its industrial relations and workplace culture are too biased towards workers (see Figure 2.19). Non-wage labour costs comprise sick leave and holiday loadings, employer contributions to superannuation and mandatory training and workers' compensation levies; they are not illegitimate imposts on employers or the economy but necessary costs of a civilized society for which responsibility must be accepted and factored into the normal process of production, rather like all other taxes. In fact, all the low unemployment countries over the post-1974 period—Sweden, Norway, Austria, Luxembourg, Switzerland and Japan—have had high-wage, high-cost economies.

As there is no relationship between real wage levels and unemployment—that is, between the price of labour and the demand for it—studies which focus on wage bargaining structures need reconsideration (see also DIR 1993a: 46–9). The paradox that good economic performance has been associated with both very centralized and very decentralized bargaining and wage fixation arrangements (see, for example, Calmfors & Driffill 1988, see also Paloheimo 1990) dissolves once it is realized that low wages do not produce high employment and high wages do not lead to high unemployment. (There certainly are connections from bargaining structures to wages growth and inflation, but not to unemployment.) Thus the push for industrial relations reform in Australia and elsewhere, in so far as it presumes unemployment is produced by excessive wage levels or that wage outcomes will be lower under enterprise-based or productivity-based arrangements, has been misconceived.

Inevitably, a high-skill, high-quality manufacturing and services sector requires a high-wage economy. The high-value-added production that leads to productivity growth and prosperity is directly associated with such wage levels. High wage rates contribute positively to the rationalization of industry through the substitution of capital for labour or through elimination of firms which might otherwise rely excessively on low-cost labour (Committee on Employment Opportunities 1993b: 29). Since high wages are usually associated with high skills, innovative managerial and production strategies will be facilitated in such an environment.

It is not sensible to argue that, in the interests of economic recovery, real wages ought to fall. In fact, as Keynes insisted during the 1930s, wage reductions and weak labour may be detrimental to economic activity (see also Grieve Smith 1996: 10–13). Restraints on profits are more likely to achieve efficacious results than restraints on labour. During the 1980s, profit rates in the low-unemployment countries were 9.5 per cent, compared with 12.3 per cent in seven of the high-unemployment countries (OECD 1994a: A26) (although as the low-unemployment countries' unemployment rates increase, this discrepancy is eroding). This confirms that the distribution of national income is always more uneven during times of crisis than during times of full employment. The distribution of income is more closely related to the level of income, to the stage of the cycle, than to the activities or intentions of labour and capital. Consequently, labour has a greater interest in good macroeconomic performance than is commonly presumed. High wages are conducive to good economic outcomes as well as to the political preferences of labour. To the extent that organized labour can restrain price 'mark-ups' in industries with a high degree of monopoly:

> a wage rise showing an increase in the trade union power leads—contrary to the precepts of classical economics—to an increase

in employment. And conversely, a fall in wages showing a weakening in their bargaining power leads to a decline in employment. The weakness of trade unions in a depression manifested in permitting wage cuts contributes to a deepening of unemployment rather than to relieving it (Kalecki 1971: 163).

Wages are a component of consumption as well as of costs, so high wages will have a positive effect on overall profits as they permit higher levels of aggregate demand, aggregate spending, economic activity and production. A high level of employment, especially well-remunerated employment, is an important guarantor of an equitable distribution of income; income distribution is determined more by the level of activity in the economy than by bargaining over wages and profits. Hence an important responsibility of sensible economic management ought to be to maintain stable and high levels of employment and incomes.

In capitalist economies generally, the 'wages as costs' dimension of economic activity is always a less important factor than the 'wages as contributor to expanding output' dimension. An unevenly skewed class distribution of income produces detrimental effects for total employment and total income; equality increases the overall level of activity (Kalecki 1971). This is because the biases in the system are towards less activity than is technically possible; it is always harder to increase than to reduce production and incomes and employment. In addition, the factors which determine the distribution of income between profits and wages (institutionalized class conflict) are independent of those which determine the level of activity (investment decisions). The pertinence of these analytical propositions has been borne out by the increased disparities in income that have emerged in the high-unemployment countries since the 1970s. Income inequalities have worsened in the countries where orthodox disregard for unemployment has been most pronounced; in most other countries inequalities have narrowed over the past two decades (see Table 3.7). Both a lower wages structure and a higher degree of wage dispersion are likely to worsen overall economic performance, indicating that the recession is largely policy-induced.

It is also unreasonable to argue that an inegalitarian wages structure provides incentives for labour mobility and the transmission of productivity gains. The expediency argument for income inequality has been ridiculed on many occasions by John Kenneth Galbraith: 'It always boils down to the slightly improbable case that the rich are not working because they have too little income, the poor because they have too much' (1998: 24, see also 1992: 46).

A long-time objective of labour movements and of policy processes has been the elimination of market incentives where they appear to cause more social and economic disruption than is warranted by the resulting inequalities. As the ACTU has noted, it is important that the credibility of the wages determination system be preserved, by maintaining minimum wages and standards of work. Otherwise, flexibility may be achieved at the cost of higher, and inflationary, aggregate outcomes (1993: vi). Organized labour's efforts to preserve wage and employment standards should not be seen as a defensive or irresponsible imposition of sectional indifference to the societal whole. Labour does not seek to impose the costs of its own benefit diffusely on everyone else; rather, it bases its strategy on a view of contemporary capitalist development that is highly sceptical of the equilibrium tendencies of markets and emphasizes the need for institutional management of the economy. The Department of Industrial Relations seems to have come to a similar conclusion: 'Some commentators in the past have suggested that the award system has imposed rigid relativities between industries and occupations, and that this has impeded efficient labour market adjustment. If this were ever true, it is clearly not today' (DIR 1993a: 84–5).

Despite its hesitant advocacy of decentralization, the DIR seems aware that the reforms might lead to a loss of capacity for public economic management: 'a more decentralized wages system will inevitably involve a reduction in the degree of control over aggregate wages outcomes. In such a system, responsibility for wage outcomes and their consequent effect on inflation and unemployment rests much more directly with the parties themselves' (1993a: 9).

Although it might be argued that, in a period of economic recovery, aggregate wage outcomes will not get seriously out of alignment with those desired by a regulated system, the extension of inequalities may frustrate any return to high employment. This will be particularly likely if, in the event of inflationary pressures, government is cajoled into a further round of deflationary 'stop–go' policy.

Table 3.7 offers a possible depiction of the extent to which income inequalities have widened in Australia since the recession began and economic policy began to increase the gap between actual and potential levels of economic activity. Since the recession, the countries with the most orthodox policy responses

Table 3.7: Income Inequality, 1980s

Ratio of Income Shares (Top 20% to Bottom 20%)		Inequality after Taxation and Redistributive Transfers
UK	9.6	(High)
Australia	9.6	
USA	8.9	
New Zealand	8.8	Switzerland
Switzerland	8.6	Canada
France	7.5	USA
Canada	7.1	Australia
Denmark	7.1	UK
Italy	6.0	France
Finland	6.0	Netherlands
Norway	5.9	Germany
Germany	5.8	Norway
Sweden	4.6	Sweden
Belgium	4.6	
Holland	4.5	
Japan	4.3	(Low)

Sources: World Bank (1996: 196–7, Table 5); Castles & Mitchell (1993: 110) (based on examination of LIS data)

have displaced the previously inegalitarian countries as those with the widest gaps between rich and poor. These new inequalities exacerbate the recession and make spontaneous 'recovery' less likely. The richest 20 per cent now earns almost ten times the income earned by the poorest 20 per cent; in countries which have not pursued deregulatory policies, the ratio of rich to poor people's incomes is less than five times. Even when the effects of Australia's tightly targeted social security system are taken into account, it remains one of the most inegalitarian of the group of OECD countries. These social effects of recession (and of recession-inducing economic policies) can also be gauged from other indicators such as crime, disillusionment and electoral backlash. It seems that general and socially sanctioned hypocrisy must be added to Australia's inadequate political structure.

From the economics to the politics of unemployment

Misperceptions of the essential features of economic recession, and therefore of the causes of unemployment, may undermine what might reasonably be done about it. An obvious problem with much of the policy effort of the 1980s and 1990s which, in accordance with a semi-official OECD model of micro-economic policy reform, was apparently oriented to reasserting a role for market 'fundamentals' is that there were no mechanisms for generating new or regenerating old activities. Recovery is presumed to be spontaneous; the role of policy is relegated to eliminating the impact of policy preference or discretion. The tendency is to favour 'solutions' that eliminate inefficient activity without generating replacement activities. Policy is renounced in favour of wishful thinking based on abstract notions of self-correcting propensities in market systems.

Additional indications of the unwillingness of the policy process to concede the nature and role of economic recession are to be found in the frequent presumption that economic normality can be restored provided the conditions for high growth, low inflation or labour market flexibility are restored. These three variations on the orthodox approach are surrogates for anti-recessionary policy. They presume that new wealth and employment-generating activity can emerge without deliberated consideration of its content, form, quality, location or linkages to existing industry. Undifferentiated economic growth, background conditions like low inflation or microeconomic changes in areas such as the labour market seem to be the preferred focus of policy precisely because they encompass neither selective interventions nor institutional transformation of the decision-making environment.

The argument is not that economic growth or low inflation are undesirable but that, even without studying any specific economy or industry, it is possible to imagine high growth, for example from a low base, which is not associated with low unemployment or good macroeconomic performance. Similarly, low inflation may well be associated with poor performance, inequality, poverty and stagnation. And microeconomic reform is likely to be the least hopeful of all strategies for industrial regeneration, if in practice it means only the diminution of a nation's productive capacities. Some public strategies seem to be favoured only because they allow structural problems to be kept off the public agenda. Waiting for growth does not redress the structural imbalances that deteriorated or dismantled industries represent; achieving or maintaining low inflation does not guarantee renewed investment; the elimination of inefficiency does not imply the creation of a viable long-term pattern of national development or even the prioritization of macro-economic criteria. It is therefore possible to detect policies, based on partial understandings of the nature of recession, which produce outcomes which effectively worsen it. All such misunderstandings constitute unnecessary economic limits to economic prosperity.

Full employment, as a social objective of government, has been abandoned during the past twenty-five years in the name of economic necessity and reality. With the demise of this goal, there has emerged an apparent loss of respect for the institutions of government. But the political malaise in Australia is constructed on a base of state capacity that has been underdeveloped for a long time. In the Anglo-Saxon polities, governments are charged with responsibility for economic management but are given too few mechanisms to achieve it. Then, when governments implement policies which make things worse, they are blamed and suffer electoral retribution. The weakness is with politics, and political weakness operates through official hostility to certain policy possibilities. The next chapter explores a particular aspect of this discursive phenomenon—the relationship between unemployment and policy measures such as taxation, welfare state expenditures, labour market policies and the public sector's role in infrastructure provision. It can be shown that much of the conventional wisdom on the inadvisability of political intervention lacks empirical support. Policies are ineffective because parts of the policy process are designed to keep them so. Polities like Australia's do not have the capacity to recognize when extra-market institutional development is needed.

For the moment, however, the lesson that can be drawn is that unemployment is only initially an economic phenomenon. Its continuation depends on the unwillingness of the political process to do something about it, rather than on an inexorable economic logic. Institutional controls are imaginable. Nonetheless, the development of economic management in the so-called Keynesian era has made some aspects of economic management more difficult than they once were. The inability of Anglo-Saxon regimes to institutionalize the commitment to full employment along Keynesian lines has led not only to the recurrence of unemployment but also to the discrediting of public economic management. Institutional initiatives directed towards full employment were politically contentious and technically difficult even in the 1930s when liberal discourse was at its nadir; in the late 1990s, it is difficult to sponsor even debate over the changing nature of capitalism and the role of policy in it. Institutional transformation was effected during the boom in many countries but, even there, severe problems of economic management remain.

Recessions are now shallower than they were, because of welfare state supports and the effects of anti-cyclical activity associated with larger public sectors. But they may well be institutionally more intractable, even with the requisite political will. It seems to be the case that far greater policy effort is required now to eliminate unemployment only half or a third as high as it was in the 1930s. Many of the easy solutions, such as those associated with general or undirected increases in demand and government expenditures, have been adopted. The reforms needed now to guarantee economic activity sufficient to recreate full employment invite a much stronger confrontation with liberalism than was the case a generation ago. Recession and unemployment, without appropriate policy responses, may well last thirty years compared with the shorter, though more socially disruptive, slump of sixty years ago. Figure 3.2 postulates cycles with decreasing amplitude which conceal the need for more intensified policy effort which, in a time of global hostility to regulatory innovation, is unlikely to be attempted. This issue is addressed further in the final chapter.

If this depiction of the long recession is correct, and no special action is taken by government to guarantee a stronger sectoral and industrial basis for the Australian economy, then the 'recovery' will be a long time coming and will not necessarily generate the level or quality of employment that is required and is possible.

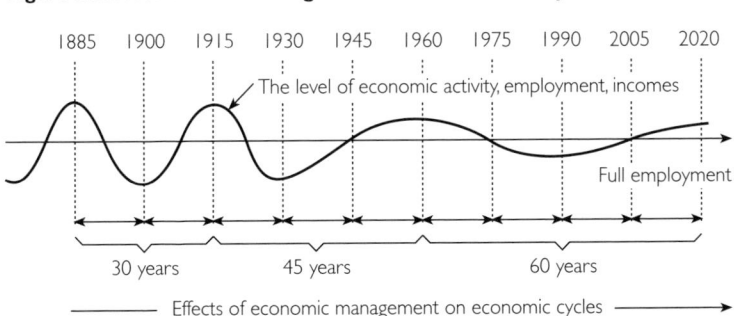

Figure 3.2: Postulated Increasing Institutional Intractability of Recessions

Problems that are notionally simpler have become institutionally more difficult, but they are not beyond the reach of national policy. Full employment has always been a matter of political contention; the current experience does not imply that there is nothing that can be done in Australia to regenerate full employment. But Australia needs to develop a new range of political capacities. The struggle for full employment and civility at the end of the twentieth century is really the same struggle to achieve democratic autonomy that has been fought (and lost) many times before. The continuing refusal by polities to perform the tasks that they were always intended to, progressively increases the costs of failure and abrogation. Governments now face cynical electorates because the governments have been falsely persuaded that they are impotent. The evidence does not endorse that conclusion. But if Australia is to take the challenge of full employment seriously, it must develop an appropriate statecraft. It must push the transition from market control to political control of the economy further and faster than it is occurring spontaneously. This is a project that will shunt Australia in a very different political direction from that to which it has become accustomed, but it is necessitated by the need to relearn lessons that have been there for the knowing for some time. The next chapter examines the policy options appropriate to such a different political direction.

Chapter 4
Policy options

Economics is always really politics. If an economy is never simply a market phenomenon, policy designed to replicate in reality an abstract version of reality is bound to become a utopian project. Even apart from the social and political dimensions of economic activity, which need to be understood on their own terms rather than as distortions to be eliminated, economies seem to evolve in such a way that the balance between regulated and unregulated spheres changes. Political failure to understand the changing relationship between the economic and political aspects of capitalism has led to misguided policy, and hence to poor performance, over the past twenty years. Chapter 3 provided evidence supporting the argument that economic activity does not respond to economic stimuli in the way that conventional wisdom supposes. We have shown that policies oriented to undifferentiated economic growth, policies which rely on monetary policy to reduce inflation, policies which presume that an increase in unemployment will help to control inflation, policies which allow structural and sectoral change to dismantle manufacturing capacities and manufacturing employment without consciously generating new industrial or value-added activity, policies which assume a direct connection between wage costs and unemployment and policies which allow inequalities to increase are all policies which abrogate or ignore the role that policy can play in directing, shaping and improving national economic performances. They have all played an important part in exacerbating the long recession. Unemployment, and recession itself, since 1974, has been largely policy-induced. That there are policy alternatives is apparent both from the comparative experience of unemployment discussed in previous chapters and from an examination of policy possibilities and policy mistakes.

An initial indication of the extent to which policy can influence economic activity—the possibilities of policy—is the growth of government. Even in the countries where expansion of state activity is resisted most fiercely, government has continued to grow during the recession. In the OECD economies as a whole, the share of GDP accounted for by government spending has increased from about 10 per cent at the turn of the century to 28 per cent in 1960 to 48 per cent now (OECD 1997b: 72). The figure has ranged from 31 per cent (Japan) to 73 per cent (Sweden) in the 1990s. In Australia government has been comparatively small throughout the century and the gap between the level of government spending and the OECD average has increased by half since the 1970s. It is unreasonable to assume that government spending captures all that needs to be known about the policy role and responsibilities of government—Japan, for example, has notionally small but substantively influential government. The state can also influence the economy through regulatory or organizational arrangements. Nonetheless, the large spending role of government indicates at least the potential for the policy process to assert leverage over economic outcomes, even if only in so far as public spending acts as an automatic stabilizer. Though the tenor and rhetoric of the 1990s is deregulatory and considerable effort has been expended by the policy process in an attempt to reduce or eliminate its discretionary and interventionist role, it is important to acknowledge the increased influence of political decisions on the level and content of economic activity.

To understate the situation somewhat, the policy process has become rather discredited in recent years. This is despite the manifest growth of government and what would otherwise be the accompanying need to incorporate an awareness of non-market determinations of economic conditions into understanding the economy and its problems. Depoliticization of economic management is a response to the unpopularity of policy among erstwhile policy-makers. Nonetheless, the evidence concerning the impact of government on economic outcomes does not support the conclusions of those who have assigned responsibility for poor performance to excessive or inefficient government. This chapter identifies three aspects of the policy process that have had a detrimental effect on unemployment: the confused state of knowledge of how capitalist economies have changed as a result of the century-long increase in the economic role and responsibilities of government; the empirical effects of the contemporary retreat from policy and regulation that contributes significantly to the inefficacy of public policy; and the institutional developments that are implied by a policy process more devoted to the goal that policy-makers once struggled to imagine—permanent full employment.

Public policy and state capacity

Policy is always necessary to economic activity; economies and societies need some modification of the anarchic patterns of activity that would result from its absence. Much government activity, especially in liberal polities, is the result of a principled commitment to the minimization of policy's disruption of market outcomes. However, even in these circumstances, the evolution of the policy process allows governments a capacity to regulate the economy, although they do so only unevenly and with varying degrees of success. The development of these 'state capacities' reflects both the autonomous, or unintended, degree to which economies require economic management, even without a principled commitment to it, and the extent to which governments, or political forces able to influence government, have been willing or able to consciously expand the public determination of economic performance. State capacity thus differs from economy to economy both because of the level of policy involvement (whether intended or not) and the level of deliberate and volitional capability in the political system to encourage the authority of politics.

The links between policies and state capacities can be illustrated by demarcating different clusters of policies and phases in the evolution of the public sector's ability to exploit them.

Policy activities of government can be classified as developmental, Keynesian or social democratic. Some types of interventionist or regulatory activity are resisted more than others, presumably because they disrupt the defining characteristics of the market system more than others. The policy responsibilities governments accept vary accordingly.

Developmental aspects of government activity are the large-scale infrastructure commitments accepted by government in capitalist economies, especially at early stages of their economic development, to sponsor the conditions for national economic development or capital accumulation. They are generally compatible with the policy preferences of liberals because the functions of the state can be justified in terms of national development (or 'natural monopoly'). The state activities often embraced by liberal democratic regimes—provision of railways, roads, ports, power generation, communications, legal and administrative systems, perhaps scientific and educational facilities—are sometimes referred to as the 'forces of production'. This term implies that infrastructure is both an outcome of prior development and a precondition for ongoing capital accumulation or capitalist economic development under market auspices. This type of state policy was probably essential in establishing markets and their legal underpinnings, so developmental aspects of public provision do not interfere with market behaviour. And they do require periodic renewal.

Keynesian aspects of state intervention are those which form the basis of 'economic management'. They are intended to redress the effects of market-induced cycles in economic activity, to reduce market-derived inefficiencies (unemployment or underutilized capacity) or to prevent market-based inequities and inequality, even where they are compatible with efficiency. This rationale for government activity is counter-cyclical; it has sometimes legitimized a significant degree of state intervention, including some welfare state measures, without seriously infringing upon capitalist control of the economy. To the extent that the essential nature of capitalism was not challenged, Keynesian policies were considered acceptable in otherwise liberal policy regimes and the idea of the 'mixed economy' emerged to accommodate the enhanced policy role of government. However, in so far as this type of state activity has apparently embraced the policy goal of full employment and the associated desire to increase economic activity beyond the level given by the market, a certain hostility to economic management in principle has emerged. Liberalism is thus ambivalent about this type of intervention, recognizing both the desirable increased profitability and developmental potential attending high levels of employment and activity and the less desirable scope for political influence over the content of employment and activity.

The institutions of economic management in the postwar mixed economy were therefore less robust than might have been expected, and the policy commitments were commensurately less interventionist and effective than would have been necessary. The postwar decades were more a period of 'bastard Keynesianism', an anodyne version of what was required to deliver economic stability, than of true Keynesianism, which would have required what John Maynard Keynes foresaw as 'a somewhat comprehensive socialization of investment'. Liberal regimes only grudgingly endorsed the principle of counter-cyclical macroeconomic management (subsequently stabilization policy) and eschewed anti-recessionary policies, policy-guided restructuring and even systematic anti-inflationary policy all through the long boom. It was after the boom of the 1945–74 period that Keynesian policy was necessary, not during it. As if to mirror the inability of an unregulated market economy to operate at full capacity, Keynesian aspects of state activity demarcate policy interventions which are abrogated as often as they are accepted.

The third cluster of policies can be referred to as *social democratic* aspects of public provision. Potentially much more politicized, and politically contentious, than other policy possibilities, social democratic forms of public activity typically involve cross-subsidization. Cross-subsidization disarticulates contribution and reward, service provision and ability to pay; it is a politically generated recognition that many activities are desirable regardless of the extent to which they can attract market support. Cross-subsidization of regions (from urban to rural), of activities (from technology-intensive to labour-intensive), of organizations (from revenue-generating to revenue-deficient), or of individuals (from successful to unsuccessful) emphatically violates the proscriptions of economic liberalism. Social democratic elements in public sector activity also involve the development of public criteria in accordance with anti-market principles and therefore imply a higher level of state capacity than developmental or Keynesian policies. For this reason, cross-subsidization has had a precarious place in public policy, prone to reversal when demands for efficiency, competitiveness, flexibility or market-led restructuring grab the policy-making imagination.

Social democratic policy presumes that not all aspects of all activities need to be self-sufficient or self-funding. It is inappropriate to apply private sector financing principles to public sector activities. Public sector activities extend entitlements that are independent of individual ability to pay. Political decisions and collectivist principles allow the assertion of a substantive rationality which would be impossible if private or individual criteria alone determined what were to prevail. Under such circumstances, principles for social activity and reward can readily be developed in, for example, wage fixing, urban amenity or housing standards. Social democratic policy prioritizes security over freedom, especially social security over entrepreneurial freedoms.

This differentiation shows that policy possibilities range from the benign to the potentially transformative. The gradual advance of policy interference with market allocative principles has occurred for both structural and volitional reasons. Structural circumstances leading to a broadening of policy responsibilities include the exigencies and internal requirements of the economy and society which tend to demand regulation irrespective of political and ideological preference; volitional circumstances are those of deliberate decisions and politically conscious choices.

The former were anticipated before the twentieth-century process of expanding government began. In the 1880s, German economist Adolph Wagner postulated a 'law of expanding state activity' which formalized observations that demands on the public sphere increased inexorably with urbanization, industrialization, modernization and social complexity because of increases in social problems requiring public responses. At the same time, national wealth provided the requisite financial resources; a distinctive discipline—public finance—emerged. The capacity of government to respond to problems, on a basis different to that which determines private financing arrangements, emerged at the same time as did distinctive problems. Government could be expected to account for an increasing proportion of national income and resources the more mature and wealthy societies became.

Despite the preference in liberal capitalism for weak and insubstantial states, growth in publicly provided services can be expected to continue, if Wagner's reasoning holds, even if growth in GDP slows, because mandated state activity depends on the level, not the rate of growth, of incomes. Wagner's hypothesis leads to the suggestion that there are increasing limits on the capacity of private sector decisions to generate private sector employment at a sufficient rate to meet developmental and societal expectations (for full employment and affluence). This reasoning is partly justified by Friedrich List's espousal in the 1840s of a developmental role for government under the auspices of 'national economy' (List 1841; Levi-Faur 1997). In consequence, as the OECD has admitted, low growth in countries with well-developed public sectors could cause public expenditures to pass 70 per cent of GDP by 2025 (OECD 1990b: 69).

The contemporary expansion of policy can therefore be explained by processes and capacities that are part of the development of capitalism itself. The consolidation of markets, private property and capitalist relations of production in the nineteenth century was always shadowed by 'another great principle'—the transition from individualist to collectivist mandates for production. The sequential adoption of developmental and then

Keynesian counter-cyclical responsibilities illustrates in embryonic form this new principle; the more gradual acceptance of the ability to cross-subsidize illustrates its contentiousness.

Public policy can be seen as 'indispensable to the whole economic life of the community', as 'a great many things have to be done otherwise than in private enterprise' (Wagner 1883: 2–5). A consistent, and perhaps irremediable, divergence between private and public financing principles has emerged. The former is constrained by market demand and voluntary payments, the latter by the state's capacity to levy compulsory taxes. Therefore states may initiate particular activities (or constraints on activity) for political reasons, independently of market demand for the activity and even independently of the means that would need to be solicited to finance it. Since Wagner, it has been realized that with public finance each activity undertaken or service provided need not be self-financing. Policy exists to alter the pattern of economic activities that would be produced by purely market arrangements. General taxation can be used to finance state activity even to the extent of disrupting the congruence of those who pay with those who benefit.

It is more than the existence of taxation-financed services that distinguish public provision. As Wagner noted, 'the state is free to define its own tasks, the manner of their discharge and thus the amount and kind of services to be provided for the people, without reference to their demand for these services' (1883: 5–8). As a result, the 'economic principle' loses some of its pertinence, to be replaced by a 'proper organic view' of how states ought to evaluate the prudence of assuming new and maintaining old responsibilities.

Wagner's 'law of expanding state activity' contained a prescriptive element, not just the enunciation of an inevitable shift from a permissive to a propulsive state, but also the assertion of the principle that the state ought to provide social benefits: 'such measures as conduce to the moral, intellectual, sanitary, physical, economic and social advancement of the mass of the people . . . so far as may seem necessary and expedient' (1887: 156–7).

Yet understanding the principles underlying policy formulation (and institutions for its implementation) has been plagued from the beginning by resistance to what was technically possible. The tradition of state analysis that followed Wagner recognized the political conflicts implied by the development of a policy acumen. German sociologist Rudolph Goldscheid argued that the transition from absolutism to a more democratic state could be thwarted:

> As feudalism broke down and the people gained control over the state, it came to be in the interest of the propertied class to render the state impotent. As a result, the state became impoverished. If the state is to be rendered a useful instrument in the hands of the people, the lost wealth must be reconstituted to the state, so that it can meet its welfare functions (Musgrave & Peacock 1958: xviii).

It has long been recognized in public policy analysis that, in so far as policy is constrained for political reasons, the building up of state capacities will never simply result from waiting for the exigencies of the situation to demand political solution. The state could be prevented from consolidating its own economic resources. State-building would be necessary for the advocates of a policy role before the state could fulfil its potential as a nation-building state. If ineffectual, this process could produce a 'caricature of the state' and thus become a source of tension between two potential paths to community development, 'capitalist economy and socially productive public economy' (Goldscheid 1925: 211–12).

In accordance with these warnings or anticipations, the liberal state became one which was intentionally 'poor on principle' (Goldscheid 1925: 204), and the struggle against extended state activity, increased taxation, government spending, innovative forms of policy development, state-sponsored infrastructure investment and publicly determined constraints on production has given the capitalist state much of its distinctiveness. For these reasons, there is a difference between liberal and conservative attitudes to the state. Conservatives prefer a state that is 'to some extent politically and economically strong' (1925: 207), prefiguring an aphorism by Oliver Wendell Holmes Jr that has since characterized the social democratic approach to policy possibilities of government: 'taxes are what we pay for a civilized society' (Musgrave 1985: 25).

Does taxation affect unemployment?

The social democratic assertion that state capacity can and ought to be expanded to enable modern societies to respond to problems which have not been part of the liberal worldview is supported not only by the analytical contributions of Wagner and Goldscheid but also by contemporary evidence. The implications of the argument presented so far are that more public activity, financed by higher taxation, and reduced private discretionary income, are both inevitable for social and logistical reasons and necessary to good economic outcomes in a post-liberal environment.

From the orthodox liberal viewpoint, taxation and public spending are important registers of government intervention and therefore of how, in their absence, economic performance can be affected detrimentally. A series of casual assumptions, with close resonances in common sense, expects that taxation stifles private incentives sufficiently to misallocate resources, reduce employment creation and unnecessarily prolong unemployment. The evidence analysed here, from sixteen OECD countries, does not support these conventional views of the consequences of government interference. Table 4.1 shows the relationship between taxation and unemployment where taxation—government receipts as a percentage of GDP—is divided into 'low' (below 35 per cent of GDP), 'medium' (35–50 per cent of GDP) and 'high' (above 50 per cent of GDP). Australia, the United States, Switzerland and Japan were low-tax countries in the period under consideration; Sweden, Norway, the Netherlands and Denmark high-tax countries.

Table 4.1: Taxation and Unemployment in 16 OECD Countries, since 1974

	Taxation			
	Low (%)	Medium (%)	High (%)	Total (%)
Low unemployment	44.7	13.6	36.1	26.1
Medium unemployment	30.3	39.5	31.2	35.4
High unemployment	25.0	46.9	32.7	38.5
Number of cases	76	162	61	299

It can be noted initially that Sweden and Japan, two of the low-unemployment countries, are the nations with the highest and lowest levels of taxation respectively. Table 4.1 indicates that in both the low- and high-taxation categories, the most likely concomitant is low unemployment. Although medium levels of taxation are associated with higher rather than lower levels of unemployment (suggesting a bell-shaped distribution), Austria stands out as an example of a country with medium taxation and low unemployment levels. It is clear that the traditional view of the effect of taxation on unemployment is not endorsed by the evidence. High rates of taxation do not appear to have the effects on performance that those who ignore the impact of policy typically suppose; 'incentives' to good economic performance are less important than has been conventionally imagined. Australia, with the third-lowest taxation over the period, has experienced comparatively high unemployment. The economic effect of taxation depends on what it finances.

Similarly, the empirical relationship between government expenditure, another indicator of 'government interference', and unemployment does not match theoretical expectations of the market perspective. Table 4.2 depicts the relation between government expenditure and unemployment, with government expenditure defined as total government outlays as a percentage

Table 4.2: Government Expenditure and Unemployment in 16 OECD Countries, since 1974

	Government Expenditure		
	Low (%)	High (%)	Total (%)
Low unemployment	33.6	20.7	26.1
Medium unemployment	41.6	31.0	35.4
High unemployment	24.8	48.3	38.5
Number of cases	125	174	299

of GDP. Expenditure below the OECD average of 45 per cent of GDP is 'low', while expenditure above 45 per cent of GDP is 'high'. Table 4.2 shows that higher government expenditure is generally associated with higher unemployment levels, an apparent endorsement of the orthodox perspective. Examination of individual nations, however, shows that only Japan (31.2 per cent) and Switzerland (29.8 per cent) of the low-unemployment countries had expenditure levels in the low category while Norway (48.4 per cent), Austria (49.2 per cent) and Sweden (59.8 per cent) all had comparatively high levels of government expenditure and low levels of unemployment. Once again Australia, with the fourth-lowest average level of government expenditure of the sixteen countries, experienced comparatively bad unemployment for the period reviewed.

Figure 4.1 adds a further dimension to the suggestion that public interference may be effectively counter-cyclical, rather than necessarily detrimental to unemployment. Private consumption expenditure as a percentage of GDP has in general been falling for the past thirty years, in accordance with Wagner's expectations. Where privately determined spending is highest, in the Anglo-Saxon nations, comparatively high unemployment has prevailed. By contrast, private consumption is lower in all the low-unemployment countries included—Norway, Sweden

Figure 4.1: Private Consumption Expenditure as Percentage of GDP in OECD and 10 Countries, 1960–1995

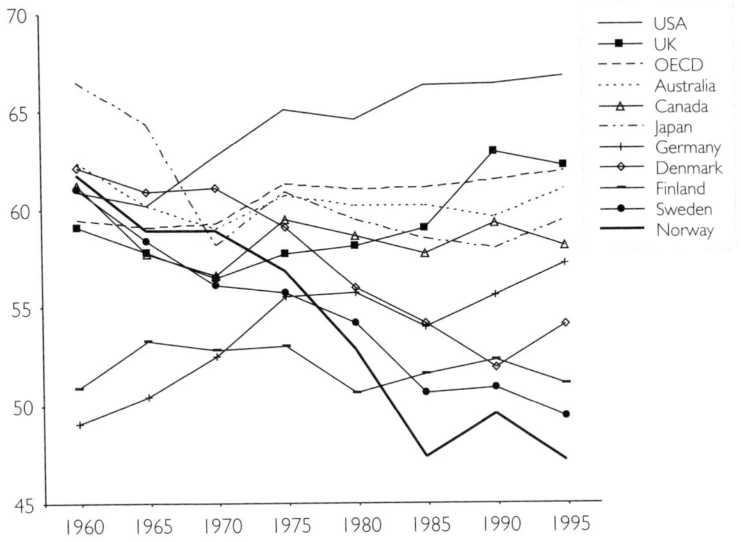

[Line graph showing private consumption expenditure as percentage of GDP from 1960 to 1995 for USA, UK, OECD, Australia, Canada, Japan, Germany, Denmark, Finland, Sweden, and Norway. Y-axis ranges from 45 to 70.]

Source: OECD (1997)

and Japan. Private consumption expenditures, far from being the mainstay of sound and sustainable economic activity, seem instead to be associated with economic volatility. In the United States, the United Kingdom, Australia and Canada, where efforts have been made to expand the role of individual initiative since the recession began, economic performance has remained bad. In the more successful nations, private initiative has generally been curtailed. The 'decommodification' of economic activity has, in those countries, been endorsed in official policy. There is reason to conclude from this evidence that the recent decline of policy-derived economic activity may be more responsible for the recession than the decline of incentives.

Australia's levels of public sector expenditure and taxation are extremely low (after social security contributions by employers, which are part of general revenue collections in Australia, are taken into account). Because of this, a significant range of mechanisms for using policy to transform economic performance is denied the Australian polity. The role of government is constrained rather than excessive. Much of the loss of social civility in the past quarter-century in Australia can be ascribed to the bipartisan tendency to reduce taxation and thus the ability to influence the economy. From a low base, state capacities have been reduced. The conventional insistence that contemporary policy trends towards marketization, deregulation and privatization will establish the 'correct economic settings' is part of a policy milieu that is worsening rather than improving economic performance. There is clearly a misapprehension of the extent of state activity in Australia. Simultaneously, liberal preconceptions have ceased to reflect empirically the forces that actually operate in contemporary capitalist economies.

Does the welfare state create unemployment?

It is conventionally considered that social welfare systems, especially generous systems, discourage employment (for example, Lindbeck 1988; Hughes 1994: 16). Though the low level of wages would seem to be a reasonable a focus for criticism if welfare payments were close to the amount that could be earned in employment, it is often presumed that unemployment benefits erode work incentives for unemployed people if the benefits are too generous and/or available for extended periods of time. In addition, the taxation to fund income compensation is considered to distort the normal operation of market forces and sometimes to compromise international competitiveness. Consequently, welfare systems have been held responsible, directly and indirectly, for unemployment. The support for these contentions, however, is often flimsy and based on unreliable statistical analysis (see, for example, Layard, Nickell & Jackman 1991: 55; Korpi 1996).

Superficial knowledge of the coincidence of generous income replacement arrangements with high rates of labour force participation and low unemployment over a long period provide grounds for considerable scepticism about prejudice concerning the linkages. It is possible to examine the relationships through quantitative analysis. In Table 4.3, the nexus between social welfare and unemployment in the sixteen OECD countries (pooled data only) is explored: 'low' levels of social security transfers are those less than 13 per cent of GDP, those between 13 per cent and 19 per cent are 'medium' and those above 19 per cent are 'high'. Clearly, countries with high social security transfers have higher rather than lower rates of unemployment. In fact, over half the cases with high levels of welfare also have high levels of unemployment; only 12 per cent were associated with low rates of unemployment. However, the low-welfare cases were also associated with medium and high levels of unemployment (40 per cent and 33 per cent respectively) rather than with low unemployment rates (26 per cent); medium levels of welfare are also associated more with lower levels of unemployment. The evidence is thus ambiguous, although it certainly does not systematically support the conventional view that welfare is bad for unemployment.

Of course, it has long been realized that high unemployment accounts for high levels of social security transfers. A more detailed look at the nature of the relationship on a nation by nation basis, with recourse to structural features of unemployment benefit systems, helps clarify the picture.

Table 4.3: Social Security Transfers and Unemployment in 16 OECD Countries, since 1974

	Social Security Transfers			
	Low (%)	Medium (%)	High (%)	Total (%)
Low unemployment	26.4	37.8	12.0	27.4
Medium unemployment	40.6	29.5	34.7	34.6
High unemployment	33.0	32.7	53.3	38.0
Number of cases	106	122	75	303

Table 4.4 presents the data used above in a different way. As anticipated by the data in Figure 2.1, Australia belongs to a group of countries (including the United States, the United Kingdom and Canada) which, although possessing above-average levels of unemployment, have a level of transfers below the OECD average. Australia's deviation from the OECD average, with the lowest level of transfers of any country in the group, is particularly pronounced. By contrast, all countries with significantly lower unemployment than Australia have higher levels of social security transfers, especially Switzerland, Sweden, Norway, Austria and Germany. There is no relationship between social security and unemployment, in either direction.

Table 4.4: Unemployment and Social Security Transfers in 16 OECD Countries

	Unemployment 1974–1992 (%)	Social Security 1970s–1980s (% GDP)
Switzerland	0.6	13.0
Japan	2.3	9.9
Sweden	2.4	17.3
Austria	2.7	19.1
Norway	2.9	14.8
Germany	4.9	16.7
Finland	5.2	9.6
USA	6.9	10.8
Australia	7.0	8.9
France	7.7	19.6
Netherlands	7.8	25.7
Denmark	8.0	15.7
UK	8.2	12.2
Italy	8.7	16.0
Canada	8.7	10.9
Belgium	8.8	20.7
OECD average	6.5	15.1

Source: OECD Economic Outlook (various issues); OECD Historical Statistics 1960–1988

Table 4.4 confirms Australia's small and undeveloped welfare commitment. Australia is decidedly mean in terms of providing such assistance, much meaner than nations with less need to be so, though Castles (1997b) and Castles and Shirley (1997) have argued that once home-ownership and compulsory contributions to superannuation are considered, the situation may be mitigated.

Analysis of comparative evidence concerning ease of access to and longevity of welfare benefits similarly reveals that there is no systematic relationship between welfare generosity and unemployment. Table 4.5 shows, for sixteen nations in the 1980s, the duration of unemployment benefits as well as the replacement rates at which they were provided. That is, it indicates the length of time the stipulated percentage of the previous income of now-unemployed people could be provided from public revenues as a matter of right.

Table 4.5: Duration of Unemployment Benefits and Replacement Ratios in 16 OECD Countries, 1980s

	Duration (Years)	Replacement Ratio (%)
Switzerland	1.0	70
Japan	0.6	60
Sweden	1.2	80
Austria	indefinite	60
Norway	1.5	65
Germany	indefinite	63
Finland	indefinite	75
USA	0.5	50
Australia	indefinite	39
France	3.75	57
Netherlands	indefinite	70
Denmark	2.5	90
UK	indefinite	36
Italy	0.5	2
Canada	0.5	60
Belgium	indefinite	60

Source: OECD Employment Outlook

The data show that the nations with lower unemployment are not those with the least generous benefit systems (lower replacement ratios), even though duration of benefits (at the high replacement rate) is comparatively limited for the top four nations. The Reserve Bank has argued that the rise in the level of unemployment benefits from 15 to around 30 per cent of average wages since the mid-1960s has coincided with the increase in structural unemployment after the early 1970s (RBA 1993: 21). However, this disingenuous argument is an artefact of the time-series research design the Reserve Bank uses, unemployment benefits having risen everywhere during the postwar years. (Comparative analysis is a prophylactic against spurious conclusions derived from the experience of only one nation.) In any case, Australia's income compensation/replacement rate is the third lowest of the countries listed. While recognizing this, the Reserve Bank has nevertheless continued to insist that 'unlike many countries, Australia's benefits are paid out for an indefinite duration, which may contribute to the incidence of longer-term unemployment' (1993: 21). The case remains unconvincing. Australia is far from alone in this respect. Austria, Finland and Germany all have benefits of an indefinite duration, at higher rates of replacement, and yet lower unemployment levels for the period under investigation. Sweden's system could also hardly be regarded as endorsing a loss of benefits after a specified period: after unemployment benefits have been exhausted, people are guaranteed work in the public sector after many other labour market measures have been activated. In addition, although most higher unemployment nations have benefits of considerable duration, the United States, Canada and Italy are all notably ungenerous, with benefits terminating after six months.

The comparative evidence indicates strongly, therefore, that reduced generosity in unemployment compensation will not reduce unemployment but will exacerbate social problems (see, for example, Friedland & Sanders 1986; Gordon 1988; Korpi 1985, 1991; Pierson 1991: 162–3; Saunders 1985; Schmidt 1982a, 1982b, 1983a, 1983b, 1987; Thurow 1981; Wilensky 1981). Unemployment is not, after all, voluntary, but macroeconomic and mainly structural. As Paul Ormerod noted in the context of the European experience:

> regulations on . . . unemployment benefit have changed only slowly, if at all, in the various European Community countries during the past twenty years. If anything, regulations have been tightened against the recipients of benefit, making it more difficult for them to draw it for long periods. Yet unemployment now is typically four times higher in the European countries than it was two decades ago. Despite this seemingly intractable empirical difficulty for the argument that tightening the rules for drawing unemployment benefit is crucial to reducing unemployment, the idea persists and has influence with policy makers (1994: 125).

The Australian government's emphasis on the deleterious effects on the long-term unemployed of a lengthy absence from the labour market reinforces the point that welfare is far from detrimental, although the way in which it is delivered may matter a great deal.

Overall, then, the argument that government interference in the economy, in the form of welfare, reduces efficiency, competitiveness and productivity by imposing extra taxes and costs on the private sector, is based on an economic view which has always been criticized. The positive effects on economic activity of social policies, even if not directly productive or efficient, needs to be more seriously addressed. In the terms raised by Wagner, it is entirely inappropriate to judge all economic activity by the criterion of efficiency if societal development is high enough to allow other determinants of desirable and undesirable activity to be applied. It is well established that higher levels of education, health and general welfare are associated with higher levels of employee productivity. Even if this were not so, an increasing proportion of the total economy can be expected to consist of decommodified and low-productivity activity in rich economies, especially as social democratic aspects of policy are realized.

The abstract focus of economics, which defines itself in terms of the 'economic problem' (scarcity) rather than in terms of how actual economies, with differing levels of development, degrees of resource availability and productive possibilities, deploy their actual and potential resources, has dominated economic analysis for more than a century. But there are other traditions of economic analysis, including institutional studies, which do not ascribe ideal or equilibrating tendencies to market economies. Markets are not eternally or inviolably legitimate, but only in so far as they deliver national prosperity in a non-cyclical and socially acceptable way. For developmental, counter-cyclical and political reasons, institutions may be constructed to curtail the influence of market criteria. Welfare systems do this, although not with equal degrees of commitment to anti-market principles. Even where the market principle is deemed to be appropriate, exogenous or foundational, political interference may be required to create the conditions necessary for liberalized economic activity, as Karl Polanyi has insisted.

A heterodox approach to economic management and welfare systems is almost inevitable in Australia because it is in a vast, sparsely settled continent that the developmental and the cross-subsidization potential of national economic policy have most to offer. Australians will probably always need to pay more per person for some services to meet the standard prevailing in more closely settled continents where per capita costs are lower. Prosperity can depend on the aspects of policy, such as taxation-funded government spending and welfare transfers, that maintain demand, incomes and affluence. Yet, paradoxically, despite its very small public sector, Australia experienced the welfare state 'backlash' as early as 1975. As Hugh Stretton has said, Australia got the backlash before it got the welfare state (1980).

Do labour market policies affect unemployment?

Examination of labour market programmes allows a detailed understanding of how welfare systems and public policy affect unemployment. The institutional mechanisms for delivery of market-compensating welfare measures have important consequences for economic performance. The most exhaustive comparative analysis of welfare states has argued:

> the modern, advanced welfare state has deliberately abandoned the minimalist philosophy (that social policy should cater only for those unable or unfit to work), and espouses entirely new principles with regard to its proper role in the life-cycle, now often committing itself to optimise people's capacities to work, to find work, and even to count on a good job with good pay and working environment. The goal is to allow individuals to harmonize working life with familyhood, to square the dilemmas of having children and working, and to combine productive activity with meaningful and rewarding leisure. In some countries, at least, this philosophy has buttressed recent decades of social-policy development; indeed, it often underpins the legitimacy and common understanding of many contemporary welfare states (Esping-Andersen 1990: 141).

Because full employment is an important component in this 'modern, advanced welfare state philosophy' (see, for example, Meidner 1980; Dow 1993), active labour market programmes are a central institutional requirement. It is therefore necessary to evaluate the types and role of labour market policy and the degree to which it contributes to reducing unemployment.

In defiance of those bodies of thought—conservative as well as social democratic—which have regarded the establishment of 'labour markets' as a wholly undesirable accomplishment of liberalism, the conventional approach is that full employment is the normal and expected outcome of freely operating labour markets. If unemployment exists, it must result from imperfections in the market; hence the policy focus on deregulation, on removal of the institutional characteristics of labour markets in particular. However, a more contextual attitude to the effects of labour market programmes can be imagined and some economists have endorsed activism in this area (see, for example,

Layard, Nickell & Jackman 1991; OECD 1990a). Whereas some strands of labour market analysis recognize that markets alone cannot successfully retrain and reallocate the working population to the sectors and regions where new and different employment is required, others strands argue that they should not. In times of mass unemployment such as has been experienced in the OECD countries for the past twenty-five years, both strands of academic argument can be heard. When patterns of economic activity are changing, economies are being restructured and economic policy is facing contradictory pressures (often with inadequate institutional means), the crucial analytical issue is deciding the mix of policy intervention and market adjustment that can best deal with underutilized labour, the most important symptom of structural transformation.

Systematic data for labour market programmes is not available for the entire period studied. Data is available since 1985, however, allowing us to draw some conclusions about the effects of various types of labour market programmes. Table 4.6 presents this data. 'Total' expenditure is the sum of all labour market programme expenditures as a percentage of GDP. The 'active/passive' ratio is the ratio of public employment services and administration, labour market training, youth measures, subsidized employment and measures for the disabled (OECD 1992a: 89–90), to unemployment compensation or early retirement for labour market reasons. It has been argued that passive programmes are the least effective mechanisms for dealing with unemployment (Korpi 1991).

Table 4.6 shows that the ranking of countries' unemployment for the latter part of the recession (1985–92) is remarkably similar to that for the post-1974 period. Although two low-unemployment countries (Austria and Norway) for the post-1974 period have medium levels after 1985, their comparative position remains the same. The only other major difference is the altered ranking for the United States (medium after 1985). This is evidence that the domestic mode of regulation of these economies has remained relatively constant, indicating in turn the possibility of national autonomy. In the case of the bad

Table 4.6: Active and Passive Labour Market Programmes and Unemployment in 16 OECD Countries, 1985–1992

	Unemployment	Total Labour Market Expenditures (% GDP)	Active/Passive Measures
Switzerland	1.0	0.43	0.95
Sweden	2.4	3.48	2.03
Japan	2.4	0.44	0.52
Austria	3.5	1.35	0.30
Norway	3.9	1.59	0.89
Germany	5.8	2.27	0.75
Finland	5.9	2.86	0.63
USA	6.3	0.75	0.50
Australia	8.1	1.53	0.28
Netherlands	8.6	3.83	0.40
Belgium	9.2	4.19	0.38
Canada	9.2	2.45	0.31
Denmark	9.2	5.63	0.29
UK	9.2	2.17	0.49
France	9.9	2.87	0.37
Italy	10.5	1.54	0.79

Source: OECD Employment Outlook

performers, the persistence of domestic policy unable or unwilling to compensate for adverse international economic circumstances is demonstrated. In these cases, the mode of regulation may have facilitated international adjustment but not domestic prosperity.

At first glance, the table appears not to provide any clear relationship between labour market programmes and unemployment. Switzerland and Japan as low-unemployment nations, for example, have minuscule proportions of GDP devoted to total labour market programme expenditure compared to Sweden's considerable 3.48 per cent and its good economic performance. Of the bad performers, Denmark spends a remarkable 5.63 per cent of GDP while the United States and Australia spend among the lowest of the OECD countries. The situation seems to be that high levels of unemployment compensation expenditures are not necessary for low unemployment and do not secure it.

A closer look at the way programmes are structured, however, reveals important patterns. The low- and medium-unemployment countries, except Austria, all have labour market programmes in which at least half the spending is active. That most of these nations have comparatively high levels of social security transfers indicates that generosity is often discharged in the context of an active, policy-driven, approach to labour market adjustment. Even when total expenditure is not comparatively high, as in Switzerland and Japan, active measures still occupy a significant proportion of the effort, though many people would regard some active measures as undesirable or discriminatory (Katzenstein 1984: ch. 4). The high-unemployment countries have comparatively higher levels of expenditure but they all (except Italy) have systems in which passive measures predominate. Australia stands out as having a comparatively low level of total labour market expenditure and the lowest proportion of active measures.

By comparative standards, then, Australia lags well behind the effort of other nations to create a more activist policy, even though there are recurrent suggestions that its effort in this area is already excessive: an *Australian Financial Review* editorial asserted in December 1993 that 'labour market programs are a poor substitute for removing the artificial barriers in the labour market to the unemployed getting a job'. This is the official sentiment that has driven the moves for 'labour market reform' through the late 1990s. The ACTU once estimated that simply maintaining current labour market programme expenditure levels would result in a reduction of only 50 000 in the extent of long-term unemployment by 1995–96 (leaving 300 000). It identified a number of ways in which labour market programmes could be enhanced in a more activist direction (1993: 7, 48–61). A similarly expansionist position has urged that direct job creation, particularly in community services, could reinstate the virtuous trends of the postwar period, contribute to the government's efficiency and welfare objectives and be conducive to promoting a labour-intensive recovery unlikely to fuel excessive imports (for example, Quiggin 1993; Langmore & Quiggin 1994). But alongside these few positive endorsements of more active labour market policy is the negativity derived from commentators who foist conventional wisdom on the policy-makers and so constrain Australia's public capacities. Even modest expansionary measures were rejected or postponed in the 1994 *Working Nation* White Paper, an official statement that had been heralded as a turning-point in the way Australia approached its economic problems.

Once again, then, the comparative evidence shows that public debates over labour market programmes within Australia are dramatically misconceived. First, policy directions that are only minimally developed are constantly castigated, even though the evidence suggests that they are necessary for improved economic performance. Second, Australia does not have the institutional mechanisms to develop a more effective series of economic policies. The theme of this book is not just that comparative economic analysis provides knowledge more conducive to appropriate policy responses to Australia's current predicament, but that public capacities need to be expanded to allow expansion of economic capacities. Orthodox views of the economy stifle debate while institutional underdevelopment stifles the re-generation of the economy itself.

Does investment matter?

Labour market policy includes training, retraining, job placement, special arrangements for disadvantaged workers, special arrangements for disadvantaged regions or sectors, troubleshooting to identify impending problems or to pre-empt skill imbalances, labour-hoarding measures if problems are expected to be only temporary and wholesale geographic or sectoral relocation of affected parts of the workforce. Many of these measures will be uncontroversial, some will be controversial. It is accepted, though, by both proponents and opponents of active labour market policy, that labour market policy alone cannot eliminate recession. Enhancing the ability of the currently unemployed to obtain work will reshuffle the unemployment queue rather than reduce it. Ultimately, active programmes can succeed only if new investment generates new economic activity. With rising population and rising participation rates, the level of employment must be expanded, with many more new jobs needed than the number of currently unemployed. If part of the problem is the movement of activity off-shore, the level of domestic employment needs to increase. Investment is critical in influencing the level of employment and unemployment. If there is too little capacity to keep up with demand, industries have disappeared, technological change has reduced the amount of labour required in production or imports have increased as a result of increased domestic wealth generation, only investment in new activity will be able to redress the problems. Lead times may be long in arranging for new productive capacity to come 'on stream', but no other course of action actually addresses the problem of economic downturn.

We hope that the following analysis makes a more forceful contribution to the debate over what ought to be done in times of recession than either the standard advocacy of more market flexibility or the periodic recourse to deflationary and contractionary policy whenever levels of economic activity do begin to increase.

Table 4.7 tests one of the most notorious claims of orthodox economic analysis—that only private sector investment can generate 'real' employment. Private investment, it is said, is the key to economic recovery; government investment only crowds out private sector activity rather than provides the basis for higher or more sustainable levels of economic performance. The table presents the relationship between public sector capital investment (net of the investment undertaken by public enterprises) and unemployment. 'Low' public capital expenditure is defined as below the OECD average of 3.3 per cent of GDP; expenditure above this level is characterized as 'high'. The relationship is remarkably clear—high levels of government capital expenditure are associated with much lower levels of unemployment. Well

Policy options **137**

Table 4.7: Government Capital Expenditure and Unemployment in 16 OECD Countries, since 1974

	Government Capital Expenditure		
	Low (%)	High (%)	Total (%)
Low unemployment	6.5	46.1	22.5
Medium unemployment	34.3	40.9	37.0
High unemployment	59.2	13.0	40.5
Number of cases	169	115	284

over half the cases of low public capital expenditure (almost 60 per cent) are associated with high levels of unemployment and almost half of the high government capital investment cases (46 per cent) are linked with low rates of unemployment. Very few cases support the counter-proposition that government capital investment impedes economic performance.

No doubt, some variants of the conventional wisdom accept that government investment does contribute to better employment outcomes. However, it is more commonly claimed that private sector investment is of far greater importance. Table 4.8 examines this thesis by revealing the effect of private capital

Table 4.8: Private Capital Expenditure and Unemployment in 16 OECD Countries, since 1974

	Private Capital Expenditure		
	Low (%)	High (%)	Total (%)
Low unemployment	11.0	38.0	22.5
Medium unemployment	33.8	41.3	37.0
High unemployment	55.2	20.7	40.5
Number of cases	163	121	284

expenditure on unemployment. 'Low' private capital expenditure is below the OECD average of 19 per cent of GDP and 'high' private investment expenditure is above that figure. The relationship is certainly the same in terms of the positive effect of private investment on (lower) levels of unemployment. However, contrary to orthodox predictions, the relationship is not as strong as that between government capital expenditure and unemployment. The cases are distributed much more evenly across the different categories, indicating that the connection here is less marked than that in Table 4.7.

The comparison is clearer in the graphical presentation of the same (pooled) data in Figure 4.2. When unemployment rates are plotted against private and public capital spending, the

Figure 4.2: Relation between Investment and Unemployment: Private and Public Sectors in 15 OECD Countries, 1970s and 1980s

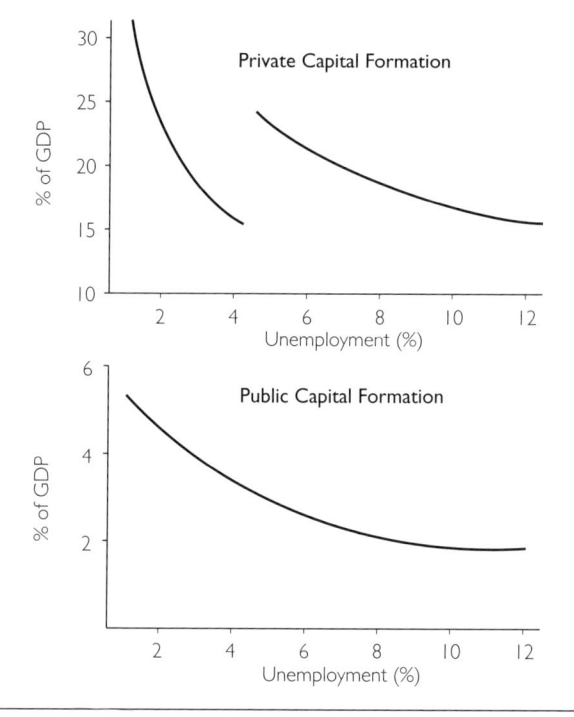

Source: OECD National Accounts, OECD Economic Outlook *(various issues) and pooled data from Labour & Industry Research Unit, University of Queensland*

country/year readings cluster around the curves. The data reveal that very small increases in public investment have had dramatic effects on unemployment, even at very low rates of unemployment. An increase in public capital formation from 2 to 4 per cent of GDP seems to result in unemployment reduced from around 10 per cent to 2.5 per cent—an enormous reduction that effectively wipes out recession. Although this is pooled data from fifteen OECD countries and may not represent the economy of any of them, there is reason to accept that the economies are sufficiently similar to provide a valuable guide to public policy in each. On average across the OECD, it seems that about 4.5 per cent of GDP spent by government (each year) on capital investment projects would eliminate unemployment. In Australia, this would amount to about $25 billion, about half as much again as it has spent annually in the past two decades. Even for nations where unemployment is already low, only a small increase in public capital expenditure is required to make a relatively large inroad into unemployment. In contrast, for private sector capital formation, the pattern differs between the high-unemployment and low-unemployment countries, although in both cases a much larger augmentation of (private rather than public) investment is required to have similar effects on unemployment.

A further dimension of the relationship between government and private capital expenditure is shown in Table 4.9. The categories are the same as defined above. The data indicate that

Table 4.9: Public and Private Capital Investment in 16 OECD Countries, 1970s–1980s

	Private Investment		
	Low (%)	High (%)	Total (%)
Low public investment	67.3	39.8	54.3
High public investment	32.7	60.2	45.7
Number of cases	110	98	208

government sector expenditure does not crowd out private economic activity. Each is high when the other is high. In other words, public investment has the benefit of making private investment more effective; investing in public infrastructure directly augments private sector production possibilities. This is theoretically consistent with critical and Keynesian suggestions that the economy functions effectively only in the context of regulations and infrastructural support. This need not be provided by government, but traditionally it has been, and these data reveal its efficacy. The self-regulation presumed of markets does exist but it is not as beneficial as publicly based regulation, if permanent full employment, stable standards of living and a capacity to develop civilized values are political goals. Japan, with its strong tradition of government intervention, bases its success on a compatible philosophy: Japan's average level of public investment over the 1974–92 period was 6.3 per cent of GDP, almost double the level of capital spending by Australia's public sector. In general terms, only the countries which have developed larger public services have been able to provide quality employment opportunities at a time when manufacturing's significance is in universal decline (Esping-Andersen 1990).

It has been well documented that government capital expenditure (as a percentage of government outlays) has been declining in Australia since 1974. This decrease in the provision of public infrastructure means that productivity, employment and incomes are all lower than would otherwise have been the case. In fact, of fifteen of the OECD countries examined here (data for Switzerland was unavailable), only Italy and Norway did not have lower levels of public capital formation in 1988 than in 1974 and only Australia and the United Kingdom had higher levels of private sector investment in 1988. Table 4.10 shows levels of public sector capital investment for the period 1974–92.

Given the importance of government investment in its own right as well as for private capital formation, just maintaining 1974 levels of investment would have eased the OECD unemployment situation dramatically. The implication is that

Table 4.10: Public Sector Capital Investment as Percentage of GDP in 15 OECD Countries, annual average 1974–1992

Japan	5.4
Austria	4.0
Norway	3.8
Sweden	3.5
Finland	3.5
France	3.2
Australia	3.0
Netherlands	3.0
Germany	2.9
Canada	2.8
Italy	2.7
Belgium	2.7
UK	2.6
Denmark	2.6
USA	1.7

Source: OECD National Accounts Main Aggregates: Vol. 2 *(various issues)*

even though national distinctiveness has eroded during the globalization of economic activity, most nation-states have helped undermine their autonomy by failing to preserve quite normal levels of public responsibility for economic development.

These findings have clear implications for governments' budget strategies, especially the fiscal consolidation and deficit reduction strategies the OECD has recently advised. The Australian government's commitment to a reduced budget deficit (or even to ongoing surpluses) is particularly arbitrary and foolish in light of the evidence presented here. The extent of government spending should never be judged by whether it contributes to a deficit (which in any case depends on taxation receipts and the willingness to impose taxes as much as on spending decisions) but by whether it sponsors something useful. The only possible consequence of deficit fetishism is the reduction of public capacity. Contraction of revenue-raising possibilities, tightening of spending, the sale of public assets, reformed administrative criteria along private sector lines, or all of these together, could well induce permanent structural incapacities for the public sphere and the nation.

It remains unreasonable for new public sector investment to be financed through a budget deficit, especially in a nation such as Australia whose taxation levels are so low. Although one register of the impoverishment of contemporary politics is the unwillingness of politicians to advocate tax increases, their lack of gumption or Machiavellianism in trying to step around obstacles to what ought to be done, it is possible to calculate the approximate fiscal requirement for a full employment level of public expenditures to be secured. On the basis of the figures above, if all of Australia's 9.3 million taxpayers paid an extra $800–1000 per year taxation and if this were invested in public sector infrastructure, full employment could be achieved. This is not a minor increment to overall levels of taxation, but community sentiment in Australia in the last years of the 1990s has hardly rewarded the efforts of governments trying to reduce their public 'burden'. Evidence from other countries suggests both that public endorsement of public courage is readily available if the results are higher levels of security and that a more civilized sentiment is thereby achievable. It is a shame the level of statecraft in Australia is so low that a comparatively effortless solution to one of the greatest tragedies of modern times—unnecessary unemployment—is not even considered (see Dow 1997a). Current trends can only damage economic performance in the countries that embrace them—unemployment being the starkest register of poor performance and the resulting insecurity a worrying indicator of societal disintegration.

It is frequently claimed that a major obstacle to recovery is national indebtedness. In popular renditions, this is often presented as a direct government responsibility and occasionally as if public debt were the main contributor. Figure 4.3 shows that, like most of the other journalistic propositions examined, this view is wrong. As indicated, Australia has by far the lowest level of gross public debt of the nine countries included. Sweden and Japan, two low-unemployment countries, have considerably higher levels of public debt. In any case, public debt is a problem

Figure 4.3: Gross Public Debt in 9 OECD Countries (% GDP), 1980–1993

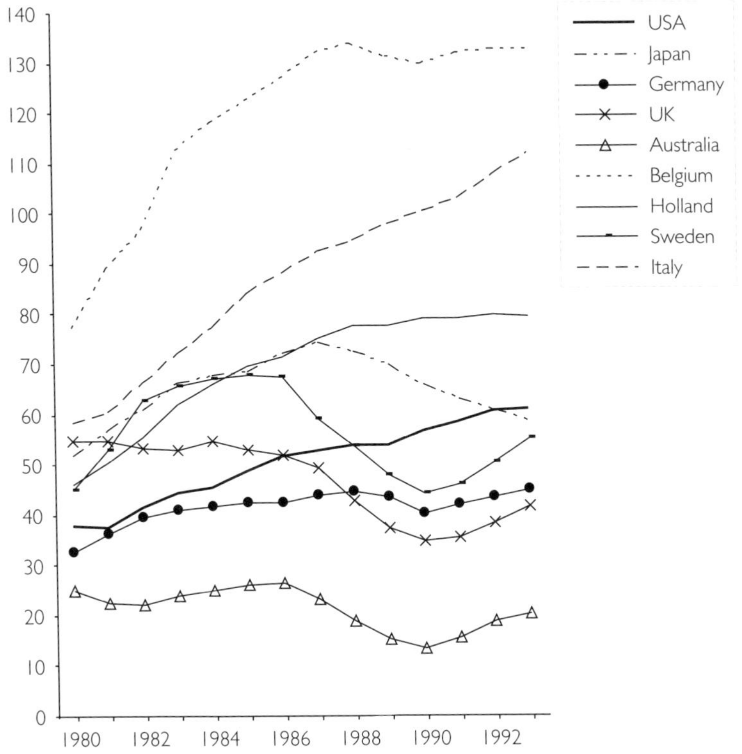

Source: OECD (1988b, 1992b)

only if the funds borrowed are not deployed prudently. If used as public capital formation or as a central part of a reflationary economic strategy, or even to prevent the unproductive diversion of existing capital into existing assets, the debt is entirely legitimate; it might even be argued that to have such low public debt at a time of serious erosion of national capacities is irresponsible. Privatization of national communications networks is clearly accompanied by the likelihood that parts of the network will be dismantled or deteriorate technologically.

An additional contention is that the public sector's demand for capital needs to be minimized in order to re-establish an appropriate level of national savings. The Fitzgerald Report

(1993) was the major document in this respect, suggesting that savings were too low because of excessive private and public consumption. The conventional view is now that continued reductions in public sector expenditure would allow savings to increase and hence make funds available for productive private investment. The evidence presented here does not allow such a conclusion, and in any case it should be realized that attempts to increase savings directly are more likely to lead to a reduction in savings as demand, incomes, purchasing power and activity dry up. The conventional argument has been floated for most of the 1990s, but in 1997 it became the basis for an extraordinary budget decision to reduce taxation rates for unearned income, thus substantially reasserting a nineteenth-century class bias for only symbolic advantage.

Savings are always low in recession because a substantial portion of the workforce is without income. Increases in savings follow, not precede, increases in investment and activity. Society must decide to increase its level of investment, not to increase its savings in the hope that a spontaneous generation of investment will follow. Investment decisions themselves will generate increased incomes, and therefore savings; macroeconomic management should not proceed from attempts to control savings (Keynes 1932). In any case, as the 1980s demonstrated, savings do not automatically lead to new investment, or the investment that is desirable or required.

Even the level of demand is not the major factor in investment decisions because public sector investment can proceed irrespective of overall economic conditions. The empirical evidence of the last thirty years in Australia clearly shows that the decline in national savings has followed deterioration in economic growth and investment rates rather than being the cause of poor performance (Sicklen 1994). In other words, savings should be considered to be a function of levels of economic activity. Investment needs to be stimulated directly by decisions to generate or regenerate particular industry sectors or activities; it should not be left to uncoordinated or unconcerned forces in the market. There is probably no more important lesson to be learned from Keynes' writings than that national economic performance depends on social control of investment. For this lesson to be translated into practical policy new political institutions, with a specific charter to oversee investment and industrial development, are necessary.

New political institutions

In its early stages, unregulated market-driven capitalist development was in its own terms fairly successful. It may be conceded that there was then no socially acceptable alternative path from subsistence to affluence, despite moral objections, manifest inequalities and unnecessary sufferings. It might reasonably be argued that self-interest and individualism played a progressive role historically, temporarily excusing the limitations on democratic development imposed by the capacity-to-pay doctrine. But it is not reasonable to conclude from this that more advanced societies are best managed according to the same principles. With complexity comes not only a range of problems which need non-market solutions, but the opportunity and societal capacity to develop those solutions. Institutional and discursive arrangements being what they are, however, the development of effective policy responses to recession is impeded more by ignorance, bloody-mindedness and the absence of suitable mechanisms than by the logistical difficulty of the task. In short, there are not the appropriate institutional structures to formally commit the political process to full employment, and the most powerful institutions that do exist have recurrently mobilized very effectively to ensure that more interventionist arrangements, with better-developed policy capacities, do not come into being. Treasuries and Finance departments, for example, have in many countries since the 1930s devoted much of their intellectual and political resources to the promotion of policies that mutate the policy process. The dominant lines of discussion concern not how to achieve permanent full employment but how to avoid violation of the market principle.

If more substantive goals are to be activated, more deliberative capacity needs to be created in the political system. New political institutions need to be created to expand the possibilities of democracy and to manage the economy in such a way that undemocratic, inefficient or inegalitarian outcomes are minimized. In other words, institutional management of the economy envisions superior economic performance in the form of lower unemployment, more guided sectoral change in industry and non-authoritarian anti-inflationary and anti-recessionary strategies; at the same time the possibility of direct political input into the processes of macroeconomic management, for reasons not commensurate with conventional evaluations of economic performance, is retained. The most characteristic political goal in this respect would be full employment, but public, institutional, democratic or deliberated mechanisms for its attainment might well impose other criteria such as environmental sustainability, regional viability, workplace equity or enhanced social rights (higher levels of public provision). As indicated earlier, it can reasonably be expected that mature or well-developed economies have an increasing capacity and need to devote resources to activities that would once have been regarded as unproductive, inefficient or unnecessary. One of the concerns of this chapter has been to point out that such reductions in scope for the market principle do not necessarily imply less desirable economic outcomes, though they might well alter the political and institutional environment.

There are well-established intellectual traditions that have for a century or more postulated the emergence of a more institutionally or politically controlled economy which nonetheless remains in other respects emphatically capitalist. Most well known is Keynes' advocacy in 1936 of some significant institutional control of investment (based on suggestions he made earlier in the 1930s for a National Investment Board). With no political agenda beyond the revitalization of the economy that had been struck by immense sectoral transformation requiring new industrial developments and by economic policies which worsened existing conditions, Keynes argued that private expectations were so low (and volatile) that they could not be relied upon to produce an acceptable (non-cyclical) pattern of economic activity in good times or bad. The chief responsibility of national controls over investment:

> would be to maintain the level at a high enough rate to ensure the optimum level of employment. Without such an instrumentality, we may be sure that the disastrous fluctuations in the volume of employment will continue in the future as severely as in the past (1932: 137).

> I conceive, therefore, that a somewhat comprehensive socialization of investment will prove the only means of securing an approximation to full employment (1936: 378).

Though the institutional proposals remain somewhat undeveloped in Keynes' writings, it is clear from subsequent and contemporary experience that investment must be controlled because investment decisions determine the macroeconomic structure. It is the weakening of a nation's industrial structure—a pattern of industrial activity that has become anachronistic in terms of the domestic or export demands for its output—that constitutes the essence of recession. Such situations may develop in association with similar transformations of other economies, or they may result from technological change, corporate strategies or managerial competences nationally or internationally. The point of the Keynesian contribution to economic analysis is that investment is the key to the operations (level and structure) of any economy. If investment can be controlled, so can recession and unemployment. There has always been political resistance to this kind of economic control, but if it is not achieved economic performance remains sub-optimal. The substance of the Keynesian proposals, like those of the German statist theorists but unlike those of the Marxists, is that it is possible to manage the process of structural transition using appropriately developed political institutions.

Since the mid-1970s, inflation has accompanied unemployment to such an extent that simultaneous unemployment and inflation can now be said to characterize the current recession. Inflation in recession initially appeared to be inexplicable and the conventional responses were more appropriate to boom-time inflation. They therefore tended to depress economic activity and to worsen the economic downturn. From a Keynesian and post-Keynesian viewpoint both the distributive conflicts that give rise to inflation and the inappropriate policy responses were entirely predictable. Wage rises, if met by price rises, cause inflation. A key determinant of the extent to which a national economy experiences inflation is, therefore, the extent to which labour movement organizations are able to demand and receive wage increases. Although it was conventionally thought that bargaining capacity was muted during times of unemployment, the postwar era witnessed a steady expansion in the organizational strength and acumen of trade unions. Corporate power also increased, enhancing its capacity to increase prices even during times of economic downturn. As revenues tended to be maintained by companies (even at the expense of higher mark-ups) and real wages tended to be maintained by trade unions (even though the demand for labour was declining), inflation, reflecting the economic and industrial power of capital and labour, increased. This is precisely the kind of inflation anticipated by post-Keynesian writers such as Michal Kalecki in the 1940s. Its solution demands another institutional innovation—societal control over the distributive struggle involving profits and wages. This is usually referred to as incomes policy. Incomes policy institutions are of many kinds, ranging from state controls over prices and/or incomes, to voluntary centralized bargaining between capital and labour, to compulsory forms of conciliation and arbitration. These are all the antithesis of the monetarist and neoclassical response to inflation, which is to decrease the level of economic activity in the hope of reducing the amount of money available to flow through into higher prices.

Institutionalized control of wages and profits does not eliminate the class conflict underlying inflation in recession, but institutionalization of the conflict is crucial to controlling this sort of inflation. Now that labour and capital are institutionally strong, the controls need to be permanent. Inflationary conflicts persist in times of high employment. The point is that full employment will always be unstable and a potential source of inflation if it is not accompanied by institutional developments sufficient to control income distribution. Inflation is an inevitable outcome of full employment only if nothing is done to secure an institutionally effective incomes policy.

One of the great merits of the Australian system of centralized wage fixation is that it has provided the policy process with a mechanism for implementing national incomes policy. Were arbitration to be dismantled, the potential to subject the distribution of income to the policy process would be lost and policy would then resort to other, less effective, less appropriate and more draconian anti-inflationary measures.

The third institutional innovation required for permanent full employment is the set of organizational arrangements usually encapsulated in the term 'labour market policy'. The purpose of labour market institutions is primarily to prevent the 'labour market' from operating according to market principles. The most long-standing objections to the liberal institutional transformations that underwrote the development of capitalist economies were concerned with the emergence of a labour market, treating people as if they were commodities. Both conservative and social democratic/Marxist traditions have criticized wage labour, the commodification of people's living standards and the resort to unemployment as a way of dealing with fluctuations in the level of economic activity. Since the 1930s, affluent societies have increasingly been able to afford public financial commitments to policies designed to remove some of the market characteristics of a labour market: income replacement, assistance with occupational and geographic mobility, job placement services, pre-emptive trouble-shooting, training and retraining schemes, special assistance to disadvantaged workers, public employment, subsidized employment, labour hoarding, standby projects and infrastructure spending.

Labour market programmes can be very expensive and, as noted earlier, do not really deal with the root cause of unemployment, which is economic downturn. Nonetheless, because the advocates of post-liberal policy institutions have always opposed the liberal commodification of labour, the effort and cost associated with directly trying to reduce unemployment is considered essential. Consequently, it is impossible to imagine permanent full employment without strong and well-funded labour market policy.

Together, these three institutional developments are necessary in any country with pretensions to long-term full employment. Fundamental to political management of the economy is public control of investment. There have been many attempts to develop such arrangements in the past sixty years (from New Deal and public works projects to counter-cyclical investment funds and politicized deployment of accumulated pension funds) and many attempts to deny their legitimacy.

Embryonic forms of these post-liberal institutional arrangements probably exist in most capitalist economies. However much they disrupt the conventional view that only privately mandated economic activity ought to govern national economic performance, such institutional developments seem to be increasingly necessary. The institutional mechanisms to control investment need to be buttressed by ancillary institutions to control income distribution and to usurp some aspects of the labour market. These proposals are summarized in Table 4.11.

The objective of this chapter has been to demonstrate the inaccuracy of many of the views which underlie current economic policy formation. In the OECD economies during the recession, taxes have not been a barrier to good economic performance and there is reason to think that Australia should increase its general levels of taxation not as a way of dampening demand but as a way of shifting the locus of decision-making from the market arena to the political sphere so that the overall level of activity can be increased, avoiding the damaging contemporary tendency for weak states like Australia's to adopt contractionary instead of expansionary policy options. Government

Table 4.11: New Political Institutions for Expanded State Capacity: Policy Implications of Post-Keynesian Political Economy

Type of Institution Required	Object of Intervention	Theoretical Rationale
Tripartite decision-making body (business, unions, government)	Investment	Keynes: to control cycles
A court system (compulsory arbitration); national wage negotiation and determination	Income distribution	Kalecki: to control inflation at full employment
Active labour market policy (training, retraining, relocation assistance, trouble-shooting)	'Labour market'	Marx and the social democratic and communitarian traditions

spending can increase a nation's productive capacities, both directly through contributions to demand and indirectly through the multiplier effects of the increased, politically motivated spending. These are the dynamic tendencies that give to the policy process its potential not just for economic management but for democratic guidance of the entire process of national development and national adjustment to changing sectoral conditions. Meanwhile, Australia's policy process continues to be dominated by a cohort of public administrators who deny the legitimacy of policy autonomy, people entrusted with public office who have lost any sense of the meaning and potential of public responsibility. They are urging Australia to adapt to a model which embodies unattainable and unnecessary elements of the liberal experiment which was proven unworkable in the 1930s.

The lessons are, first, that the potential of the policy process to do more than integrate the domestic economy with other economies has not been well recognized in Australia and, second, that Australia has not developed the institutional arrangements to achieve that potential. This is a political problem of major dimensions. It is to the politics of economic management that the next chapter turns.

Chapter 5
Political possibilities

Structural unemployment is a political problem because prolonged recession is not technically necessary. It persists because the political system has been unwilling and unable to activate anti-recessionary strategies that have been available for at least half a century. Further, the depoliticization of politics since the 1970s has made the problem worse. Latent democratic capabilities in most modern economies have remained unheralded, their potential unrecognized. The political system has become impoverished, not only resistant to the extension of its own capacities but unable, for doctrinaire reasons, to utilize even those mechanisms within its grasp. State institutions have refused to influence, in an expansionary direction, the level or content of economic activity. We have already indicated that structural tendencies have caused an expansion of the part of the total economy operating under non-market auspices. This could have combined with volitional forces to produce the full employment economies that were envisaged in the 1930s and 1940s. The structural forces, if understood and exploited, could have facilitated political control over recession, whereby full employment could be genuinely reprioritized. Both the long-standing liberal principles which once purported to explain how, why and with what effects national economic development occurred, and the currently fashionable strains of liberal sentiment which insist that development is not a state responsibility and that it is normally illegitimate to impose political criteria onto market processes, are now prolonging the recession. Impotence is not really a new phenomenon; it has been nascent in the form and rationale of liberal polities and economies from their beginning.

The depoliticization of politics has resulted in a loss of productive and administrative capacities. Yet it has been urged upon most western governments, for over two decades now, by an economics profession whose control of the central discourses of social and economic analysis has been abetted by compliant and commensurate developments in other fields of public management. The available critiques of economics are many. It will suffice to mention two aspects of the debates that are presumed in what follows here. First, economics as a discipline has such well-developed conceptual models of how a well-ordered economy would operate (if all the assumptions made in the model held), that it has a tendency to criticize as unreasonable any social or political conditions that render those presumptions inoperative. We do not think the world is wrong if it does not conform to the model. Second, economics presumes that the fundamental problem for all humankind is scarcity—unlimited demand for limited resources. Yet in times of recession many resources are left unused; there is an institutional incapacity to use what is available or to do what can be done. This is the political aspect of full employment.

Despite worsening unemployment, income inequality, societal security, public and private capacities and respect for government, these discursive understandings within liberal polities lead to great economic damage. They drive a political agenda that has become increasingly immune to the substantive preoccupations of the first few postwar decades—national development, problem-solving, institution-building, public morality, civil decency and political principle. Unemployment is therefore a specifically political problem because it results from an underdevelopment of political will.

Liberalism's claim to democratic intent was initially based on fear of the abuses of state power. But this is no longer convincing; its strictures now impede both democratic and material development. Maintaining the political structures and inhibitions of the past, in an era when the pre-liberal excesses have disappeared from most advanced capitalist democracies, underestimates the damage wrought in the liberal era by weak and underdeveloped states and constrains the reconstructive possibilities of the present. It is by choice, not necessity, that public political processes have insufficient resources to deal with unemployment. For the polities and societies that have been experiencing unemployment since 1974, a key question is why the polity, under neo-liberal auspices, has become so willing to provoke supporters and constituents by undoing past accomplishments but seems incapable of facing the struggles necessary to reassert a role for institutionalized, politicized, publicly guided, substantively rational and democratic determination of its economic outcomes. In this chapter, we discuss some explanations that have been presented by major theorists of capitalism over the past century. They all devolve to a recognition that political objections to full employment persist because a return to full employment would not be universally welcomed; it would produce and depend upon significant shifts in the balance of political power between labour and capital. Organizations of capital typically prefer the preservation of liberal prerogatives, perversely, to keep intact the non-interventionist principles that appeared to be the basis of the political strength of capital in the past, even though capital would benefit materially from the prosperity that high levels of economic activity imply.

There are many reasons for thinking that the conditions favourable to national economic progress in the past have changed dramatically. Yet much policy is still formulated in circumstances where such transformations in the nature of economic management cannot be easily considered. Consequently, in many countries, the form and content of policy advice contributes to the problems policy is supposed to resolve. So, although the time is now ripe to embrace both the shift in the relative roles of markets and politics (towards the latter) that policies for full employment imply and the political battles involved, such developments are more likely in some places than others. The chapter discusses the different combinations of politics and markets and the various modes of economic regulation that have already emerged in OECD countries. It also discusses whether past patterns of policy capability indicate countries' abilities to assert an independent political will in the future.

Finally, the chapter presents additional data indicating the positive economic consequences of our recommended changes in the institutional and power arrangements of capitalist economies. In other words, there is already evidence that where unorthodox or post-liberal institutions have been developed, or where trade unions have been able to forge a permanent place in macroeconomic decision-making, overall levels of economic activity have been higher and less volatile, living standards higher and more secure, and sectoral adaptability more manageable and less traumatic.

From markets to politics

To understand the role played by markets in a capitalist economy it has always been necessary to understand the role of social and political conditions—integral parts of the same phenomenon. Initially, capitalist development, as opposed to capricious and slow improvements in living standards, became possible only because there had emerged a social class with a new social role and a political environment conducive to its prerogatives. As capitalist development began to produce capitalist societies, as something more than isolated capitalist activity, it relied on the existence of a class of capitalists, with the power, resources and motivation to create an economic order, and a class of wage labourers, whose conditions of existence depended almost entirely on the decisions of others and on economic outcomes that were the unintended consequence of others' decisions. The inherent politics took a long time to unfold and to acquire nationally specific contours, but its essential features were the principled elevation of private property and property ownership to positions of economic significance, on the one hand, and attempts to thwart this process, on the other.

Capital's 'historic mission' was to create the institutions and arrangements that would become corollaries of an economy based on private ownership. These include the assertion of profitability (rather than arbitrary or personal preference) as the main criterion by which economic activity is decided; the assertion of market mechanisms (rather than administrative or authoritative fiat) to govern the allocation of resources; a system of commodity production, including the creation of a labour market (rather than production for need and treating people as having distinctive needs); and control of the production and labour process by owners or entrepreneurs (rather than by the workers or any more democratic constituency).

The creation and maintenance of these social conditions was an intensely political, and confrontational, process. There is still political conflict in asserting the legitimacy or illegitimacy of these 'social relations' of capitalism. Contemporary conflicts over work conditions, wage rates, principles for wage fixation, taxation, economic management, social welfare (not only the level of benefits but their scope), the extent of public provision, the rights of management, the rights of trade unions, the role of competition, the role of government and the extension of democracy to workplaces or to economic issues are all examples of the political nature of the economy. Political parties and political systems tend either to support or to seek alternatives to these characteristic features of market society.

Over time, movements have emerged to challenge the supremacy of some of the key features of the liberal ideal. There have been suggestions, for example, that the progressive role of market forces would be transitory, rather than permanent. The growth of government has always allowed the potential for explicitly political decisions to be made, or retained, concerning what economies ought to do. Relentless application of privately based rules for calculating benefits and costs has occasionally been considered inappropriate. Economic management on a national scale has emerged as a possibility and, with it, rules and argument concerning the desirability of market intervention by state agencies. The efficacy of private control of the economy has been questioned where success breeds corporate power. Institutional means of subverting the market in the name of communitarian, social, egalitarian or traditional ideals have sometimes been championed; the one guaranteed outcome of competition—a class of losers—has not always been endorsed as socially desirable. Commensurate with the role adopted by capital in the eighteenth and nineteenth centuries, and as a result of the changes needed to ensure the continuation of the productive possibilities of the capitalist economy, it is 'labour's mission' to repoliticize economic decisions. Labour, through its political parties, workplace organizations, policy-making bodies and influence in corporatist institutions, can readily embrace a social democratic project to displace capitalist social relations of production as they become redundant or as opportunities for more democratic influence on the economy arise. An anti-liberal or, more correctly, a post-liberal politics can be expected to emerge as the labour movement asserts its prerogatives over the macro-economy—partly because of the moral hostility labour feels towards labour markets and partly as a continuation of the critique of the limited rationality of capitalism (recurrent unemployment) that has always worried labour. To activate its mission to create institutions capable of decommodifying labour and managing the economy, labour needs to develop both an internal competence that is more than oppositional and the external mechanisms whereby existing societal forces can assume social responsibilities. This is likely to be such a long process that initially labour will be unable to act alone; it will need to manipulate those resources that could be commanded by labour and social democratic governments.

Labour's expanded role, both as an expression of enhanced democratic potential in advanced societies and as an embodiment of an expanded rationality, will of course be resisted. This will continue to make unemployment a political matter.

Theories and doctrines of liberalism have for some time played an important role in preventing the emergence of non-prescriptive solutions to the problems of a competitive market economy. Their dominance in policy advice, for example, seems to be responsible for the inadequacy of industry policy in most countries; for the strength of national institutions devoted to balanced budgets and small government as a point of principle;

for the failure of the 'Keynesian revolution' in most countries; for ongoing opposition to full employment policies and institutions; for inability to recognize that the post-1974 inflation was not primarily demand–pull, but cost–push; for the weakness of national incomes policies in most countries; for the frailty of corporatist institutions in the past two decades; and for the constant official pressure to make labour markets work more 'flexibly', that is, like other markets.

There is little evidence in most capitalist societies in the 1990s of a vibrant intellectual tradition identifying current problems for the policy process to address. Instead, a more or less doctrinaire set of responses, the same solution for each and every problem, is rehearsed in each country, regardless of circumstances, need or ability to survive the medicine.

Discussion of contemporary unemployment should include serious reflection on these long-term issues, involving consideration of how and with what purpose a capitalist economy ought to exist. The types of institutions prefigured in chapter 4 should by now be the subject of public debate. That this has not occurred indicates an impoverished ability to properly examine and understand the changes that have occurred in economies, and an unwillingness to make the requisite institutional changes. For these reasons, the framework within which economic activity is organized is a political matter in both good times and hard times.

The contributions of a number of key schools of political economy to these debates are summarized in Figure 5.1 on pages 160–1.

When conditions are buoyant, there are pressures from labour and social democratic movements to expand the sphere of the economy subject to democratic determination, for example by extending the proportion of production provided and mandated outside the market, for direct distribution to users. Forms of such decommodified production, as shown in Figure 4.1, include not only improved or expanded welfare entitlements but also the public and collective consumption embodied in expenditures on urban amenity, public infrastructure investment and public sector employment. New or reconstructed institutions will need to develop their own charters, rules, procedures and forms of defence against anticipatable criticisms. Though each will involve a politicization of crucial aspects of the economy, they need not imply expansion of the powers of government. Labour and capital, for example, might negotiate outcomes and reach compromise without any explicit political direction—yet the decisions will be different from those that would obtain under more procedurally orthodox auspices.

Current unemployment demonstrates that political dispute over the economy is especially intense during recession because it is then that the inadequacies of traditional laissez-faire arrangements and the need for institutional reform are most apparent. The recession of the past quarter-century has led to spirited and successful reassertion of liberal discourse affecting economic policy, so it cannot really be said that knowledge of failure and societal discontent results in progressive or defensible responses. When recession is combined with long-term evolutionary tendencies in the economy, the dimensions of political resistance to the changes necessary to restore full employment are substantial.

Modes of regulation

The argument that market modes of regulation have become less capable of delivering prosperity or stable levels of economic activity depends on analysis of how capitalist economies have developed. We hope that previous chapters have demonstrated that the solution to contemporary unemployment depends not merely on a change of policy but on the creation of new political institutions (or radical adaptation of existing institutional mechanisms) to allow politicized control of the economy. Capitalist economic development already relies on institutional control of the economy; in all countries government intervention has existed throughout the postwar era. But, as the data in chapters 2, 3 and 4 demonstrated, there is variation. As we have

Figure 5.1: From Markets to Politics: Changing Modes of Regulation

Karl Marx	Development of the 'forces of production' (productive capacities) in capitalist societies is initially facilitated by capitalist 'social relations' of production. However, at higher stages of development, these defining social relations become impediments to further material development and need to be transformed into 'post-capitalist' (non-market) relations if progress is to continue. If capital concedes its prerogatives and allows new post-liberal relations of production, based on political control of the economy, to emerge, production and progressive development will continue, albeit with erosion of the distinctively capitalist nature of the economy.
Adolph Wagner	As industrialization and societal complexity proceed, problems emerge which require societal resolution (initially urban sanitation, later public administration etc.). These costs to society are easily met because income and wealth are simultaneously increasing. But they represent a shift from private to public criteria for activity, higher taxes, an expanding state and therefore a change in the balance between markets and politics.
Emile Durkheim	'Non-contractual elements of contract', non-economic bases of economic activity, are inevitable. Market society produces societal dislocations that warrant redress through organizational, communitarian or ethical arrangements.
Max Weber	Capitalist rationality is defined and facilitated by the possibility of formal rules for calculating benefits and costs, profits and losses. This allows relentless application of formal criteria to decisions concerning desirable economic activity. However, it is likely that recurrent pursuit of formally rational procedures (based on enterprise calculation) will eventually result in substantively irrational outcomes. Resources might be allocated to more profitable but less useful activity. Polities must retain the right to assert explicit (publicly debated) outcomes (such as the long-term sustainability of the national economy) if necessary.

John Maynard Keynes	Structural crises in the economy (of which the clearest manifestation is unemployment) can be averted by state intervention to control ('socialize') investment decisions. Continued prosperity (full employment) would require permanent institutions to shift the entrepreneurs' traditional function (investment decisions) to the public sphere.
Michal Kalecki	The post-Keynesian writers agreed with Keynes, while insisting that rational economic management (in liberal polities) would be resisted by governments and business. If full employment is not generally welcomed, new institutions will be required to institutionalize the conflicts over these aspects of economic policy (for example, inflationary conflicts over income distribution). Inequality is incompatible with high levels of income and employment.
Joseph Schumpeter	Competition and individual innovation initially result in entrepreneurial success. But the resulting 'bigness' and market domination lead to monopoly, which requires bureaucratized (routine) innovation. Unfortunately but inevitably, capitalism would assume more of the features of a planned or negotiated economy and lose its distinctive entrepreneurial character.
Karl Polanyi	Market society is not natural, therefore most societies produce arrangements (such as trade unions, governments) to protect citizens from the adverse effects (risk, uncertainty, inequality, societal dislocation) of the market.
C. B. Macpherson	Liberal economic management has been marred by the contradiction between its espousal of political equality and tolerance of large economic inequalities. Post-liberal interventions are warranted to reconcile political and economic principles.
Joan Robinson	The 'Keynesian revolution' was 'bastardized'; orthodox policy advice triumphed, resulting in policies which unnecessarily prolong recession. Full employment (without inflation) is possible only by reactivating the sentiments and vision of the era of postwar reconstruction, and by recognizing the paradox that private control now impedes private profitability and public prosperity.

indicated, the Australian economy is regulated in a distinctively liberal way and has an industrial structure reflecting its non-interventionist policies. Japan and Germany, on the other hand, have different industries, dependent upon different forms of economic management.

Given the different degrees of government intervention, the different combinations of politics and markets, it is possible to refer to different 'modes of regulation' or different modes of economic governance. These different modes of regulation imply differing political capacities, differing responses to unemployment, different opportunities for the political process to influence economic activity. In short, the development of institutions such as those outlined towards the end of chapter 4 has begun almost everywhere but has proceeded unevenly. Control of the economy that was formerly 'unregulated' (that is, regulated by markets) is now more bargained or negotiated. Some complex manufacturing industries seem to depend upon such a shift; where traditional and less thorough forms of regulation have been retained, manufacturing has been less successful. Both industrial structure and institutional structure are affected by political conditions.

Outlining the concept of the 'negotiated economy', Nielsen and Pedersen have claimed that 'negotiation-based economic processes are conducted partially and, to an increasing extent, within a discursive framework created by institutions, whose aims are to achieve systematic accumulation of experience, to shape opinions and to influence attitudes' (1988: 83). Australia's wage-fixing system, when it was based upon compulsory arbitration and national wage determinations that were binding in all sectors and regions, conformed with this view of a negotiated economy. Australia also has institutions, such as the Treasury, whose experience and influence has been less interventionist. An important instance of political bias in liberal polities is the dominance of institutions like Treasury devoted to a weak state. Nonetheless, as the ninety-year history of the arbitration system shows, there are other possibilities.

It is possible to imagine similar systems of national bargaining, backed by institutions that become repositories of knowledge and expertise, able to influence not only economic outcomes but discussion of outcomes, in respect to aspects of macro-economic policy apart from wages policy. The model provided by compulsory arbitration of disputes between labour and capital could well be applied to disputes over investment practices, if labour aggressively developed its competences and thus asserted a macropolitical role in industry development. Analogous arrangements exist with respect to Japan's industry policy, Germany's system of industrial banking and Sweden's active labour market policy. French and Italian public enterprises, though less successful, provide further examples of modes of regulation designed to influence national industrial structures. Of course, no country yet seems to have a complete system of public economic management based on the principle that political control of investment, income distribution and the labour market is necessary for permanent full employment.

Clearly, unemployment is a less intractable problem in some countries than in others. The differences do not really result from deliberate intention or political volition, but are more or less accidental. They reflect historical differences in the extent to which statist institutions or their pre-capitalist precursors had achieved community legitimacy and therefore encountered less resistance when new tasks were assumed, than in the more explicitly liberal regimes. 'In reality, this is less a question of purely ideological choices between laissez faire and dirigisme than of solutions invented under the pressure of necessity with the aim of bringing social conflict and the accidents of the accumulation process under control' (Boyer 1990: 75).

It may be concluded that some mode of regulation always underwrites capitalist activity, which thereby may be classified as a 'regime of accumulation'; even a market liberal system amounts to a mode of regulation because of its regulation and rationalization through competition. 'Integration through markets' seems to be the current political project of the European Union. Since the recession began, the market mode of regulation has become resurgent, with international competitiveness cited as the major criterion on which economic activity is decided.

Although commitment to some level of public responsibility, however contested and incomplete, has emerged in all advanced capitalist countries in the post-1945 period (Deane 1989: ch. 9), the tasks of economic management are rarely specified. They can be inferred: to generate a high level of economic activity, to maintain it without excessive social or environmental dislocation and to provide effective mechanisms for its restructuring when necessary. Orthodoxy would add external balance and low inflation to the list; social democratic approaches see these as embodied in the three parts of the general prescription, thereby affirming their reluctance to have high levels of activity sacrificed or deferred for more symbolic goals. The Anglo-Saxon countries have institutions that have interpreted the principles of public economic management minimally and austerely, while others have turned them into a more open-ended charter and even a political challenge.

By regulating market behaviour, and thereby constituting the actual economy, institutions and organizations make each economy different from the theoretical model of an economy. It is regulation that converts abstract market principles or laws of accumulation into an economy with real industries and problems: 'The system constituted by such "modes of regulation" defines a particular "regime of accumulation"' (Clarke 1988: 62). Pure economic analysis, in both liberal and Marxist forms, has become redundant because it has been unwilling to acknowledge the extent to which its preferred object of enquiry—market behaviour—differs from the phenomenon we are investigating—the actual economy. It has become apparent that modes of regulation, increasingly though not inherently state-instigated, are crucial to the definition of capitalist economies. Expansion of the tasks of macroeconomic management, like the growth of state activity more generally, marked a distinctive form of regulation. Corporatist institutions mark another. Retreats from previous regulatory arrangements signify further forms of regulation.

By studying regulation, studying the institutional forms that constitute the economy, the long-term changes in the links between capitalism's underlying social relations and the patterns and consequences of accumulation may be examined: 'institutional forms sometimes favour the continuation of the prevailing logic of accumulation, and sometimes undergo a change of orientation and develop along new lines' (Boyer 1990: 68). An Australian example is the conversion of the dispute settlement functions of the arbitration system into a national incomes policy arrangement during the 1980s. Institutions are not independent; they have purposes, logics, origins and phases of maturity and degeneration (Boyer 1990: xxvi).

In some European countries, institutions with considerable authority over economic activity have existed for some time, many becoming unable to maintain the good performance they promised or delivered earlier. The majority of European polities have begun to exemplify, it has been said, a type of 'flawed statism' that has sometimes been referred to as 'Eurosclerosis', whereby national specificities have frustrated effective institutional interlockings (between, for example, finance capital and industrial investment) (Cox 1986: 16–48). So a negotiated economy does not guarantee economic success; it is a necessary rather than a sufficient condition for low unemployment.

Institutions are not permanent. In fact, corporatist forms of regulation were never properly developed, even in the countries where such experiments were pushed furthest. Swedish corporatism remained unfinished, even at its peak in the 1960s, because of the absence of an explicit industry policy, the fragile nature of its wage regulation (dependent on employer complicity) and the lack of intellectual consensus over even such well-developed elements as the Rehn–Meidner model. Swedish experience since the mid-1980s shows how easy it can be to dismantle politicized economic management. Pressure for retreat to liberal modes of regulation must be expected even when the macroeconomic consequences are disastrous.

The distinctiveness of Australia's economic management can be highlighted by reference to other OECD countries' political and economic conditions since the 1970s. Figure 5.2 shows that economic and political conditions together constitute distinctive modes of regulation. Over the past twenty years, some countries

Figure 5.2: Political Divergence and Modes of Regulation

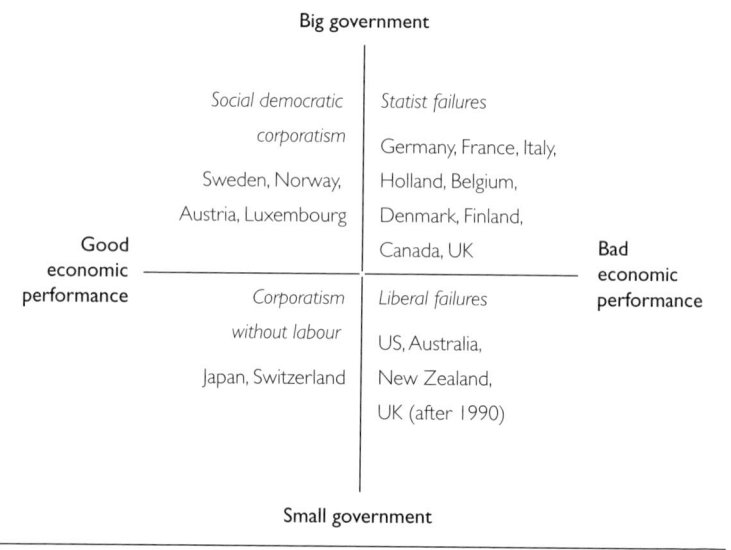

	Big government	
	Social democratic corporatism	Statist failures
	Sweden, Norway,	Germany, France, Italy,
	Austria, Luxembourg	Holland, Belgium,
Good economic performance		Denmark, Finland, Canada, UK	Bad economic performance
	Corporatism without labour	Liberal failures
	Japan, Switzerland	US, Australia, New Zealand, UK (after 1990)
	Small government	

Source: Derived from data in OECD Economic Outlook (various issues)

have enjoyed good economic performance (low unemployment) alongside big government; some have experienced poor performance despite big government. Some have experienced bad performance (high unemployment) and small government; a fourth category has had both small government and good performance. The clusters identify the configurations of 'politics versus markets' during the recession, and hence provide a means of specifying the parameters of important political conflicts that may be said to underwrite successful and unsuccessful economies.

Four modes of regulation, derived from clusterings of institutional management of the economy and macroeconomic outcomes, can be identified as follows.

Social democratic corporatism

Good performance (low unemployment since 1974) is attributable to institutional arrangements. The unusual political institutions result not really from what governments have done but more from tripartite bargaining, conflict-management or cooperation between labour, capital and the state. Sometimes, as with wage bargaining in Sweden, the corporatist arrangements are not tripartite but bipartite; the state is uninvolved. Corporatist institutions do not eliminate conflict; they institutionalize it. Incomes policies and industry policies are the most important forms of corporatist economic policy arrangements, but labour market policy and a range of low-level issues (for example, a crisis in the health care or education system) can be handled this way too. The economic and institutional situation in some of these countries has changed considerably in the 1990s, but after 1974 reasonably coherent forms of macrocorporatism did exist. A consequence of the well-developed policy institutions is that policy weaknesses or failures in one area can be compensated for by capacities in other areas (for example, Sweden's lack of industry policy was partly compensated for by the trade unions' solidarity wages policy which operated as a de facto method of industrial rationalization at least during the 1960s). There need be no 'cumulative causation'. Nonetheless there is probably no enduring 'path dependency' either, since institutional arrangements, even well-entrenched and long-standing ones, can readily be reversed if the balance of class power alters, as happened in Sweden in the 1980s.

Statist failures

A large group of countries with big government has nonetheless experienced poor performance (high unemployment) over the past twenty years. There has been ineffective corporatist development in these countries mainly because of splits on the left of politics between socialist and communist parties (France, Italy) or between socialist and religious or linguistically based trade union confederations (Germany, the Netherlands, Belgium) which prevented the degree of co-involvement in macro-economic policy-making that was achieved in, say, Sweden. Until the end of the 1980s, the United Kingdom was in the group, although it has become less statist. Since the 1990s, it would be in the category of liberal failures. In this group, despite policy attempts to maximize rates of accumulation, the absence of an intellectual commitment to Keynesian policy seems to have been part of the policy environment.

Liberal failures

In this category sit most Anglo-Saxon countries where small government (and the implied underdevelopment of state capacities) is responsible for poor performance. These countries simply do not have the institutional capacities for such management of the macroeconomy as is implied by full employment, counter-cyclical development or politically guided sectoral adjustment. Typically, sectoral change and structural adjustment mean not the creation of new industries but the movement off-shore of existing ones. State-sponsored brakes on the pace of structural change (until circumstances are more propitious for full employment) would normally be regarded as illegitimate. Australia is a partial exception due to its centralized wage fixation which allowed, especially in the 1980s, a de facto incomes policy; this too was dismantled in the 1990s in favour of a more decentralized, inflation-prone, inequality-inducing, unregulatable liberal system. In these circumstances, there is cumulative causation—failure breeds further failure.

Corporatism without labour

This group of countries is small; Japan is really the only case. 'Creative conservatism', 'authoritarian success' and 'creative defeat' are other terms that have been used to refer to the conservative commitment to full employment and the strong institutions needed to activate it. Strong links between government and the private sector, bordering on what would elsewhere be called corrupt (that is, Japan's distinctive and anti-liberal industry and trade policies), have been responsible for economic success. The statist prioritization of national development ahead of free trade is undisputed. There are recurrent pressures from the international community for such regimes to liberalize their successful (and principled) policies—if these pressures succeed, corporate success will be achieved at the cost of national decline.

Permanent institutions for political control of the economy would change behaviour, just as changed behaviour (by capital, labour and the state) would be necessary to make new institutions possible and effective. But they do not and ought not imply an increase in the power of the state as much as an increase in the range of economic decisions made according to public rather than private calculation. Not only are governments unreliable, but state institutions have diverse goals and policy instruments. Such a corporatist state is then without power or interests of its own (Jessop 1988: 152, 1990: 256), but it might still be expected to mobilize productive forces in accordance with transformed productive relations towards an end (prosperity and security) that liberal regimes notionally endorse but are always incapable of delivering.

In times of structural crisis, when discretionary intervention by the state is necessary to reconstitute regulatory institutions, strategic political and social choices have a role to play in restructuring the economy. It seems likely, therefore, that an alternative, social democratic regime of economic activity needs to be conceptualized or constructed. This would require focus on the links between the economic and non-economic aspects of accumulation.

Regeneration of full employment will require the dismantling of strategies, institutions and policy preferences that are prone to reducing national capacities in times of economic crisis. The manifestations, in the state sphere, of individual entrepreneurs' propensity to endorse policies that undermine economic performance and profitability include:

- refusals to subject industry development to policy (thereby consolidating fluctuations in investment and activity);
- monetarist responses to inflation (which reduce economic activity, thus exacerbating the distributional conflicts that underlie inflation in recession);
- deregulatory wage-fixing arrangements (which impose flexibility and therefore inequality instead of income determination in accordance with citizenship entitlements);
- deflationary responses to balance of payments problems (hence reducing instead of expanding national capacities);

- over-enthusiastic acceptance of internationalized criteria, such as competitiveness or global mobility, for both private and public sector activity, resulting in the forfeit of national capacities without guarantees that new activity or employment will be generated to compensate for that lost;
- general austerity policies (because of orthodox belief that public debt is necessarily bad, that too much growth causes too little growth, that economies can be overheated even with unutilized capacity, that productive capacity cannot be publicly mandated, that national economies cannot afford recovery, or that people need to be poorer in order to be richer).

Data endorsing the need for alternatives to these policy preferences were presented in previous chapters.

It is likely that some critics of liberalism are reluctant to endorse the identification of the state with particular economic interests (see Offe 1984: 134–45). As Figure 5.2 makes clear, states in general have an ambiguous record of economic management unless they recognize and accommodate the conflicts involved in their displacement of the market mode of adjustment. Nonetheless, political control of the economy is likely to favour manufacturing activity more than market regulation is. Selectivity is inevitable if the political process is to assert its right to determine, even partially, which economic activities receive or are denied public sanction. It is because attempts to regenerate economic activity conflict with the market principle, that pro-capitalist and anti-capitalist purposes increasingly coincide. Without such an anti-capitalist or anti-liberal rationale, the fate of our times seems to be state adoption of policies that do not facilitate material development, rather than the bias in policies that do.

Trade unions and post-liberal politics

The kinds of institutions mentioned thus far, those constitutive of changing modes of regulation, represent a potential 'post-liberal' politics. Post-liberalism is pro-liberal to the extent that it maintains liberalism's democratic achievements, but anti-liberal in so far as it recognizes the limitations that liberalism has imposed on the democratic impulse. In particular, post-liberalism opens up to democratic process the decisions made behind the anonymity and uncertainty of the marketplace. Just as we maintain that unemployment is the most policy-relevant indicator of recession, we are also convinced that corporatist arrangements exemplify a practical and effective post-liberal polity. Before elaborating our empirical model, it is necessary to indicate why trade union participation is crucial to the successful development of corporatist institutions.

Institutions with corporatist features in OECD countries began to be noticed in the early 1970s, although they had a much longer lineage in some (Schmitter 1974). The label was applied to developments which involved what are often termed the major functional interest groups—employer associations and trade unions—in key decision-making or policy-formulation processes. The significance and consequence of these institutions will always be contentious. The corporatist literature is both extensive and ambiguous and will not be reviewed here. (Literature confirming the impact of corporatist arrangements on economic outcomes includes Calmfors & Driffill 1988; Cameron 1984; Clegg, Boreham & Dow 1986; Dow, Clegg & Boreham 1984; Henley & Tsakalotos 1993; Hicks 1988a, 1988b; Keman 1984; Korpi 1991; Schmidt 1982b, 1984, 1987; Tarantelli 1986). It is instructive, however, to demarcate our argument from a number of other hypotheses. In particular, we develop one of the three approaches identified and classified by Therborn (1987) as representative of the major strands of analysis.

The first approach is a concept of class harmony and organic unity secured through the incorporation of the various functional groups, especially capital and labour, into a strong central state. Facilitating these arrangements is an ideology of consensus of social partnership, manifested politically through low levels of industrial conflict (Crouch 1985; Schmidt 1982a; McCallum 1986). The major economic actors are 'manipulated by the state to disengage from class conflict and to achieve a compromise which freezes the balance of class power' (Held 1989: 66). The higher aims which are at the heart of this compromise are concerned with economic stability and maintaining the conditions of capital accumulation. For the labour movement this requires commitment to crisis management over the structural or redistributive measures of macroeconomic policy.

A second and related approach views corporatism as limited to a more restricted policy domain in which market wages are reduced by a combination of incomes policies and an increased social wage designed to induce labour quiescence. In essence, as Cameron (1984: 146) put it, corporatism in this concept constitutes a system of institutionalized incomes policy, in which labour movements act responsibly and voluntarily participate in, and legitimize, the administration of wage restraint to their members. The argument advanced by proponents of this view is that corporatist incomes policies reduce unit labour costs which, in turn, influence employment levels. This view has been subject to both theoretical (Clegg, Boreham & Dow 1986: 316–18) and empirical critique, including the view expressed strongly by Therborn on the basis of his analysis of labour costs in the OECD countries that 'the development of unemployment has become completely disassociated from changes in labour cost' (1986: 61).

An alternative concept of corporatism, the one which interests us, involves institutional arrangements which allow the effective participation of labour organizations in the formulation and implementation of policy 'across those interdependent policy areas that are of central importance for the management of the economy' (Lehmbruch 1984: 66). Two aspects differentiate this view of corporatism from the other approaches. First, there are policy issues that are much more susceptible to public resolution when collective criteria are applied than when relegated to entrepreneurial or parliamentary processes. Hence there is an explicitly democratic rationale for the post-liberal arrangements discussed and advocated throughout this book. In addition, as private investment decisions have public and long-lasting consequences, there is an economic as well as a normative rationale for subjecting them to democratic deliberation. In other words, trade unions have a direct interest in accepting a public role and participating in these institutions; they do not merely become instruments of an authoritarian state (Higgins 1985). The labour movement can benefit organizationally, by taking on legitimate public functions, as well as materially, in terms of delivering better economic conditions for members and non-members.

The second and closely related aspect is the inevitably conflictual nature of the issues to be resolved by these institutions. The participation of trade unions and business associations in macropolicy processes does not imply either a search for, or the achievement of, consensus. What is achieved in such decision-making forums is a decision, not necessarily a consensual decision. Given the conflicts that corporatist policy forums are intended to resolve (structural changes in the economy, distributive conflicts that lead to inflation, the development of principles to prevent uncoordinated displacement of labour), compromise may be possible, but consensus and unanimity will be rare. This is not because the autonomous organizations have different perspectives, but because the issues are inherently unyielding to consensus. The rationale for these policy processes is not to eliminate the conflict but to secure decisions different from those that would be made as a result of deliberation in boardrooms, the stock exchange or industrial arenas. Corporatist institutions do not eliminate uncertainty and chance, but they do provide the opportunity for deliberated, principled and managed change rather than the outcomes resulting from market fluctuations alone.

It is likely, however, that trade union organizations' structural position in capitalist societies induces them to hold a substantive policy outlook similar to that we have advanced. That is, trade unions' preference for full employment and equality is not really a contingent or even strategic choice, as much as the logical growth of their fundamental rationale—to undermine market determination of social and economic conditions (see Polanyi 1944). If they are periodically lured away from their 'anti-capitalist' mission, it must be on terms which eventually create tensions with its constituency, which recognizes its objectives have been displaced. On the one hand, private capitalists are locked into what Karpik (1978) once termed a 'profitability logic of action'. They are principally concerned with short-term profits and the microeconomic dimensions of capital accumulation, so they are likely to neglect other aspects of industrial production in their decision-making. Workers, on the other hand, are dependent for the maintenance and development of their way of life on a broad range of factors involved in production. These include job security and enterprise viability, the quality of the working environment, the development of career paths, skills formation, wages and a socially meaningful relationship between work and leisure. It would seem that workers and the organizations which represent them are subject to a wider range of concerns than individual owners of capital. For these structural reasons, the rationality of labour is multidimensional, in contrast to the one-dimensional rationality of private entrepreneurs.

Our preference for the retention and further development of corporatist arrangements does not guarantee that full, secure and well-remunerated employment will ensue. New political decision-making arrangements are a necessary though not a sufficient condition for improved economic outcomes. We do not dispute that in specific instances (for example, if liberal governments and employer associations were to obstruct principled wage-setting or politicized control of investment) corporatist decisions may damage labour's objectives. But weakness of labour and the bias against full employment would not be perpetuated as a legitimate point of economic governance. Trade unions may not always win, but their routine participation in policy-making will inevitably make a difference. So will the participation of employers' political organizations.

A model of unemployment

The remaining part of this chapter, tests the corporatist argument that good economic performance depends increasingly on labour movements' adoption of a role in economic policy-making that changes the form of contemporary political conflict. It applies the same pooled time-series statistics used earlier but with the additional political variables we suggest are important. We employ an 'Ordinary Least Squares' (OLS) regression procedure that can account for the relative influence of the different independent variables on levels of unemployment. In general, the purpose of a regression procedure is to understand the relative importance of a number of the potential determinants of some phenomenon (here, unemployment). The present objective is to determine the importance of corporatist political arrangements in accounting for levels of unemployment in relation to other variables like the inflation rate and the level of government expenditure. Statistical analysis like this, especially when it is applied to a large number of cases as is the situation here (a pooled time-series data set from sixteen countries over nineteen years, 304 cases), is more reliable than most other forms of empirical investigation. We can be confident that the findings are consistent and accurate. The model of unemployment developed is explained further below. Technical aspects of the procedure are included as an appendix.

A number of the variables included in the model have already been considered in earlier chapters. They are government capital expenditure (GOVTCAP), private capital expenditure (PRIVCAP), extent of the industrial labour force (IND), size of the labour force (LAB), economic growth (GROWTH), openness (trade dependence) of the economy (OPEN), inflation (INFLAT), and government expenditure (GOVTEXP). The relationships between these variables and unemployment can be expected to be consistent with the conclusions reached earlier. Of the variables considered earlier, social security expenditures and taxation were not included in the model because of extreme multicolinearity effects—for this reason, taxation, social security expenditures and government expenditure can be regarded as the same variable for statistical purposes. It should also be noted that all variables were lagged one year to ensure the direction of causality.

The model is completed by two additional variables informed by the theoretical argument elaborated above. The first seeks to operationalize the extent to which trade unions participate in general economic policy formulation (LABEC) to test the central hypothesis of this chapter, that union involvement in economic policy development is associated with significantly lower levels of unemployment. It should be noted that the extent of union involvement in economic policy is closely associated with the participation of employer associations, so that the variable can reasonably be used as a proxy for corporatist arrangements more generally.

The variable is constructed according to the extent to which union confederations were formally involved in negotiations with government in broader policy formulation, particularly macroeconomic policy, industry policy, social welfare policy and labour market/employment policy. For each country, all confederations representing more than 10 per cent of the unionized workforce were examined. The most important factor determining the allocation of scores was whether union confederations were formally included in policy formulation. This required participation based on an expectation of routine and regular, not ad hoc, involvement. The variable is scored on a 10-point scale with highest scores allocated to confederations which formally participated in policy formulation in three or more of the above areas. The next highest scores were allocated where major confederations formally participated in a more limited range (one or two) of policy areas. Lower scores were allocated where some consultations took place with trade union confederations over policy but no formal policy-making role was accorded to them. Lowest scores were allocated where some unions were involved in policy consultations but input was not sought from the major confederations. The way in which countries differ on this variable can be seen in Tables 5.2 and 5.3 (in the appendix).

A second variable is included which is often put forward as an explanation of comparative levels of unemployment in political terms. 'WAGE' operationalizes the extent to which unions participate in the processes of collective wage bargaining only. This argument holds that, because peak confederations are able to moderate wage demands, unemployment is lowered through the generation of lower levels of wages and inflation than would otherwise have been the case (see, for example, Calmfors & Driffill 1988). Unions play a limited role—that of constraining wage growth. Given the lack of empirical support for a relationship between either wages or inflation and unemployment, it is not expected that WAGE has any appreciable impact on unemployment.

WAGE is also scored on a 10-point scale. The most important factor in the allocation of scores was whether union confederations were formally included in wage-setting arrangements. Two other factors which were taken into account in assigning scores within categories were the extent to which wage-setting was determined by centralized negotiations (as opposed to lower levels of collective bargaining) and coverage, that is, the proportion of the labour force covered by centralized agreements. Individual country details are in the appendix.

Table 5.1 sets out the results and provides considerable evidence for the propositions developed here. First, it can be noted that the model fit, shown by the adjusted R^2 of 0.71, is quite high. This means that 71 per cent of the variation in unemployment (for the countries and time period examined) is explained by the variables included in the regression model. We can therefore be confident that many of the important influences

Table 5.1: Unemployment Model in 16 OECD Countries, 1974–1988

Variable	Parameter estimate	Significance
LABEC	−0.66	0.0001
WAGE	0.08	0.2457
GOVTCAP	−1.10	0.0001
PRIVCAP	−0.13	0.0087
IND	−0.12	0.0003
LAB	−0.10	0.0037
GROWTH	−0.24	0.0001
OPEN	0.01	0.0247
INFLAT	−0.01	0.7339
GOVTEXP	0.05	0.0439

Adjusted $R^2 = 0.71$
N = 209

on unemployment levels have been taken into account (see appendix).

Second, the findings reached in the earlier chapters are confirmed, even when their relative effects are taken into account. Government capital expenditure, private capital expenditure and a healthy industrial labour force all lead to lower levels of unemployment. Government capital expenditure stands out as the most effective way to reduce the unemployment rate. The data show that an increase in government capital expenditure of 1 per cent of GDP is associated with a reduction in unemployment of about 1.1 per cent. (The significance level of 0.0001 means that there is only a 0.01 per cent chance that the relationship does not actually hold.) We emphasize that this finding is of particular relevance to Australia, where levels of public investment have fallen since the 1970s, from a comparatively low base.

We noted earlier that economic growth does not necessarily reduce unemployment. Inflation, trade dependence (openness) and government expenditure all have very small and insignificant effects on unemployment (that is, there is no relationship). WAGE, one of the new variables, also has a small and insignificant effect. This confirms the existing evidence that even where wage bargaining structures lower wage levels, investment and lower unemployment do not necessarily result, although lower levels of inflation may (see Przeworski & Wallerstein 1982).

Third, and finally, the most interesting finding concerns the LABEC variable. The participation of unions (and therefore employer associations) in the formation of economic policy clearly has a very high, significant and negative effect on levels of unemployment. A 1-point increase in the participation index results in a decrease in unemployment of around 0.66 per cent. This is strong evidence in favour of the argument developed in this book. The construction of a different 'politics of the economy' has vital ramifications for countries' ability to achieve social and economic objectives, particularly low levels of unemployment. For this reason we endorse the development of a social democratic corporatist mode of regulation wherever possible (see also Boreham & Compston 1992; Dow 1997b).

Barriers to full employment

Investment is the key to economic performance. Investment decisions have public and long-term effects. First, they determine future production, employment, income and living standards. Second, investment fluctuations reduce production, employment, income and living standards. It is therefore important that investment not fluctuate, not be unduly influenced by private calculations based on business expectations. Investment needs to be coordinated with the needs of the macroeconomy—delayed or brought forward as required for permanent counter-cyclical management and permanent control of structural change. Effective politicization of investment cannot occur without policies dealing with infrastructure, incomes, labour markets, welfare and the balance between regulated and unregulated activity. The integration of such a wide-ranging economic strategy clearly implies a new form of state and requires the involvement of labour and capital, if not their cooperation (Parker 1996). Conflict is inevitable, but it is better for the conflict to be institutionalized no matter how complicated, costly, awkward and unwelcome the institutionalization of political control of the economy will be. The objective is not just lower unemployment, but more stable patterns of economic development and the extension of democracy at both government and workplace levels (Boreham & Hall 1994; Mahon 1987). Equality and wealth are not contradictory. To imagine that economic performance and social objectives conflict is an unwarranted legacy of the successful diffusion of orthodox economic ideas.

Economic management should not be a matter of administering painful economic medicine or of taking hard decisions. It is not necessary to reduce government spending, purchasing power, wages or activity to eliminate unemployment; the intuitive sense that such responses exacerbate the problem they are allegedly trying to remove, a sentiment which has reached socially damaging levels in the late 1990s, is correct. This is precisely the sort of policy stance that concerned Keynes in the 1930s: conventional policy was a 'hateful and disastrous' way of dealing with a 'decreased capacity to produce wealth'—'a policy the country would never permit if it knew what was being done' (Keynes 1925: 248, 268, 270). In the 1980s and 1990s, it has produced the long recession. This is not the first time governments have been 'misled by experts'. Attempts to restore market conditions are tantamount to a great social experiment, an attempt to impose a generalized solution based on wishful thinking (and on one among many strands of economic theory) rather than upon analysis of how economies actually operate. As we have indicated, the solution to the problem of declining production and declining employment is the generation of more activity. The fear of expansion which has been the hallmark of liberal policy-making for most of this century and intensified during the past quarter-century is unnecessary and fatalistic. Sustained recessionary cycles are avoidable.

The comparative evidence indicates that only a permanent, institutionalized commitment to full employment by a reconstructed political apparatus will produce full employment. This was the conclusion reached by Keynes when the world was prepared to elevate substantive goals like prosperity and security to political prominence. There existed then a class of intellectuals, often without formal training, who were able to carry the full employment project to the point where public efforts to create appropriate national and international institutions based on common sense rather than liberal doctrine were successful. Full employment cannot be achieved through proxy goals such as growth, low inflation, international harmonization, deregulation or the removal of rigidities. A full-employment economy brings about efficiencies rather than the other way around, but it also allows the political process to retain such inefficient and unproductive activities as it deems desirable. This policy goal is more legitimate than the tried and disproven neo-liberal insistence on flexibility.

The barriers to these alternative economic ideas and to the institutional changes they imply are and always have been political in character.

Technical appendix

Diagnostic analysis of the data revealed some problems regarding its reliability. Investigation of residuals showed a marked tendency for country effects to show up as bunched autocorrelated errors, although no countries were invariably above or below the regression line. This was one reason why we did not consider it necessary to control for between-country differences in the level of the dependent variable. The other reason was theoretical: we are just as interested in explaining between-country differences in unemployment as accounting for within-country changes in unemployment. Controlling away between-country differences would make this impossible. From our theoretical perspective, the regression estimates are not biased for failing to control for between-country differences in unemployment. However, although coefficients remain unbiased and the adjusted R^2 is still valid, coefficient variances are biased, so that coefficient standard errors and significance tests are biased in the direction of giving a false sense of significance (Kmenta 1971: 273–82). Since we regard our dataset as a population and not a sample, however, significance levels are not relevant. This opened the way for two different approaches, which both confirmed the reliability of our results.

The first was to retain the OLS coefficients, ignore significance levels and treat the problem of reliability as a problem of stability. That is, we examined whether the coefficients, especially their signs, were stable or unduly influenced by outliers. Sensitivity to the inclusion of particular countries was tested by omitting each country in turn and rerunning the regression for the remaining 14 countries (a jackknife procedure) to see whether the omission of any particular country had a disproportionate effect on the regression estimates. The regressions were then jacknifed by year, as an extra check. This procedure showed the coefficients to be reliable; their signs remained the same for all jackknife regressions.

The second procedure involved retaining significance tests as important indicators of reliability. With time-series data the number of cases, important to statistical significance, is artificially inflated.

Table 5.2: Trade Union Confederation Participation in Economic Policy (LABEC), 1970–1992[a]

	1970	71	72	73	74	75	76	77	78	79	80	81	82	83	84	85	86	87	88	89	90	91	92
Australia	2	2	2	6	6	6	4	4	4	4	4	4	4	8	8	8	8	6	6	6	6	6	6
Austria	8	10	10	10	10	10	10	10	10	10	10	10	10	10	10	10	10	10	10	10	10	10	10
Canada	3	3	3	3	3	3	3	3	3	3	3	3	3	3	3	3	3	3	3	3	3	3	3
Denmark	7	7	7	7	7	7	7	7	7	7	7	7	7	7	8	8	8	8	8	8	8	8	8
Finland	7	7	7	7	7	7	7	7	7	7	7	7	7	7	7	7	7	7	7	7	7	6	6
France	5	5	5	4	4	4	4	4	4	4	4	4	4	4	4	4	4	4	4	4	4	4	4
Germany	8	8	8	8	8	8	8	8	8	8	8	8	8	6	6	6	6	6	6	6	8	8	8
Holland	7	7	7	7	7	7	7	7	7	7	7	7	7	7	7	7	7	7	7	7	7	7	7
Italy	4	6	6	6	6	6	6	6	6	6	6	6	6	6	6	6	6	6	6	6	6	6	6
Japan	4	4	4	4	4	4	4	4	4	4	4	4	4	4	4	4	4	4	4	4	4	4	4
Norway	10	10	10	10	10	10	10	10	10	10	10	10	6	6	6	6	6	10	10	10	10	10	10
Sweden	10	10	10	10	10	10	10	10	10	10	10	10	10	10	10	10	8	8	8	8	8	7	6
Switzerland	5	5	5	5	5	5	5	5	5	5	5	5	5	5	5	5	5	5	5	5	5	5	5
UK	3	2	2	4	6	6	6	6	6	4	4	4	4	4	4	4	4	4	4	4	4	4	4
USA	4	4	4	4	4	4	4	4	4	4	2	2	2	2	2	4	4	4	4	4	4	4	4

[a] Participation measures constructed by the authors on the basis of individual country studies—see text (0 is low, 10 is high)

Source: Individual country studies by authors. Political Economy of the Advanced Societies data set

Table 5.3: Trade Union Confederation Participation in Wage Bargaining (WAGE), 1970–1992[a]

	1970	71	72	73	74	75	76	77	78	79	80	81	82	83	84	85	86	87	88	89	90	91	92
Australia	9	9	9	10	10	10	10	10	10	10	10	10	8	10	10	10	10	10	10	10	10	9	8
Austria	10	10	10	10	10	10	10	10	10	10	10	10	10	10	10	10	10	10	10	10	10	10	10
Canada	2	2	2	2	2	2	2	2	2	2	2	2	2	2	2	2	2	2	2	2	2	2	2
Denmark	7	7	7	7	7	7	7	7	7	7	7	6	6	6	6	6	6	6	6	6	6	6	6
Finland	10	10	10	10	10	10	10	10	10	10	10	10	10	10	10	10	10	10	10	10	10	10	10
France	6	6	6	6	6	6	6	6	6	6	6	6	6	5	5	5	5	5	5	5	5	5	5
Germany	6	6	6	6	6	6	6	6	6	6	6	6	6	6	6	6	6	6	6	6	6	6	6
Holland	7	7	7	7	7	7	7	7	7	7	7	7	7	7	7	7	7	7	7	7	7	7	7
Italy	7	7	7	7	7	8	8	8	8	8	8	8	8	8	7	7	7	7	7	7	7	7	6
Japan	2	2	2	2	2	2	2	2	2	2	2	2	2	2	2	2	2	2	2	2	2	2	2
Norway	9	9	9	9	9	9	9	9	9	9	9	9	8	8	8	8	8	9	9	9	9	9	9
Sweden	10	10	10	10	10	10	10	10	10	10	10	10	10	10	10	10	10	10	8	9	9	8	8
Switzerland	4	4	4	4	4	4	4	4	4	4	4	4	4	4	4	4	4	4	4	4	4	4	4
UK	4	4	4	4	4	10	10	10	4	4	4	4	4	4	4	4	4	4	4	4	3	3	3
USA	2	3	3	3	3	3	2	2	2	2	2	2	2	2	2	2	2	2	2	2	2	2	2

a Participation measures constructed by the authors on the basis of individual country studies—see text (0 is low, 10 is high)

Source: Individual country studies by authors. Political Economy of the Advanced Societies data set

Small differences from year to year for any particular country result in strong correlations between values and the equivalent figure for previous years. To ensure that the results of the OLS procedure are not misleading, tests can be undertaken. To obtain estimates for which the coefficient variances and significance tests were unbiased, we employed a GLS-ARMA regression procedure based on a method outlined by Kmenta (1971: 512–14). Thus, SAS PROC TSCSREG begins by obtaining for each country an autoregression coefficient by regressing the residual on its lagged value, then renders the data non-autoregressive by subtracting from each observation the product of the autocorrelation coefficient and the observation's lagged value; finally, it re-estimates the transformed data using OLS regression. PROC TSCSREG also adjusts for heteroskedasticity by dividing the values of all observations by the standard deviation of the residual, and adjusts for contemporaneous correlation by incorporating this information into the variance–covariance matrix. The results of the TSCSREG procedure improved significance levels and therefore confirmed the results of the OLS model.

Chapter 6

The political path to full employment in Australia

Australia's inability to embed policies to secure and guarantee full employment is a defining feature of its liberal political system, but it is not unique. Australia shares its public incompetence with other countries where the political process cannot effect outcomes different from the industrial structure that market adjustments would produce. This reflects the liberal biases in Australia's polity; biases which have historical and discursive preconditions that may forever preclude effective policy interventions to achieve the levels of activity that are technically possible but recurrently thwarted. Liberal biases exist in all polities underwritten by capitalist economies but to an unequal extent, as shown by the social democratic corporatist and authoritarian successes of recent decades. Resistance to full employment is embedded in the Australian polity, but it is corrigible. In this final chapter, we discuss the nature of the political challenge to the internationalist liberalism that must be mounted in Australia and we evaluate, more in hope than in expectation, the likelihood of a politically effective post-liberal strategy for ongoing economic management and development oriented to full employment.

Full employment requires the extension of policy competences, rather than the adoption of 'correct' policies. For this reason, we have argued that the attainment of full employment, with the attendant levels of civic amenity and national autonomy, is a political problem rather than a technical one. More often than not in this century, political battles to extend the scope of democratic determination of social and economic outcomes have been lost, or won only briefly, before being followed by longer periods of reversal. Economic liberalism has remained hegemonic both when conditions have been buoyant and when they have deteriorated (towards high unemployment, low-quality employment, industrial decline, increasing inequality and social insecurity). That is, both when there has been reason to think that policy sufficiently controlled development to take credit for stability and when the policy process had to bear much of the responsibility for instability, the dominant presumption has been that market outcomes constitute the norm. Even countries such as Sweden or Japan, not characterized by liberal approaches to economic management and structural adjustment, have been effectively pressured to liberalize, to wind back precisely the institutional mechanisms responsible for past successes in favour of the policies preferred by countries with a sustained record of past failure (Bienefeld 1994: 120–1).

The politics of political capacity

The central outcome of the data we have presented is the vindication of interventionist traditions in political economy, both conservative and post-liberal. Accordingly, we have urged the polity to reclaim the tradition of economic analysis and policy-making which has been lost from recent public debates in Australia. Though interventionist prescriptions can be derived from Marxist, statist or post-liberal traditions, we recommend the last as the most conducive to solving the problems faced in Australia at this stage of its economic development. The post-Keynesian tradition of analysis and policy advice has long recognized the importance of politics and institutions for good economic performance. It is therefore also aware of the political and intellectual resistance to be overcome if the quest for efficiency and competitiveness is to be subordinated to substantive goals of full employment, societal cohesion, socially responsible structural change and the most democratic and equitable spread of the benefits of economic activity.

The major traditions of political analysis—Marxism, statism and liberalism—have hardly produced a greater cumulative understanding of the role of politics in the economy than has economic analysis, particularly in Australia. So the characteristic weaknesses in each of the major bodies of political doctrine need to be identified and redressed before we can begin to specify the task of reconstructing political capacities to the extent required for a national full employment programme. The strengths and weaknesses of these three traditions are now considered.

Marxian theories of the state, those deriving from political economy in the classical tradition, are generally sceptical of the possibility that the state (government or public sector) can or ought to act in a progressive manner. Marxism's common conclusions (concerning the omnipotence, oppressiveness or functionality of politics) emphasize the resistance to policies designed to impose national or deliberated criteria upon economic activity. However, Marxism remains unconvincing as a general proposition asserting the impossibility of systematic governance of the processes of accumulation. From Marxian political economy it is reasonable, and usual, to conclude that the state may act to facilitate the logic of market-driven flows of capital and economic activity. However, in view of the continuing diversity in national modes of regulation, there are equally valid Marxian reasons for expecting the state's role in capital accumulation to increase (and generate good macroeconomic outcomes) as there are reasons to expect it to be class-biased (against labour) or biased against particular national interests in favour of international imperatives. Contrary to Marxism's orthodox positions, then, it is possible to derive from the logic of Marxian analysis the expectation of a larger political and policy role for the organizations and parties of labour and for political struggle to be based on resistance to this expansion (Dow 1998).

Arguments for and against an expanding state have become the key discursive form of contemporary political and class conflict. In fact, conflicts concerning the relative desirability of public and private auspices for economic activity are really instances of class politics, conflicts between labour and capital— the class-based tensions over the criteria, auspices or principles that should apply to economic management. Yet neither the expectation of an increasing politicization of economic decision-making nor the empirical investigation of its implications has been well received in Marxist literature or in political science understandings of the state generally. Our concern in this chapter is to show how these 'reformist' (and post-liberal) aspects of political theory can be developed to contribute to understanding how and why state capacities ought to expand and the limits or resistances to these 'possibilities of politics'.

The Marxian orientation to politics can be reconfigured, without losing its integrity, to stress the barriers to full employment (in the absence of policy interventions that transform the normal political and social relations underlying the market economy). Its analysis would thus not be of an economy which presumed that capital accumulation is a market phenomenon, but of one which indicated the directions in which politicization and democratization could proceed once the appropriate conditions (successive waves of crisis and crisis-resolution interventions) had been experienced and exploited.

Such a post-liberal political agenda could also be derived from post-Keynesian political economy. As indicated in chapter 4, post-Keynesianism postulates that economic recession (including aspects resulting from global restructuring) can be effectively subjected to policy at the national level. This requires institutional control of investment, presumably via corporatist decision-making arrangements which require the organizations of both labour and capital to routinely participate in the policy process, control of inflation via institutional control of conflicts over the distribution of income through incomes policies (both at full employment and during periods of unemployment) and usurpation of the labour market by institutionalized (active) labour market policies. At the limit, government can be expected to become an 'employer of last resort'. While post-Keynesianism therefore prefigures the intellectual legitimacy of interventions that will simultaneously transcend the market and improve national economic performance, Marxism provides an awareness of the dimensions of the post-liberal project and the nature of the political resistances to it. These policy proposals have begun to occur, though ad hoc and somewhat unanticipated, rather than in response to their theoretical rationale. It is clear that the political theory derived from Marxian and Keynesian critiques of capitalist economies is underdeveloped—it has not sufficiently incorporated real political developments into the current corpus of knowledge about the possibilities of politics (Clegg, Boreham & Dow 1986; Das 1996; Dow 1996; Jessop 1994; Thelen 1994).

Weberian theories of the state, those deriving from a more 'statist' (or 'society-centred') perspective, emphasize the autonomy of political processes (from external and internal influence) and the capacity of the government (especially through bureaucratic organization, the development of 'rational' procedures and the capacity to 'coordinate' non-state activities) to expand its capacities for effective governance, or to reduce impediments to governability. This tradition implicitly accepts a logic of political development, that is, an argument that political competence, governability and the legitimate scope of state activity are all prone to increase (the 'law of expanding state activity'). Much of the statist literature derives from conservative and anti-liberal strands of political thought advocating the need for the national polity to maintain social solidarity in the face of market-induced uncertainties; it is critical of the Marxian claims that polities are fatally constrained by the class biases of private ownership. There is much in this body of theorizing, which includes nineteenth-century German writers such as Friedrich List and Adolph Wagner, which deserves to be reintegrated into a contemporary state theory. It is often claimed that the (sometimes authoritarian) economic success of the non-liberal Asian industrializers owes much to the influence of this concept of statism (Weiss & Hobson 1995; Weiss 1998). However, much of this work lacks a well-developed sense of the opposition to statist activity, not only internal objections but also those from the international institutions that have been persuading individual governments to adopt free trade, deregulatory and competition-enhancing stances. It is clear, for example, that business groups tend to resist even those attempts at state politicization of the economy that are destined to serve them well in the long run; capital cannot act rationally (Kalecki 1943). In other words, one of the legacies of the liberal era is that collective or political activity and competences are difficult to engineer and perpetually prone to reversal.

It is nonetheless important to retrieve what is tenable from the conservative, statist literature on politics, supplement it with an understanding of the hostilities towards political intervention (even where the ultimate outcomes are desirable) and forge from the statist viewpoint and other analytical traditions conceptions of what states ought to do (Bell 1994; Evans 1992; Goldscheid 1925; Jones 1994, 1995; Krabbe 1996; Levi-Faur 1997; Riha 1985; Rueschemeyer & Evans 1985; Skocpol 1985; Weiss & Hobson 1995).

Perhaps the most important observation from statist theory is that individual, entrepreneurial and economic capacities are 'embedded' in the society; they need to be. The idea of embeddedness derives from Durkheimian and Polanyian arguments that the 'non-contractual elements of contract' or the 'non-bureaucratic elements of bureaucracy' play crucial roles in any economy and that attempts to eliminate them would be misguided (Evans 1992, 1995). In other words, economies are constituted by more than market mechanisms; morality, trust, law and a reasonable level of societal stability all seem to be necessary for a functioning economy (Stretton 1995: 13; Krygier 1997: 99–130; Streeck 1997: 197–219). So too are protective responses to risk, insecurity, competition and loss. The statist tradition declares that economic development depends on state capacities which can be effected through rational and competent bureaucracies sufficiently insulated from societal pressures to be strategic and selective in channelling assistance, particularly capital, to industries deemed central to the industrialization project, but sufficiently tied to the community to orient private behaviour towards the public or national interest. Distinctive state–capital relations can be forged, allowing ongoing negotiation and renegotiation of goals and principles, so that the state shapes capital accumulation, not the other way around. Durable public institutions facilitate both the autonomy of the developmental responsibilities of the state and the embeddedness of its required mechanisms in organic patterns of solidarity, discipline and societal legitimacy (Evans 1992).

Some of these anti-liberal and pro-national sentiments were voiced by Keynes in his 1933 essay on national self-sufficiency. There, Keynes argued that nations ought to minimize rather than maximize their integration with other countries' economies, that the costs of protection and autonomy were a small price to pay for the freedom from insecurity and risk that a nation-first strategy would involve, and that, as almost everything could be made almost everywhere, nations were entitled to experiment with policy institutions and arrangements that would secure full employment and national development. In short, his call could be depicted as 'as much free trade as possible but as much national autonomy as necessary' to achieve politically desirable objectives. This was also the tenor of the anti-liberal and historical German political economy that preceded the Keynesian contributions (Reinert 1995). In the statist tradition, national development of the forces of production, overseen by the state and involving public provision of infrastructure, education, sectoral co-ordination and a viable manufacturing base constituted the public interest (Levi-Faur 1997). The principal role of the state would therefore be to reduce or eliminate the opposition to and constraints upon national development that could be expected to accompany liberalization of economic activity (by maintaining national strategies for development and adjustment to change) and to redress the destructive effects of market outcomes (by establishing domestic linkages and socializing risks internally) (Boyer & Drache 1996: 9–12; Weiss 1998).

The statist tradition in practice has been less concerned with democratic protocols and more concerned to tolerate and preserve the historical structures which have constituted national distinctiveness (List 1841; Wagner 1883, 1887). Despite conservatism's disdain for market-produced inequalities, status differences remain and there is reason to believe that countries without a statist history stretching back into the pre-capitalist era would offer infertile grounds for experiments so late in the day. Although the examples of late industrialization being facilitated by statist forms of governance in the development period may provide a sound institutional basis for effective regulation and structural change during periods of maturity, in the Australian context it seems probable that the institutional developments foreshadowed in chapter 4 (institutions to control investment, income distribution and the labour market) are more likely under corporatist than under statist auspices.

We still conclude that sensible economic management in Australia is possible—because post-liberal, rather than pre-Keynesian, forms of institutional innovation and policy-making experiments are required to achieve the outcomes that liberals claim to want, and because there has been some recent experience, even here, with post-liberal forms of regulation. But Australia's major political priority must be to create state competences and capacities that have, with the exception of the arbitration system, been largely unknown.

Liberal theories of the state, those emphasising the desirability of limited government, provide the political development approach most compatible with current policy preferences for international (and competitive) criteria for government activity. Liberalism as a movement has left some important legacies which political development in any circumstances will probably feel obliged to respect. The achievements of liberalism, acknowledged even by its critics, include the ending of arbitrary political rule, the elevation of the principle of individual freedom and the establishment of legal guarantees of (and respect for) private property. Even where these have been eroded by the encroachment of taxation and business regulation, or supplemented by moral or communitarian or democratic codes of conduct, liberal proscriptions and protocols have been important in the emergence of civilized governance. Liberal theories, as we have seen, have been most influential in the Anglo-Saxon polities which are characterized by small government or, since the 1970s, by retreats from former commitments to social liberal interventions and poor economic performance.

A significant paradox for liberal theory is its co-existence with a century-long growth in political influence, registered through increasing levels of state expenditure, the development of corporatist forms of policy-making and ongoing decommodification of social life as a result of the expansion of the welfare state. For all the rhetoric of neo-liberalism in recent decades, the state's substantive economic role has not declined and growth has been associated with prosperity and security rather than with tyranny. Nonetheless, extending state capacity beyond the boundaries of liberal tolerance will involve many of liberalism's caveats about the risk of government (Dunn 1990; Gamble 1996; Hintze 1897; Jänicke 1990).

Our view is that liberal theories do not satisfactorily account for what is happening in mature capitalist economies, and may even be said to contribute to economic and social dislocation when used as the rationale for policy abrogations (in first, second and third world contexts). Liberalism can be said to constitute one of the key obstacles to the state accepting developmental responsibilities; it weakens links between the public and private sectors, encourages speculative activity and creates an incremental rather than strategic approach to national development and management.

The liberal retreat from governance

In the immediate postwar period, it was common for public intellectuals to speculate on the ways in which interventionist social and political arrangements could achieve full employment and equality in the developed countries and foster development in the underdeveloped parts of the world. Most commentators and activists were reasonably aware of the barriers to full employment, but there was some consensus in conservative and social democratic discourse that limitations ought to be confronted, that new institutional mechanisms for overcoming structural and technical barriers to civilized outcomes had to be constructed and that there were political responsibilities that rich nations' polities could now accept. In Australia and elsewhere, these aspirations have been bypassed by the resurgent liberal responses to the recession, essentially an internationalizing project, of the past two decades. There is now more concern for rationalization, restructuring, competitiveness, efficiency and cost reduction than for full employment, managed sectoral change, equality, civilized processes of national development and enquiry into how the costs and opportunities of affluence can best be borne. If the politicians and political institutions responsible for the neo-liberalism of the past twenty-five years had devoted as much effort to creating new industries and employment as they devoted to eliminating employment and activity, Australia would be in a better position to maintain the promises and vision of the postwar era. As John Kenneth Galbraith has claimed, the contemporary distortion of policy priorities owes much to the self-interest of those who imagine their privileges will be threatened by the altered social and administrative arrangements we have foreshadowed. 'To invent a plausible or, if necessary, moderately implausible ideology in defence of self-interest is thus a natural course. A corps of willing and talented craftsmen is available for the task' (Galbraith 1996: 5).

A modern paradox is that orthodox responses do not guarantee the outcomes desired by the custodians of the status quo, as continuing unemployment and structural uncertainty confirm. A further irony is that more and more strands of conservative thought have begun to despair at the erosion of morality, cohesion and amenity implied by the application of liberal economic doctrines (Gray 1996; see also Manne 1998).

Largely because of continuing unemployment, there is a steadily increasing perception that something has gone very wrong with western political processes (Quiggin 1996). Despite more than two decades of strident assertions of the policy parameters implied by deregulation and marketization, structural unemployment remains unaddressed and appears intractable. Not only have high levels of unemployment been accepted, but social problems like civic crime and racist violence fester, while the polity clumsily denies and sidesteps its responsibilities and culpability. Public cynicism towards professional politicians and public administrators, registered in cultural expressions as well as electoral outcomes, is matched by the practitioners' apparent indifference to ideology, principle or passion. The so-called modernization of political parties appears to have emptied them of specific content or willingness to respond imaginatively to circumstances. The opinionated seriousness of the elites which govern and advise and mediate governance seems permanently at odds with everyday realities. The decline in the quality and security of employment has been legitimized by doctrines declaring the virtue of flexibility and the need to eliminate past protections. Intellectuals have abandoned the search for solutions; in an age of cowering subservience to generic forms of managerialism, administrative rationality and competitive entrepreneurialism, there is no longer the sort of reflection that inspired the institutional reconstruction and analytical creativity of fifty years ago.

The comparative perspective developed in this book confirms the expectations of post-Keynesian analyses, which reached most of the same conclusions during the 1940s, 1950s and 1960s when the failure, of the Anglo-Saxon countries in particular, to develop appropriate institutions for managing the macroeconomy was first addressed (see Kalecki 1943; Robinson 1973). But the post-Keynesian economic policy alternative implies a post-liberal political project that is out of kilter with the prevailing political and intellectual mood in public policy. Full employment requires not just the reactivation of a vision that prioritized national development above free trade and competitive market allocation, but the political struggles necessitated by sustained opposition to current political and intellectual fashions.

Contemporary conservatism is as concerned by the lapse in nation-building and state-building as have been the social democratic critics of neo-classical orthodoxy. To conservatives like John Ralston Saul, neo-liberalism and administrative rationality have allowed the human capacity for discernment, argument, common sense, morality and memory to be hijacked by 'process-minded experts' more concerned with 'running things properly' than with debate or reflection, elevating process over substance. Formality, abstraction, expediency, technocratic rationality and amorality have replaced purpose, doubt, debate and untidiness. As a result, people in most areas of public decision-making have lost the ability to make principled judgements. There are all the signs of permanent decline: power without purpose, structures without direction, promises without fulfilment (Saul 1992). The lost sense of societal direction, the contemporary malaise that includes the misguided, if well-intentioned, belief that procedure is more important than outcome, has produced functional incapacity and policy-makers with no regard for democracy or citizens or the achievements of civilization. In no area has the damage been more pronounced than in the dismantling of public capacities urged by economists and accompanied by a declining appreciation of the need for distinctive public principles:

> It was the general creation of an effective bureaucracy which brought an end to . . . filth and disease, and the public servants did so against the desires of the mass of the middle and upper classes. The free market opposed sanitation, the rich opposed it. The civilized opposed it. Most of the educated opposed it. That is why it took a century to finish what could have been done in ten years. Put in contemporary terms, the market economy angrily and persistently opposed clean public water, sanitation, garbage collection and improved public health because they appeared to be unprofitable enterprises which, in addition, put limits on the individual's freedoms (Saul 1992: 238, 239).

If the effect of the new managerial rationality has been to obliterate public commitment to democratic procedure and policy diversity because they are thought to be inefficient, unprofessional, embarrassing, amateurish or emotional, the processes of public life have been irreparably sabotaged, emptied of what they were designed to achieve—the possibility of allowing democratic intention (politics) to override formal process (efficiency): 'Expecting business methods and market forces to do the job of government, when business and the market fought desperately against every humane and social accomplishment of government over the last two centuries, makes no sense at all' (Saul 1992: 265).

The 'reforms' of recent decades have concentrated on costs rather than on what costs (and effort) can procure. They have ignored real production and the generation of new capital and new productive capacities. Financial sectors in particular are unfazed by the decline of real economic activity, depression and the emergence of the casino society. The state has been diverted from its proper public task of creating a solid base for national administration by infantile endorsement of activities like tax evasion and currency speculation (Dow 1997a). Government now attempts to administer instead of making decisions, it confuses execution with effecting intention, it has developed management techniques rather than moral values, it rewards speed but not consideration, it asks how not why. This is why the loss of responsibility and the decline of values have gone hand in hand with substantive failure. Accomplishments cannot be attributed to economic rationalism and failure to political intervention. The opposite is true. It is time to reassert humanity's preference for untidy solutions because ultimately they will be more, not less, successful.

The contemporary conservative critique of liberalism has much in common with our call for the reactivation of political choice. It is concerned that countries have been urged to purge their cultural and institutional legacies and to embrace a universalist rationalization that will eliminate the distinctiveness of politics. Liberalism in economic advice and the non-interventionist institutions of liberal capitalism ought to be denied their pseudo moral authority; polities are entitled to retain cultural difference—the diversity of values, moralities and forms of government. Liberalism's agenda seems to be the rejection of the political project itself (Gray 1994: 732).

The evidence of the past twenty-five years, as presented in this book, reveals relationships that render contemporary mature economies distinctive. The repudiation of previously imagined relationships means that these mature economies may be commensurately impenetrable to the gaze of economics. More liberalization implies worse, not better performance; governance needs to be more sophisticated, not more minimalist; taxes need to be higher, not lower; state capacities need to be enhanced, not hollowed out; wages probably ought to be rigid rather than flexible. The costs of public provision will remain high and defensible rather than an eradicable impost onto costs to consumers or taxpayers. In the face of globalization, nations are entitled to retain as much national capacity as possible. These findings, though they derive from our research and challenge the orthodoxy of the moment, do not represent a significant departure from an alternative strategy of economic and social development that has always characterized debates in economic policy and politics. (For a concordant Australian view, see Capling, Considine & Crozier 1998; for a view which endorses the exhaustion of political possibilities, see Latham 1998). As Figure 5.1 indicated, findings which suggest that continuing improvement in national standards of living depend on more political capacities and interventions are unsurprising to most branches of social science. In all countries at all stages of development, the conditions postulated by advocates of liberalization are contested; they also seem to be accepted cyclically then abandoned. The actual fate of the economies subject to the vicissitudes of policy advice does not depend on the closeness of the approximation to a model of market rationalism but on the degree to which substantive goals can be embedded in the competences of the polity.

If political economy is to move forward, most of the conventional assumptions and ideas about how a modern economy functions need revision. So do societies' understanding of how the components of political development—policy and intervention and democratic principle—can be expected to contribute to material development. This is a more urgent task than attempting to ascertain why favoured policies seem to damage rather than benefit the economies exposed to them.

This trajectory is less designed to produce proper policy settings than it is designed to subordinate national and interventionist criteria to global imperatives, thereby divorcing structural change from national and democratic considerations. The evidence we have assembled, in conjunction with the reconstitution of neglected theoretical approaches from outside the neo-classical paradigm, has enabled us to sketch a viable, if politically contentious, alternative. It is still possible, we have argued, to secure full employment in countries such as Australia. But the attempt to do so amounts to arguing for the supremacy of deliberated over autonomous outcomes. Creating a milieu in which institutions can express the general will while developing and retaining technical competence, is a long-term political project.

Our main contention has been that politics matters; it can be seen that political responsibilities will become both more necessary and more costly in all advanced countries. Conventional policy is biased towards overemphasis on market determinants of growth and prosperity; it tends to keep economic activity at a lower level than is technically possible and therefore to exacerbate recession. The available policy options imply that structural adjustment, the transition from one 'regime of accumulation' to another, ought to be incorporated into the normal routines of national economic management in ways that reduce competitiveness, insecurity, risk, national vulnerability, flexibility and international interdependence, rather than consolidate them. Comparative analysis provides compelling evidence that only where economic and industrial restructuring has been subject to political objectives has change been managed with minimal disruption and dislocation. The significant differences in nations' economic and social performance, and the consistency with which success and failure identify corresponding policy frameworks or modes of regulation, indicate that this is possible.

Political possibilities exist; there is room to manoeuvre. Current dogma nonetheless claims that future policy priorities must be framed subservient to market modes of adjustment, that lower levels of taxation and policy intervention and higher levels of inequality are inevitable, that unemployment of 6 or 8 or 10 per cent ought to be accepted, that a nation has no right to develop policy competences in defiance of conventional economic wisdom, and that neither a diversified national economy nor a decent, politically secured standard of living are viable.

Historical potentials, missed opportunities

With the demise of the Labor regime in 1996, the long-standing bias against state initiatives in economic development and management continues. A key question is whether Australia's historical legacy as a liberal nation renders a more 'dirigiste' alternative permanently unattainable. The potential for imaginative political development has not been completely ignored in Australia. Political possibilities have sometimes emerged and, while remaining unexploited when they were most urgently needed—in the 1930s and since the mid-1970s—have proven a distinctive national capacity for challenging the limitations which have, till now, dominated public policy-making (see Battin 1996; Dow 1996; Johnson 1996; Smyth 1996; Smyth & Cass 1998).

Australia's public institutional capabilities and economic outcomes have not always been underdeveloped. Early in the century, Australia enjoyed a reputation as a 'working man's paradise'. It was well-known for state experiments in adult suffrage, pension reform and the system of compulsory arbitration of industrial disputes. Until about World War I, Australia had one of the largest public sectors in the world and its highest per capita living standards. The retreat from 'Australian exceptionalism' and from expansive political possibilities is a postwar phenomenon. This early period of Australian nation-building left an ambiguous impact on the political system. While the open-minded, but principled, 'socialism without doctrine' can claim some success in enhancing standards of living and security in Australia, the absence of a strongly institutionalized or embedded sense of why the forces of principled liberalism, nonintervention and free trade wreak such damage has prevented government from responding in the national interest on at least two occasions (the 1930s and since the mid-1970s). Changes in the global economic environment, sectoral change in domestic industry, depression and unemployment all need to be resisted. Yet embedded liberalism has always retained the strategic edge in the Australian polity and has readily defeated proposals for experimental, pragmatic or principled post-liberalism in policy.

The immediate post-1945 period and the 1980s were both times when non-doctrinaire routes to full employment were defeated by liberal biases in policy-making institutions. The 1945 White Paper, *Full Employment in Australia*, was itself a heavily compromised vision for a new social order, developed in the aftermath of war when 'no financial or other obstacles (had) been allowed to prevent the need for extra production being satisfied to the limit of our resources' (Commonwealth of Australia 1945: 3). Politicians, intellectuals, policy-makers and the general community had all recognized by 1945 that governments could and should influence levels of employment. Yet even with the collective and solidaristic national sentiment brought about by the war and the creativity of a group of 'young and progressive' intellectuals in the Department of Postwar Reconstruction, full employment never became an explicit and unequivocal government objective. The White Paper promised more, citing full employment as the government's 'obligation' to the people, but its dissipation into a commitment to demand management instead of the 'socialization of investment' was implied by the Keynesian analysis on which it was based, meant that the episode was much less 'bold and unequivocal' than the custodians of postwar reconstruction seemed to imagine (see Macintyre 1985: 81–2). The wholly anticipatable resistances to authentic Keynesian policy and to full employment were not anticipated by the Australian polity; neither were the political institutions needed for a market-transcending route to prosperity constructed. Therefore, no acumen, statecraft or integrity can be ascribed to Australian economic management in the postwar period.

The historically unique opportunity to develop political capacity was squandered. Restrictive and deflationary approaches to the economy are logical outcomes of the policy process if it is constituted by institutions hostile to political control of investment or income distribution, or eradication of the labour market. The caveats and reservations which generate this kind of transformation were mostly contained within the 1945 White Paper. Macintyre has claimed that stability, not full employment, was the key objective. 'Nugget' Coombs recognized the scepticism and ambiguity that permeated the formulation of the document: 'The final version was . . . a compromise document expressing only what could be supported by consensus and avoiding issues likely to provoke controversy . . . The need to carry Treasury with us was critical' (1981: 52). Of course, the failure to consummate the Keynesian promise into effective institutions was a liberal phenomenon rather than an Australian one. Even the collective experience of depression and war was insufficient to shift the ideological underpinnings of the Australian polity away from periodic acceptance of austerity and back towards its earlier nation-building focus. The Treasury seems to have been instrumental in restraining the state apparatus, and its managerial capacities, from expanding. Ironically, it was the sequence of events from the late 1920s to the end of the war, including the Keynesian revolution, which expanded Treasury's jurisdiction.

The expectations aroused by the 1994 White Paper fell short of those in 1945; the paper possessed a series of even more restrictive caveats and conditions (see Johnson 1996: 188–9). The period in between saw the entrenchment of a Treasury orthodoxy (reliance on restrictive fiscal and monetary policy, the reinterpretation of Keynes' message as 'demand management' and the pre-emptive exploitation of fear of inflation), following the disappearance of the countervailing emphases of the Department of Postwar Reconstruction, rejection of the Vernon Committee's 1960s' recommendations for enhanced public competences and the 1970s' flirtation with monetarism. Unions' attempts in the 1980s to use the arbitration system to integrate different arms of policy (with a pragmatic approach to economic conditions) were ignominiously sidelined after 1987, and the 1994 *Working Nation* proposals also opted for 'solutions' that would least disrupt market mechanisms, obviating any sustained resistance to internationalist liberalism. In other words, the forces responsible for the problem of unemployment were endorsed and encouraged by a policy profile ostensibly (but not realistically) designed to exacerbate them.

So, though the experience of the post-1974 recession has been important in the struggle between democracy (politics) and the capitalist economy (markets), it has been only a period of consolidation of an impotent regime of regulation, not an historical watershed. The Committee on Employment Opportunities, officially responsible for developing the broad policy framework in the lead-up to *Working Nation*, had little of the young and progressive sentiment of its 1945 predecessor. Given the state of the electorate in the 1993–96 period, and the unwillingness of either polity or populace to engage in a political struggle for progressive outcomes, perhaps the document would have been more appropriately labelled 'disillusioned nation'. An unsuccessful Opposition had even proposed removing the full employment commitment from the Reserve Bank's charter. The sentiment of the times, if not an explanation of their privations, has been expressed by Hugh Stretton:

> When most of society's expert and articulate voices agree about serious national matters it is difficult for fifty-one per cent of electors to disagree with them; and if they do, there is nothing they can do about it if they are offered no alternative leadership or policy directions at election time, and if the relevant policies are anyway introduced without warning or mandate . . . Political leaders on both sides, business and public service leaders, press and academic economists have all contributed to it. The exceptions in each of those groups have been silenced, marginalised or stereotyped as nostalgic reactionaries successfully enough to avoid any need to actually answer their arguments (1993: 62).

The discursive aspects of the current recession, whereby pessimistic or cynical evaluations of the possibilities of political reform have become the baseline for societal consideration of what is possible, are yet to be fully analysed. Carol Johnson has argued that not all accomplishments of the Keating years were negative, because significant contributions to non-doctrinaire views of citizenship seem to have resulted (see also the remarkably forgiving analyses by Frankel 1997 and Wiseman 1996). A strong thread of social and political commentary nonetheless emphasizes the departures from expected and past labourist policies after 1983 (Battin 1996; Johnson 1996; Marsh 1995; Smyth 1996). We tend to disagree with this reasoning, because the political conditions for full employment have never been properly developed by labour. As has been said of other countries, Australian Labor rarely misses an opportunity to miss an opportunity. 'New' Labor in Australia is no newer than it is in the United Kingdom; in both places the internal forces maintaining what is considered an electorally necessary distance between principle and practice have been entrenched throughout the century. Policy remains too willing to impose 'solutions' to imagined problems, such as potential inflation, which frustrate development, prosperity, politicization and democracy. A distinctive statecraft that would attempt to secure national economic and policy autonomy has never emerged. The institutional inertia of the political system has proven too great, the level of sophistication of the state apparatus too low and the impact of the Treasury too malign.

The macropolitical responsibilities of labour

Following the defeats of the mid-1970s, the Australian Labor Party and the organized labour movement did initiate two significant attempts to construct some of the strategic impetus required for a sophisticated response to the recession. In view of the failure of 'social contracts' in the United Kingdom, something imaginative and experimental was required to transcend labour's defensiveness over mass unemployment and high inflation. Radical, if flawed, attempts to change the nature of state–labour–capital relations appeared in the 1983–87 period. Unhappily, they were more derided than discussed by the Australian intelligentsia. Labour imagined the development of an explicitly political and active role for unions, in conjunction with a party at least notionally willing to facilitate the necessary processes of organizational restructuring. The ALP–ACTU Accord was a significant step towards a post-liberal response to macro-level industrial and economic management—an initially popular policy signalling the willingness of the peak council of unions to engage constructively with policies to remedy unemployment and inflation. It was influenced by the negative lessons from the United Kingdom and the potential offered by the unions' eighty-year involvement in wages policy. Though most critical appraisals of this historic experience cast labour's willing participation in the arbitration processes as 'labourist' cooptation, its potential was always much more. Principled wage fixation has always required institutions wherein criteria other than the capacity of employers to pay be allowed to operate. Developments during the 1980s even allowed wage-fixation procedures to become an occasion where all aspects of social and economic policy could be discussed, thus transcending one of the characteristics for which Australian unionism had long been criticized—its recurrent propensity to mount its militancy at an industrial rather than a political level. Ultimately, the efficacy of this strategy was undermined by an employers' offensive and government's fulsome embrace of the liberal agenda of deregulation, privatization and competition policy; that is, issues other than those agreed to in the Accord commitments were largely to blame for its subsequent loss of authority and purpose (Dow 1996: 165).

As late as 1987 labour was still prepared to try to add public responsibility (for the macroeconomy) to its public functions (involvement in production and wage-setting). Articulation of the theoretical and practical rationale for this strategic transformation of Australian labour reached its height of clarity and self-consciousness in the second initiative, *Australia Reconstructed*, the product of an ACTU 'study mission' to western Europe. It remains the most comprehensive policy proposal, with an alternative economic vision along post-Keynesian lines, ever presented in Australia, more alert to the obduracies of the full employment project than the *Full Employment in Australia* White Paper of 1945. As an 'alternative economic strategy' (see Higgins 1985; Ewer, Higgins & Stevens 1991), it envisaged a strategic effort by the peak organization of labour to impose its prerogatives on the institutional, policy and economic development of the country. *Australia Reconstructed* was developed, more than a decade after the recession began, following the abandonment of similar policy interventions (concerning a social contract, planning agreements and expansion of public enterprise) in the United Kingdom. It was an outgrowth of the specific party–union agreements embodied in the Accord, in turn based on Australia's institutionalized, and potentially statist, wage-fixing arrangements. In the context of Australia's comparatively poor post-1974 performance and recurrent adoption of ineffective liberal economic policies, it staked a claim for a post-liberal alternative, for the permanent involvement of organized labour in a full range of macroeconomic and social policy controversies. It therefore merits a claim to intellectual legitimacy as well as political boldness. *Australia Reconstructed* embodied most of the principles of post-Keynesian critique of economic policy orthodoxy, though it lacked both the insights that were derived from the statist critique of political liberalism and the sense of resistance that Marxism (and the history of labour movement struggles against capital social relations of production) provides.

Its proposals for macroeconomic policy stated the mission group's lack of faith in expansionary responses to recession; its wages policy affirmed acceptance of centralized arbitration procedures and peak level bargaining between the ACTU and the government. Its industry policy claimed selective approaches rather than blanket protection were warranted; its 'active' labour market policy implied a state–union role in job creation and retraining rather than passive income compensation. Its industrial democracy proposals asserted labour's competence in managerial matters as well as workplace reform; and finally, it wanted to develop, within the union movement, a highly policy-conscious 'strategic unionism'. Much of the strategy was justified in Kaleckian terms. It had already been shown to be effective in the mission countries, particularly Sweden, where the union movement had claimed credit and prime responsibility for very low unemployment, high standards of living and politicized decision-making of a corporatist kind for over fifty years (see Higgins 1987).

Explicit in the unions' new policy assertiveness, therefore, was the view that labour movement participation in macroeconomic policy would be permanent and beneficial for economic outcomes such as industrial restructuring and unemployment. The Keynesian prescription for social, institutional, democratic or publicly debated control over investment was a key feature of the recommendations, supported by discussion of the Swedish labour movement's (already failed) attempt to develop collective capital through wage earner funds (ACTU/TDC 1987: 14–23).

The ACTU proposals reversed union hostility (which still existed in Sweden) to incomes policy but accepted the Scandinavian preference for a high-wage and solidaristic route to full employment and equality. Once again, the post-Keynesian rationale for equality was explicit (see Meidner 1948, 1978). The solidarity principle decreed that productivity increases in the leading sectors ought to flow on to the entire workforce, and the analytical principle of Kaleckian political economy claimed this would facilitate, not constrain, high levels of economic activity and full employment (Kalecki 1971). The Australian wage-fixing system was considered more than capable of adapting to solidaristic principles even if pressure for 'flexibility' were to continue (ACTU/TDC 1987: 50–6).

On industry policy, the key recommendation concerned the need for sectorally specific policy interventions, tripartite decision-making structures and a National Development Fund to prioritize productive and non-speculative investment. As industry policy is the great unmade part of the Keynesian revolution, the ACTU was reactivating the most important omission from the 1945 White Paper. The rationale for active labour market policy is not its capacity to have a significant impact on structural unemployment or industrial decline but its importance, through the expectation that generating employment ought to be a matter of policy, in any long-term labour movement efforts to usurp the hegemony of the market principle in the deployment of labour. The industrial democracy proposals were devised not only to develop legislated 'co-determination', which was intended to enhance both the quality of worklife and workplace productivity, but to check neo-managerial techniques that would strengthen capital's undemocratic and harmful control over entrepreneurial and industrial adjustment (1987: 162–4). 'Strategic unionism' is the term applied to the altered internal arrangements and broad political objectives that the ACTU proposed. This has also been referred to as 'political unionism' (Higgins 1985) and 'democratic class struggle' (Korpi 1983). Politicization of the economy is not a new demand, but the fact that class conflict could be institutionalized—brought within democratic parliamentary and extra-parliamentary parameters—was seen as a departure from abstentionism, a possibility that the normal imbalance of power between labour and capital could be somewhat redressed.

Subsequent attempts to break through fatalism and orthodoxy were less comprehensive than *Australia Reconstructed*. The ACTU's submission to the Committee on Employment Opportunities in 1993 (the White Paper deliberations) purported to reconcile union priorities with business' and economists' demands for flexibility. As previously, the ACTU identified its three related objectives as investment, innovation and involvement, but its strategy in the 1990s was far less convincing than its 1987 strategy. It reflected resignation in the face of government intransigence and official acceptance of the business view of how to manage the structural changes that constitute the recession (see Hall & Harley 1997). It presented a banal and pointless electoralism.

While some of the analytical focus of the Accord experiment remains, the required institutional configurations are wholly underdeveloped. This is precisely the scenario that has led generations of Marxist critics to assume that the 'role' of the state was to accommodate labour and society to a market-dominated, exploitative and repressive economy. The ACTU, in the 1990s, should have known, as it appeared to in the 1980s, that the technical problem of increasing investment is less intractable than the political and institutional problem of subjecting it to democratic control. Investment is too low because the logic of accumulation has shifted the locus of economic activity elsewhere; the market is oriented elsewhere. To increase investment in Australia requires the assertion of political, national and democratic priorities over those produced by autonomous, extra-national economic processes. This in turn requires the creation of the new political institutions discussed in chapter 4. Innovation may be acceptable and desirable, but it may also be labour-displacing and too rapid for societal adaptation. Union peak councils should not be advocating innovation without a simultaneous concern to ensure sufficient employment is created. As explained in chapter 5, union involvement in economic policy-making can secure the required shifts (Boreham & Compston 1992; Boreham & Hall 1994) provided the political will exists to legitimize and accommodate the conflictual basis of the restructured policy process. Because labour's voice changes the criteria or auspices for investment decisions, and because, as a result, conflictual relationships in the economy are accorded a prominence that is normally denied, the new institutions are important not only for their functional role but for the need to manage the conflict. The ACTU's recent submissions seem neither to recognize nor to welcome the 'macropolitical responsibilities of labour' (Dow 1995).

The fate of the unions' alternative strategy for the re-generation of industry in *Australia Reconstructed* can best be explained in the light of subsequent events.

The botching of the corporatist experiment in Australia by the end of the 1980s seems to have resulted from the unions' inability to exploit one of the Hawke era's potentially positive responses to the recession early in the decade—corporatism. The Economic Planning Advisory Council (EPAC) had been a central proposal of the Accord. It had been intended as a source of medium- and long-term policy advice independent of the Treasury and as a conduit for public input to policy-making. Formally a tripartite council, but with a significant representation from non-federal levels of government, and groups without functional links to policy-making (small business, consumers and welfare recipients), EPAC was also intended to house a research bureau. As early as March 1983, however, there were adverse bureaucratic reactions. The *Australian Financial Review* anticipated Treasury's hostility: 'it is instinctual behaviour for the Department to regard itself as the rightful and dominant economic adviser to government'. Treasury would inevitably 'assert its influence early and develop a central say in the structural formation of a policy it does not believe in but which it could want to dominate'. In fact, almost a decade earlier, the Coombs Royal Commission on Australian Government Administration had anticipated 'the considerable political courage . . . [required by a] . . . government to set up such a council which would be intensely "political" and which could at times be at variance with its own pronouncements on the state of the economy and could make critical ex post evaluation of economic measures taken by the government' (RCAGA 1976: 307). The unions were not prepared for the rejection of expansionary policy, which should have been anticipated.

The political scepticism was apparent and EPAC's potential role undermined when, as Treasurer, Paul Keating set out to distance its 'planning' aims 'from any intention to give planning an ideological interpretation that associated it with strong government interference in the economy' (*Australian Financial Review*, April 1983). Treasury acted as it had in the 1930s and at the time of the 1945 White Paper, thus reconfirming the inieliminatable liberal blinkers of Australia's economic policy-making (Stutchbury 1985). Perhaps it is not surprising that EPAC (and the Accord) never fulfilled the hopes of their advocates (see Dow 1984). More surprising was the critics' propensity to regard the putative corporatist developments as exemplifications of, rather than departures from, Australia's historical liberalism (see Beilharz & Watts 1983). Admittedly, Keating's eleventh-hour recasting of EPAC as an 'Economic Round Table with a more business oriented membership' shortly before Labor's loss of government shows not only that the government's understanding of the rationale for tripartism was minimal but also that the ACTU had lost its enthusiasm for principled involvement in macropolicy.

Business, as we have noted, was influential in preventing the new tripartite institutions becoming embedded in the policy-making process. Business had always resisted the centralized aspects of arbitration, despite the demonstrable benefits in terms of a stable industrial relations environment and reasonably equitable income distribution; this kept the overall level of economic activity higher than it would otherwise have been. Yet, in what Stephen Bell has referred to as 'the rather raw exercise of the political power of business interests and wealth holders' (1997: 278), an authoritative business voice emerged in support of policy orthodoxy. Although the structural weakness of the political organizations of business—historically constituted by divisions between State associations, different factions of capital, rural–urban conflicts, export-oriented and import-dependent activity and the lack of economies of scale in some branches of Australian industry—has often been cited as an impediment to corporatist economic management, it has worked instead against the national economic interest.

This paradox expresses the key recurrent problem of modern capitalist economies. Business as a whole is unable to act rationally; it strives to protect either its political power or its profitability—it cannot do both. The Business Council of Australia was remarkably effective at shifting the centre of gravity in both industrial relations and economic policy during the 1980s and 1990s (Bell 1997: 201–7). The BCA garnered legitimacy in the eyes of its constituent members and the business sector more generally—normally a central element in successful corporatist arrangements—remarkably easily, but used it to dismantle the arrangements that might have allowed a broad-based recovery.

The policy significance of corporatist arrangements is their ability to resolve policy conflicts publicly, which does not directly require 'representation', and a possible source of instability is peak organizations' capacities to bind their membership to the decisions reached. Since the 1980s, the political influence of employer associations in Australia seems unimpaired by their inability to exert authority over all business factions. In other words, the line between participation in and resistance to public policy-making by business in Australia is fine. The gap between what's good for the economy and what business organizations think is good for the economy was noted in chapter 5. The BCA's existence is evidence of a willingness to play a policy role; its subsequent activity is evidence of labour's inability to capitalize on the institutional mood of 1983.

There certainly are external or structural conditions militating against the success of an alternative strategy in Australia. Nonetheless, the incompleteness of the left's full-employment aspirations seems to warrant more attention. Six inherent weaknesses can be identified in *Australia Reconstructed*. First, it advocated high rates of ('evenly distributed') growth without noticing either that Australia in fact has had relatively high GDP growth since 1974 without a significant impact on unemployment or that undirected growth cannot be relied on to restructure an economy towards high levels of high-quality employment. Waiting for growth is the government's way of avoiding the explicit interventions needed for a national economic management oriented to full employment. It is the liberals' response and, in Australia as elsewhere, growth does not by itself alleviate a recession. Second, much is made throughout the document of the 'consensus' approach; yet what actually happens in corporatist forums is not so much consensus as an institutionalization of conflict, particularly over the class distribution of income and control of investment. *Australia Reconstructed* also reflects the ACTU's and the ALP's repudiation of protection as a viable mechanism for ensuring a diversified economic structure.

They accepted the logic of internationalization without recognizing that any elite-endorsed shift from a 'cosseted' to a competitive economy does not guarantee success and would probably occasion significant harm. However desirable the move to a highly skilled, export-oriented productivity culture might be, Australia's resource availability, unlike that of the small European countries, gives it much greater potential for self-sufficiency and therefore less pressing need to accept the imperatives of international competitiveness and its 'shock therapy' solutions. The government's attempt to rewrite the experience of protection as part of the Liberals' 'postwar development model' belies a significant and enduring quality in Australian politics—the propensity of the ALP to stubbornly, even arrogantly, assert liberal positions as inevitable, while imagining that they were something different. The party's position on tariffs should have been as follows:

> Economists are not entitled to demand that only criteria of efficiency and competitiveness are appropriate for national economic development. Any nation's polity is entitled to prefer and to choose high-cost industry if the alternative is no industry at all, because the benefits of activity far exceed the costs of inactivity. In so far as returns from the export of unprocessed agricultural and mining products are in long-term decline, making the cost of imported manufactured items a trade and external balance problem, the first priority of policy ought to be creation of more industry locally, not the destruction of existing industry by the elimination of protection. How dare the economists and the rationalist approach to policy demand that nations are not entitled to prioritize standards of community solidarity, morality and balanced development over the performance indicators favoured by advocates of globalization? The application of market criteria should be seen as licence granted to a range of people and activities provided the benefits to society as a whole clearly outweigh the costs and provided the necessary non-economic supports for civilized life are ensured and provided the periodic fluctuations in activity and

livelihood are compensated. It should not be regarded as an authorisation to apply market principles and the profitability criterion to all parts of society or even to all parts of the economy. The role of government therefore is not to facilitate a market mode of regulation but to adjudicate between the available rationales for public management and to decide when efficiency is not the most appropriate criterion. This will necessarily involve the establishment of public institutions whose charter is to secure substantive economic and societal outcomes even, occasionally, at the cost of economic liberal procedure and the international logic of structural adjustment.

Fourth, the commitment of the leadership (party, government and unions) to the new strategic thrust seemed insincere, or sincere only so far as the unions' ideas coincided with the favoured stance of the government and the bureaucracy. This muted commitment is evident in the frontispiece statements by the Minister for Trade and the ACTU secretary. A fifth weakness derives from the document's endorsement of improved productivity without recognition of the inexorable growth of scope and need for more unproductive economic activity. This is tantamount to ignorance of the nature of modern economies, a disturbing lapse for a movement whose basic rationale had been suspicion of the capacity of market economies to unambiguously secure economic development and contempt for important moral aspects of the market principle even when material success was assured. Finally, much of what eventuated as the Business Council of Australia's counter-mobilization against the ACTU's strategy was accepted in *Australia Reconstructed* itself. The BCA's preference for flexible, initially two-tiered, but later enterprise-level, bargaining was endorsed, as were employer views on the failure of traditional forms of management, export promotion, employment growth, fiscal policy, workplace reform and debt. Should not the ACTU have anticipated both the government's lack of enthusiasm and the BCA's resistance? That it did not may be seen as an indication of the resistances to state capacity in Australia.

Managerial resistance to state capacity

Can the long-term possibilities of progressive politics be discerned from contemporary events? General reasons for the cumulative emergence of structural inability to deal with unemployment in the 1980s and 1990s can indeed be specified. The 1993 television programme *Labor in Power* (see Taylor 1993) included the observation from a long-standing Treasury official that 'Treasury got more of its agenda up in the decade of the Hawke–Keating government than the rest of the postwar period combined . . . easily'. This constitutes evidence for the view that a doctrinaire elite had become responsible for thwarting policy alternatives. But it is also evidence that the ACTU insufficiently anticipated the political and discursive problems for interventionist strategy, particularly the extent of class conflict over the auspices governing economic management.

The ACTU also insufficiently anticipated the shift in managerial strategies at the microeconomic level that effectively undermined much of the unions' macro-level focus. Strategies to expand state capacity, as we have noted, are intended to create competences in the polity that are not the responsibility of government alone but which give a public role to the political organizations of labour and capital. The role of labour in building state capacity and moulding industrial capacities seems to be crucial. So, therefore, is the role of business. Consequently, the capacity of business to frustrate the statist project must be reckoned as intrinsic to attempts to secure full employment. Without necessarily having Machiavellian intent, business in the 1980s and 1990s seems to have opted for industrial relations strategies that prioritize competitiveness over production.

Industrial relations, the issue upon which 'true believers' apparently based party allegiances in the early 1990s, had become bipartisan by the late 1990s. A distinctive approach to productivity enhancement, selected from two broad alternatives, had surfaced by the mid-1990s. The alternative 'ideal types' which now characterize national policy arrangements in industrial relations are that which is oriented to increasing profitability in the short term, and that which involves enhancing productive capacity. Figure 6.1 details the respective strategies.

It is important to stress that these diametrically opposed approaches to the importance of production and the treatment of labour are not analytical abstractions. They are broadly accurate representations of the culture of production that typifies many of the industrial nations. The 'production enhancement' strategies are those exemplified in countries such as Japan, Germany, Austria and Sweden. The 'profitability oriented' strategies characterize the United States, the United Kingdom, Australia and New Zealand. While enterprises in the latter countries show higher levels of profitability, the broader social and economic consequences involve a substantial destruction of national productive capacity, significantly higher levels of unemployment and increasing levels of poverty and social inequality. In other words, enterprises become more profitable at the same time as there are fewer of them. And, as the industrial structure changes more or less randomly, the networks and connections required for a more comprehensive system break down, further narrowing the manufacturing base.

It has even been suggested that a commitment to high-technology, high value-added manufacturing would require a policy-driven entrenchment of oligopolistic enterprises able to exploit economies of scale, rent-seeking possibilities, industrial clusters, barriers to entry and a 'collusive mode of development' (Reinert 1995) rather than the strategies recommended by neoclassical economists. The history of all industrially successful countries, as well as the requirements of structural transformation of the mature economies, suggests that synergies need not only to be created but also protected.

Australia now stands out as perhaps the key example of the profitability-oriented approach. As the pace of enterprise bargaining has quickened, so has the rate at which the institutional structures which protected production, labour and living standards been demolished. Workplace bargaining can facilitate either of the strategies depicted in Figure 6.1 (see also Boreham, Hall & Leet 1996), however, it is most unlikely that

Figure 6.1: Alternative Micro-level (Enterprise) Strategies

Profitability-oriented Strategy	Production-enhancement Strategy
Concentrates on maintaining high levels of profitability in the short-term	Has long-term focus on productive capacity and market share
Tends to restore/increase profitability through cost reductions in areas such as research and development, investment, training and maintenance	Tends to restore/increase profitability through productivity development—maintaining or increasing research and development, investment and training
Reduces costs through real wage cuts	Concentrates on a high-wage, high-skilled workforce engaged in high value-added production
Uses new technology to replace labour and to reduce labour costs by substituting lower-skilled machine operators for skilled workers	Integrates new technologies into a production process which capitalizes on a highly-skilled workforce generating high-wage jobs
Creates flexibility in employment through deregulating labour market practices, particularly with respect to employing casual workers (being able to discharge surplus employees at times of downward fluctuation in demand)	Limits turnover to maximize the return from training and experience (in Japan where these practices are widely employed, the turnover rate is only 3.5 per cent p.a.—fewer job losses in a year than the United States has in a month)
Replaces high-wage full-time workers with low-wage part-time workers	Guarantees employment security for a mainly full-time workforce to maintain organizational capacity, institutional memory and experience even if some underemployment occurs
Has low levels of investment in training and concentrates training expenditure on management	
Has hierarchical organizational structures in which managerial control is paramount and contributions from employees are devalued	Concentrates on training and skills development at all levels of the workforce, particularly the lower 50 per cent, to facilitate the implementation of high-tech processes at the workplace
Offers relatively high rewards for managers compared to the workforce, associated with high expectations placed on management performance	Has organizational arrangements which facilitate participatory practices involving most of the workforce in decisions about production processes and building employees' skill and experience into production
	Has a collective approach to enterprise decision-making, rewarding the work group rather than individual managers

employment and management changes driven from below will reorient (existing) strategies away from an exclusive focus on profitability. Australian workplaces are immersed in a milieu which places a high value on this cost-reduction approach. Only a strong and coherent national system can reinstate a productive enhancement strategy, one which emphasises long-term capital investment, research and development, training and participation—even if it is implemented through enterprise-level negotiations. Left to themselves, individual enterprises are unlikely to adopt such a method of enhancing production, especially when it contradicts established management fads.

The general trend has been a shift away from union-driven attempts to resist the extension of standard hours, to a management drive for working-time flexibility, often in the form of reduced penalty rates, an increased span of ordinary hours, variations to rostered days off, annualized salaries and weekly hours averaged over a period of several weeks (ACIRRT 1993:11). Studies of the agreements reached in the early 1990s indicate that in many a common objective was to provide greater flexibility in working hours to tailor employment conditions to the needs of business. Nearly half of the first thousand agreements, including almost 60 per cent of service sector agreements, focused on hours-of-work issues. Production enhancement measures involving redesigned jobs and workplace reorganization were introduced in fewer than 25 per cent of workplaces. Examination of workplace agreements (DIR 1993b) suggests that in many cases established working conditions are being substantially eroded for short-term economic benefits.

Production enhancement strategies based on productivity development through skill formation and training, the integration of new technologies with an experienced, high-wage workforce, formal joint consultative committees and other participatory practices, job redesign and workplace reorganization occur in only a significant minority of workplaces with enterprise bargains. Whatever outcomes result from the broad changes following the new circumstances in industrial relations, improvements in working conditions and the productive capacity of the labour force are unlikely to be among them. A large section of management in Australian enterprises is deeply embedded within the harmful philosophy of short-term profitability through cost minimization. The ability to reconstruct this approach through micro-level negotiation with enterprise management is severely, if not entirely, limited.

These enterprise-level changes affect state capacity and the macropolitical role of labour because, to the extent that the role of the arbitration system is downgraded, unions are excluded from bargaining over the issues that matter. Micro-level outcomes can be expected to be less favourable to workers and, while there is still uncertainty about the economic outcomes of enterprise bargaining, there is no ambiguity about equity questions—workplace bargaining favours those in a superior bargaining position (Peetz 1992: 343). Disparities in pay and working conditions between different groups of workers are likely to become greater, thus exacerbating poor macro-performance.

As documented in chapter 2, one of the most striking features of the Australian labour market in recent decades has been the growth of irregular employment (part-time, casual and temporary employment). Non-standard forms of work have eroded bargaining capacities and reduced the range of issues subject to bargaining. Such workers are concentrated in low-level, menial jobs which require relatively low skill. By definition, they are relatively easy to fire and can be replaced with minimal cost or difficulty. Irregular workers are less often unionized than full-time permanent workers, further reducing their bargaining resources.

So, weakening of the micro-conditions of individual workers seems to be part of the project of displacing broader political principles for inclusion of union organizations in national, democratic decision-making processes. The only social group with an objective interest in full employment and with potentially sufficient power resources to mount a struggle for full employment, is facing declining morale. One of the major achievements of the modern epoch, employment security, is being eroded for the chimera of prosperity.

The rhetoric and possibilities of politics

The apparent contradictions in the struggle for decent economic policy are not new; they are inscribed in the nature of capitalism itself. Yet the fight for full employment has become as much rhetorical as practical because much of the effort is now in discrediting, for elites, the populace or labour's own functionaries, much of the rhetoric of conventional economic policy-making and electoral reaction to economic insecurity. Now, at the end of the 1990s, there is evidence of electoral resistance to economic rationalism, though without an effective public discourse this can take horrific forms. Public disquiet with microeconomic reform led the Liberals to electoral loss in 1993, Labor to defeat in 1996 and the coalition to near break-up after 1996 (not to mention the more bizarre developments with the One Nation phenomenon in 1998 and 1999).

Our argument and evidence runs counter to the current consensus in macroeconomic management and micro-level managerial preference. Because the key economic hypotheses, policy proposals and political approaches we have developed are largely counter-intuitive, we summarize them here.

- The main conventional indicators of economic performance—inflation and economic growth—are inappropriate guides to the unemployment problem. Economic growth is neither a necessary nor a sufficient condition for full employment (nor is employment growth). Inflation and unemployment are unrelated - they have separate and independent causes. Policy can eliminate inflation and policy can eliminate unemployment; it is no longer reasonable to assume that economic forces decree that there is a meaningful relation between the two. What is important, to identify whether the generation of new industrial and economic activity is matching the displacement of older activity, is productive capacity.
- Conventional preference for restrictive policy rather than economic expansion ought to be resisted. In Australia, public

debt is low, so budget surpluses and fiscal consolidation are unwarranted. Because levels of savings and income are determined by general rates of investment, only expansionary policy can produce higher savings. Expansionary policy does not exacerbate balance of payments problems unless Australia keeps imports controls illicit. Trade and current account problems can be remedied only through industry policy, not austerity. Further, the resources necessary to fund public activities are readily available, through taxation increases from a very low base.

- The effects of government-sector activity are clearly positive. Very small increases in public investment have dramatic effects on unemployment, even at very low rates of unemployment. Public investment renders private investment more effective. The evidence supports the proposition that investment in public infrastructure directly augments private sector production.
- There is little or no relationship between real wages and unemployment. All the low-unemployment countries have been high-wage economies. Wage reduction and wage flexibility do not constitute solutions to economic recession or unemployment.
- There is no relationship between generosity of welfare benefits and unemployment. All countries with significantly lower rates of unemployment than Australia have higher, not lower, levels of social security transfers.
- There is no relationship between the labour force participation rate and unemployment. Neither high labour force participation rates nor employment growth are impediments to reduced unemployment.
- No advanced country has been successful without a strong manufacturing base. Even though the contribution of manufacturing to employment has been declining everywhere, Australia's self-inflicted deindustrialization is severe and especially damaging.
- Although they cannot deal with wholesale structural change, active labour market policies are crucial for any economy

wishing to maintain full employment. Australia has a comparatively low level of active labour market measures.
- The formulation and implementation of concrete policy measures can only take place within the democratic processes of the political system. However, such democratic procedures are not limited to parliament. Only with the establishment of extra-parliamentary organizations can social and economic policies adequate to the task of managing the economy in the public interest be imagined.
- The path towards political responsibility for unemployment is not consensual. Resistances to full employment are inevitable, even though it would benefit all in the long run. Full employment requires a political project, based on the macro-political role of unions, to develop the capacities necessary to eliminate the resistances to full employment. Orthodox economic reasoning amounts to an abrogation of political responsibility. Only a permanent, institutionalized, political commitment to full employment can result in full employment.

We have attempted to show in this book that much of the current economic crisis has not been technically necessary and that more concerted action by government and political processes generally could have alleviated it. We have argued that states have thrown away many of the capacities they had (or could have developed) to deal with recession and unemployment. Possibilities for politics have not only remained unexploited but have been intentionally suppressed. We have therefore suggested three types of state institutions that need to be created, as public spheres which can provide societies with the capacity to democratically discuss and politically control their economies. There is political room to manoeuvre.

We have concluded that many contemporary polities have become insufficiently statist. The evidence, both empirical and analytical, strongly demonstrates, as it has since the crisis and policy mistakes of the 1930s, that full employment is achievable even in a world of rapid structural change, provided appropriate mechanisms to expand and strengthen democratic possibilities are constructed. This does not imply, however, a particularly statist solution to Australia's current problems. The nation needs a more experimental approach to economic management, which can be achieved by reactivating the corporatist arrangements that were initiated, with obvious public endorsement, in the mid-1980s. The value of so-called corporatist arrangements is that they recognize the conflict that underlies normal processes of economic activity. They can ensure that conflicts—over control of investment decisions, the distribution of income and the extent to which labour is allocated by market mechanisms—are institutionalized, though not eliminated. Corporatist institutions extend the democratic impulse because they give voice to all the social forces whose activity is crucial to the economy; they improve economic performance because they prioritize actual outcomes rather than purely formal mechanisms for economic decision-making. The corporatist structure we are urging is therefore not statist, because it will not be the state that acquires the right to make decisions; it is, rather, the embodiment of an extension of the political process. Enhancement of state capacity is enhancement of the expectation that labour and capital will pursue their functions according to more politicized criteria, not that the state will decide everything. It is naturally desirable that these changes be implemented in the context of a very open and active political process.

Questions about the processes and scope of politics need to be addressed as part of a discussion of anti-recessionary macroeconomic policy. We are sceptical of many suggestions that emphasis should devolve to the unregulated, private sphere of 'civil society', because we are not convinced that the political process as such has failed. Rather, we have argued that for the past twenty-five years politics has been forced into retreat and political possibilities denied precisely when they ought to have become more effective. There is an urgent need for reconstitution of the 'publicness' of politics—a realm of enhanced and ongoing debate and discussion of alternative possibilities. Formerly private decisions of private enterprises will be politicized by the development of public forums to hear debate and make decisions about industrial investment, income distribution and the so-called labour market. The responsibility that the political process must accept is to create these forums (Goldfarb 1998). In the process, the nature of the decisions will inevitably change. Business will be forced to adopt a public role; bargaining and negotiation with trade unions and the state will disperse its former autonomy. But the policies that result in industrial structuring and restructuring will still reflect real social conditions; similar problems will be aired, but solved in different ways. Conflicts will continue but they will be democratically and institutionally resolved. The liberal political pretence that the economy ought not to be politicized, that business decisions are legitimately outside the democratic process, will be dismantled by arrangements which also make sound economic performance easier to achieve.

Business groups such as the Business Council of Australia will continue to have a legitimate voice because capital is crucial to a capitalist economy. Labour will also acquire a permanent voice in macropolicy because its normal activity is also crucial in a capitalist economy. The outcomes of decisions arrived at in this way will differ from those of capital alone and the publicness of the process will be clear. Capital and labour take on political roles because they are functionally important to the economy, not because they are merely interest groups. Interest-group politics involves organizations acting in a private capacity in a public arena. Democratic corporatism, on the other hand, occurs where a wider range of decisions is made openly and publicly, in an already constituted public arena, by actors who must act in a public capacity if they are to retain their legitimacy. Eventually, in such a context, the organizations on both sides of the class divide will routinize their public responsibilities. Parties of the left can be expected to side with labour against capital on many issues concerning the decommodification of labour and the elimination of unemployment; if parties of the right combine with business to thwart such outcomes, such is the price of democracy. Our proposals are not statist, but neither do they fall on the civil society side of the divide. They allow for political debate and politicized bargaining. They do not guarantee outcomes.

New political institutions need not become state actors nor implement state policy, but they must adopt permanent public roles and adapt the public outcomes of private behaviour, economic and otherwise. The state is required both to facilitate the process and to implement many of the macro-level decisions made in new institutional contexts. Non-state forces, particularly the political organizations of capital and peak councils of trade unions, will become, more explicitly than at present, public forces with responsibilities and rights. It is important and necessary for both economic and democratic development that the political realm be regenerated, that the abrogation of political responsibility be reversed and that political capacities be expanded.

Australia must cast aside the unreasonably pessimistic picture of the creative potential of politics in general. In the past the political process has been denied the political resources needed for the tasks it is charged with; it is then judged harshly when it fails, as it must, to cope. Our purpose, in this book, has been to show that the long recession can be countered. The suffering all citizens endure while any of them endures unemployment is not inevitable. The worm can be turned.

Bibliography

Arndt, Heinz W. 1994, *Full employment in historical perspective* (The Full Employment Project Working Paper 3/94). Melbourne: University of Melbourne & Institute of Public Affairs.

Australian Bureau of Statistics (ABS) 1991, *Labour statistics Australia, 1989* (Catalogue 6101.0). Canberra: ABS.

—— 1996, *The Labour Force, Australia* (Catalogue 6203.0), June.

—— 1997, *Australian National Accounts: national income and expenditure 1995–96* (Catalogue 5204.4). Canberra: ABS.

Australian Centre for Industrial Relations Research and Teaching (ACIRRT) 1993, *Agreements database and monitor* (Report no. 1). Sydney: ACIRRT.

Australian Council of Trade Unions/Trade Development Council (ACTU/TDC) 1987, *Australia Reconstructed*. Canberra: Australian Government Publishing Service.

Australian Council of Trade Unions (ACTU) 1993, *A program towards full employment: the ACTU's program for sustainable employment and jobs growth for the 1990s and beyond*. Canberra: Australian Government Publishing Service.

Australian Government 1994, *Working Nation: policies and programs* (presented by the prime minister to the House of Representatives). Canberra: Australian Government Publishing Service.

Australian Manufacturing Council (AMC) 1990, *The global challenge: Australian manufacturing in the 1990s* (Pappas, Carter, Evans & Koop/Telesis report). Melbourne: AMC.

Battin, Tim 1996, 'A political analysis of Australian economic debate: the place of socialist thought' in Tim Battin & Graham Maddox (eds), *Socialism in contemporary Australia*. Melbourne: Longman.

Beilharz, Peter 1994, *Transforming Labor: labour tradition and the labor decade in Australia*. Melbourne: Cambridge University Press.

Beilharz, Peter & Rob Watts 1983, 'The discovery of corporatism', *Australian Society* 2(10): 27–30.

Bell, Stephen 1994, 'Statist analysis' in Andrew Parkin, John Summers & Dennis Woodward (eds), *Government, politics, power and policy in Australia* (5th edn). Melbourne: Longman.

—— 1995, 'The collective capitalism of northeast Asia and the limits of orthodox economics', *Australian Journal of Political Science* 30(2): 264–87.

—— 1997, *Ungoverning the economy: the political economy of Australian economic policy*. Melbourne: Oxford University Press.

Berger, Suzanne & Ronald Dore (eds) 1996, *National diversity and global capitalism*. Ithaca: Cornell University Press.

Bienefeld, Manfred 1994, 'Capitalism and the nation state in the dog days of the twentieth century' in Ralph Miliband & Leo Panitch (eds), *The Socialist Register 1994: between globalism and nationalism*. London: Merlin Press.

—— 1996, 'Is a strong national economy a utopian goal at the end of the twentieth century?' in R. Boyer & D. Drache (eds), *States against markets: the limits of globalization*. London: Routledge.

Boreham, Paul & Hugh Compston 1992, 'Labour movement organization and political intervention: the politics of unemployment in the OECD countries, 1974–1986', *European Journal of Political Research* 22(2): 143–70.

Boreham, Paul & Richard Hall 1994, 'Trade union strategy in contemporary capitalism: the microeconomic and macroeconomic implications of political unionism', *Economic and Industrial Democracy* 15(3): 313–53.

Boreham, Paul, Richard Hall & Bill Harley 1996, 'Two paths to prosperity? Work organization and industrial relations decentralization in Australia', *Work, Employment & Society* 10(3): 449–68.

Boreham, Paul, Richard Hall & Martin Leet 1996, 'Labour and citizenship: the development of welfare state regimes', *Journal of Public Policy* 16(2): 203–27.

Boyer, Robert 1990, *The regulation school: a critical introduction* (trans. Craig Charney). New York: Columbia University Press.

Boyer, Robert & Daniel Drache (eds) 1996, *States against markets: the limits of globalization*. London: Routledge.

Brigden, James Bristock et al. 1929, *The Australian tariff: an economic enquiry*. Melbourne: Melbourne University Press.

Burdekin, Richard C. K. & Paul Burkett 1996, *Distributional conflict and inflation: theoretical and historical pespectives*. London: Macmillan.

Calmfors, Lars & John Driffill 1988, 'Bargaining structure, corporatism and macroeconomic performance', *Economic Policy: A European Forum* 6: 13–61.

Cameron, David 1982, 'On the limits of the public economy', *Annals of the American Academy of Political and Social Science* 459: 46–62.

—— 1984, 'Social democracy, corporatism, labour quiescence and the representation of economic interest in advanced capitalist society' in John Goldthorpe (ed.), *Order and conflict in contemporary capitalism: studies in the political economy of western European nations*. Oxford: Clarendon Press.

Capling, Ann & Brian Galligan 1992, *Beyond the protective state: the political economy of Australia's manufacturing industry policy*. Melbourne: Cambridge University Press.

Capling, Ann, Mark Considine & Michael Crozier 1998, *Australian politics in the global era*. Melbourne: Longman.

Cass, Bettina 1988, 'Income support for the unemployed in Australia: towards a more active system', *Social Security Review Issues Paper* no. 4. Canberra: Australian Government Publishing Service.

Castles, Francis G. 1985, *The working class and welfare: reflections on the political development of the welfare state in Australia and New Zealand, 1890–1980*. Sydney: Allen & Unwin.

——1988, *Australian public policy and economic vulnerability: a comparative and historical perspective*. Sydney: Allen & Unwin.

——1991, 'Why compare Australia?' in Francis Castles (ed.), *Australia compared: people, policies and politics*. Sydney: Allen & Unwin.

——1997a, 'Historical and comparative perspectives on the Australian welfare state: a response to Rob Watts', *Australian & New Zealand Journal of Sociology* 33(1): 16–20.

——1997b, 'The institutional design of the Australian welfare state', *International Social Security Review* 50(2): 25–41.

Castles, Francis & Deborah Mitchell 1992, 'Identifying welfare state regimes: the links between politics, institutions and outcomes', *Governance* 5(1): 1–26.

Castles, Francis G. & Ian F. Shirley 1997, 'Labour and social policy: gravediggers or refurbishers of the welfare state?' in Francis G. Castles et al. (eds), *The great experiment: labour parties and public policy transformation in Australia and New Zealand*. Sydney: Allen & Unwin.

Clarke, Simon 1988, 'Overaccumulation, class struggle and the regulation approach', *Capital & Class* 36: 59–92.

Clegg, Stewart, Paul Boreham & Geoff Dow 1986, *Class, politics and the economy*. London: Routledge & Kegan Paul.

Cohen, Stephen & John Zysman 1987, *Manufacturing matters: the myth of the post-industrial economy*. New York: Basic Books.

Commission on Employment Issues in Europe (Kriesky Commission) 1989, *A programme for full employment in the 1990s*. Oxford: Pergamon Press.

Committee on Employment Opportunities 1993a, *Restoring Full Employment: the issues in brief*. Canberra: Australian Government Publishing Service.

——1993b, *Restoring Full Employment: a discussion paper*. Canberra: Australian Government Publishing Service.

Commonwealth of Australia 1945, *Full Employment in Australia*. Canberra: Commonwealth Government Printer, also excerpted in John Wilson, Jane Thomson & Anthony McMahon (eds) 1996, *The Australian welfare state: key documents and themes*. Melbourne: Macmillan.

Coombs, Herbert Cole 1981, *Trial balance*. Melbourne: Macmillan.

Cox, Andrew 1986, 'State, finance and industry in comparative perspective' in Andrew Cox (ed.), *State, finance and industry: a comparative analysis of postwar trends in six advanced industrial nations*. Brighton: Wheatsheaf.

Crawford, J. R. et al. 1979, *Study group on structural adjustment (Report)*. Canberra: Australian Government Publishing Service.

Crouch, Colin 1985, 'Corporatism in industrial relations: a formal model' in Wyn Grant (ed.), *The political economy of corporatism*. London: Macmillan.

Dahrendorf, Ralf 1995, 'Preserving prosperity', *New Statesman & Society* 8(383): 36–41.

Das, Raju J. 1996, 'State theories: a critical analysis', *Science & Society* 60(1): 27–57.

Deakin, S. & F. Wilkinson, 1992, 'European integration: the implications for UK policies on labour supply and demand' in E. McLaughlin (ed.), *Understanding unemployment: new perspectives on active labour market policies*. London: Routledge.

Deane, Phyllis 1989, *The state and the economic system: an introduction to the history of political economy*. Oxford: Oxford University Press.

Department of Employment, Education and Training (DEET) 1989, *Employment, education and training: key trends and government initiatives* (submission to the Economic Planning Advisory Council). Canberra: Australian Government Publishing Service.

—— 1990, *Women in the labour market: a statistical profile*. Canberra: DEET (Women's Bureau).

—— 1991, *Australia's workforce in the year 2001*. Canberra: Australian Government Publishing Service.

Department of Industrial Relations (DIR) 1993a, *Submission to the Committee on Employment Opportunities*. Canberra: Australian Government Publishing Service.

—— 1993b, *Workplace bargaining: the first 1000 agreements*. Canberra: Australian Government Publishing Service.

Devery, Christopher 1991, *Disadvantage and crime in New South Wales*. Sydney: NSW Bureau of Crime Statistics and Research.

Dow, Geoff 1984, 'The case for corporatism', *Australian Society* 3(5): 14–16.

—— 1992, 'The economic consequences of economists', *Australian Journal of Political Science* 27(2): 258–81.

—— 1993, 'What do we know about social democracy?', *Economic and Industrial Democracy* 14(1): 11–48.

—— 1995, 'The macropolitical responsibilities of labour', paper presented to the *Second International Conference on Emerging Union Structures*. Institutet för arbetslivsforskning, Stockholm, June.

—— 1996, 'Full employment and social democratic institutions: the reconstruction of political possibilities' in Tim Battin & Graham Maddox (eds), *Socialism in contemporary Australia* Melbourne: Longman.

—— 1997a, 'Simplicity or civility? The new debate on tax reform', *Ockham's razor*, ABC Radio National, 9 February. [URL: www.abc.net.au/rn]

—— 1997b, 'Labour's mission and the capacities of politics: in defence of *Australia Reconstructed*', *Journal of Australian Political Economy* 39: 122–40.

—— 1998, 'Beyond the logic of accumulation: towards a Marxian theory of state capacity' in Geoff Dow & George Lafferty (eds) *Everlasting uncertainty: interrogating The Communist Manifesto 1848–1998*. Sydney: Pluto Press.

Dow, Geoff, Stewart Clegg & Paul Boreham 1984, 'From the politics of production to the production of politics', *Thesis Eleven* 9: 16–32.

Dunn, John (ed.) 1990, *The economic limits to modern politics*. Cambridge: Cambridge University Press.

East Asia Analytical Unit/Department of Foreign Affairs and Trade 1992, *Australia and north-east Asia in the 1990s: accelerating change*. Canberra: Australian Government Publishing Service.

Economic Policy Advisory Council (EPAC) 1991, *Competitiveness: the policy environment* (EPAC paper no. 47). Canberra: Australian Government Publishing Service.

—— 1992, *Unemployment in Australia*. Canberra: Australian Government Publishing Service.

—— 1994, *Economic effects of micro-economic reform* (Background paper no. 38). Canberra: Australian Government Publishing Service.

Emy, Hugh 1993, *Remaking Australia: the state, the market and Australia's future*. Sydney: Allen & Unwin.

Esping-Andersen, Gösta 1990, *The three worlds of welfare capitalism*. Cambridge: Polity Press.

—— 1996, 'After the golden age? Welfare state dilemmas in a global economy' in Gösta Esping-Andersen (ed.), *Welfare states in transition: national adaptations in global economies*. London: Sage.

Evans, Peter 1992, 'The state as problem and solution: predation, embedded autonomy and structural change' in Stephan Haggard & Robert R. Kaufman (eds), *The politics of economic adjustment*. Princeton: Princeton University Press.

—— 1995, *Embedded autonomy: states and industrial transformation*. Princeton: Princeton University Press.

Ewer, Peter, Winton Higgins & Annette Stevens 1987, *Unions and the future of Australian manufacturing*. Sydney: Allen & Unwin.

Ewer, Peter, Ian Hampson, Chris Lloyd, John Rainford, Stephen Rix & Meg Smith 1991, *Politics and the Accord*. Sydney: Pluto Press.

Fitzgerald, Vince 1993, *National saving: a report to the Treasurer*. Canberra: Australian Government Publishing Service.

Frankel, Boris 1997, 'Beyond labourism and socialism: how the Australian Labor Party developed the model of "New Labour"', *New Left Review* 221: 3–33.

Friedland, Roger & Jimy Sanders 1986, 'Private and social wage expansion in the advanced market economies', *Theory and Society* 15: 193–222.
Galbraith, John Kenneth 1992, *The culture of contentment*. London: Sinclair-Stevenson.
—— 1996, *The good society: the humane agenda*. Boston: Houghton Mifflin.
—— 1997, 'Preface' (to special issue: Globalization and the politics of resistance) *New Political Economy* 2(1): 5–9.
—— 1998, *The socially concerned today*. Toronto: University of Toronto Press.
Gamble, Andrew 1996, *Hayek: the iron cage of liberty*. Cambridge: Polity Press.
Garnaut, Ross 1989, *Australia and the northeast Asian ascendancy*. Canberra: Australian Government Publishing Service.
Gills, Barry (ed.) 1997, 'Globalization and the politics of resistance: special issue', *New Political Economy* 2(1).
Goldfarb, Jeffrey C. 1998, *Civility and subversion: the intellectual in democratic society*. Cambridge: Cambridge University Press.
Goldscheid, Rudolf 1925, 'A sociological approach to problems of public finance' in Richard A. Musgrave & Alan T. Peacock (eds) 1958, *Classics in the theory of public finance*, London: Macmillan.
Gordon, David 1988, 'Can we pay the piper? Linkages between the macroeconomy and the welfare state', *Politics & Society* 16: 487–502.
Gray, John 1994, 'After the new liberalism', *Social Research* 61(3): 719–35.
—— 1996, 'What liberalism cannot do', *New Statesman* 125(4301): 18–20 (20 September).
Gregory, Robert G. 1993, 'Aspects of Australian and US living standards: the disappointing decades 1970–1990', *Economic Record* 69: 61–76.
Grieve Smith, John 1996, 'Rebuilding industrial capacity' in Jonathan Michie & John Grieve Smith (eds), *Creating industrial capacity: towards full employment*. Oxford: Oxford University Press.
Hall, Richard & Bill Harley 1997, *Towards a new classification system for Australian unions*. University of Sydney: Australian Centre for Industrial Relations Research and Training (ACIRRT Working Paper no. 46)

Held, David 1989, *Political theory and the modern state*. Cambridge: Polity Press.
Henley, Andrew & Euclid Tsakalotos 1993, *Corporatism and economic performance*. London: Edward Elgar.
Hensen, P. 1990, 'Employment: the key to keeping people out of prison', paper presented to Australian Institute of Criminology Conference, Hobart.
Henwood, Doug 1997, *Wall Street: how it works and for whom*. London: Verso.
Hicks, Alexander 1988a, 'National collective action and economic performance: a review essay', *International Studies Quarterly* 32: 131–52.
—— 1988b, 'Social democratic corporatism and economic growth', *Journal of Politics* 50: 677–704.
Higgins, Winton 1985, 'Political unionism and the corporatist thesis', *Economic and Industrial Democracy* 6(3): 349–81.
—— 1987, 'Unions as bearers of industrial regeneration: reflections on the Australian case', *Economic and Industrial Democracy* 8(2): 213–36.
Hintze, Otto 1897, 'The state in historical perspective' in Reinhard Bendix (ed.) 1968, *State and society*. Berkeley: University of California Press.
Howard, Robert J. 1992, *Unemployment in Australia: the problem, its causes, policy responses*. Melbourne: VCTA.
Hughes, Helen 1994, *Achieving full employment* (Full Employment Project Discussion Paper no. 1/94). Melbourne: University of Melbourne & Institute of Public Affairs.
Hughes, J. & R. Perlman, 1984, *The economics of unemployment: a comparative analysis of Britain and the United States*. Brighton: Wheatsheaf.
Hyde, John 1994, 'How we can get back to work', *Australian*, 11 February.
Indecs (Barry Hughes et al.) 1990, *State of play: the Australian economic policy debate*. Sydney: Allen & Unwin.
Industries Assitance Commission (IAC) 1977, *Some issues in structural adjustment*. Canberra: Australian Government Publishing Service.
Industry Commission (IC) 1990, *Annual Report 1989–1990*. Canberra: Australian Government Publishing Service.
Jackson, R. Gordon et al. 1975, *Policies for the development of manufacturing industry: a green paper—volume 1 (report)*. Canberra: Australian Government Publishing Service.

Jänicke, Martin 1990, *State failure: the impotence of politics in industrial society*. Cambridge: Polity Press.
Jessop, Bob 1988, 'Regulation theory, post-fordism and the state: more than a reply to Werner Bonefeld', *Capital & Class* 34: 147–68.
—— 1990, *State theory: putting the capitalist state in its place*. Cambridge: Polity Press.
—— 1994, 'Post-Fordism and the state' in Ash Amin (ed.), *Post-Fordism: a reader*. Oxford: Basil Blackwell.
—— 1997, 'Capitalism and its future: remarks on regulation, government and governance', *Review of International Political Economy* 4(3): 561–81.
Johnson, Carol 1996, 'Broadening the political agenda: towards socialist democracy in Australia' in Tim Battin & Graham Maddox (eds), *Socialism in contemporary Australia*. Melbourne: Longman.
Jones, Barry 1989, 'After the bicentenary: where do we stand (or sit)?' in Lionel Orchard & Robert Dare (eds), *Markets, morals and public policy*. Sydney: Federation Press.
Jones, Evan 1994, 'Economists and the state', *Journal of Australian Political Economy* 33: 36–64.
—— 1995, 'Economists and the neglected spirit of reform', *Journal of Australian Political Economy* 35: 62–86.
Junankar, P. N. & Cezarny A. Kapuscinski 1992, *The costs of unemployment in Australia* (Office of EPAC background paper). Canberra: Australian Government Publishing Service.
Kalecki, Michal 1943, 'Political aspects of full employment', *Political Quarterly* 14(4): 322–31.
—— 1971, 'Class struggle and the distribution of national income' in *Selected essays on the dynamics of the capitalist economy 1933–1971*. Cambridge: Cambridge University Press.
Karpik, Lucien 1978, 'Organizations, institutions and history' in Lucien Karpik (ed.), *Organization and environment: theory, issues and reality*. Beverley Hills: Sage.
Katzenstein, Peter J. 1984, *Corporatism and change: Austria, Switzerland and the politics of industry*. Ithaca: Cornell University Press.
—— 1985, *Small states in world markets: industrial policy in Europe*. Ithaca: Cornell University Press.
Keating, Michael & Geoff Dixon 1989, *Making economic policy in Australia 1983–1988*. Melbourne: Longman Cheshire.
Kelly, Paul 1992, *The end of certainty: the story of the 1980s*. Sydney: Allen & Unwin.

Keman, Hans 1984, 'Politics, policies and consequences: a cross-national analysis of public policy-formation in advanced capitalist democracies (1967–1981)', *European Journal of Political Research* 12: 147–70.

Keynes, John Maynard 1925, 'The economic consequences of Mr Churchill' in *Essays in persuasion*. New York: W. W. Norton, 1963.

—— 1932, 'Cheap money, wise spending and the means to prosperity' in Donald Moggeridge (ed.), *The collected writings of John Maynard Keynes, volume 21: activities 1931–1939—world crises and policies in Britain and America*. London: Macmillan & Cambridge University Press (Royal Economic Society).

—— 1933, 'National self-sufficiency' in Donald Moggeridge (ed.), *The Collected Writings of John Maynard Keynes, volume 21: Activities 1931–1939—— World crises and policies in Britain and America*. London: Macmillan & Cambridge University Press (Royal Economic Society).

—— 1936, *The general theory of employment, interest and money*. London: Macmillan.

King, John E. 1994, 'Kurt Rothschild and the alternative Austrian economics', *Cambridge Journal of Economics* 18: 431–45.

Kitson, Michael & Jonathan Michie 1996, 'Manufacturing capacity, investment and employment' in Jonathan Michie & John Grieve Smith (eds), *Creating industrial capacity: towards full employment*. Oxford: Oxford University Press.

Kmenta, Jan 1971, *Elements of econometrics*. New York: Macmillan.

Korpi, Walter 1983, *The democratic class struggle*. London: Routledge & Kegan Paul.

—— 1985, 'Economic growth and the welfare state: leaky bucket or irrigation system?', *European Sociological Review* 1(2): 97–118.

—— 1991, 'Political and economic explanations for unemployment: a cross-national and long-term analysis', *British Journal of Political Science* 21(3): 315–48.

—— 1996, 'Euroclerosos and the sclerosis of objectivity: on the role of values among economic policy experts', *Economic Journal* 106: 1727–46.

Krabbe, Jacob Jan 1996, *Historicism and organicism in economics: the evolution of economic thought*. Dordrecht (NL): Kluwer Academic Publishers.

Krudinski, J. 1977, *Attempted suicide: report to the Victorian Minister for Health*. Melbourne: Victorian Mental Health Authority.

Krugman, Paul 1986, *Strategic trade policy and the new international economics*. Cambridge: Massachusetts Institute of Technology Press.

Krygier, Matrin 1997, *Between fear and hope: hybrid thoughts on public issues*. Sydney: ABC Books.

Langmore, John & John Quiggin 1994, *Work for all: full employment in the nineties*. Melbourne: Melbourne University Press.

Latham, Mark 1998, *Civilising global capital: new thinking for Australian Labor*. Sydney: Allen & Unwin.

Layard, Richard, Stephen Nickell & Richard Jackman 1991, *Unemployment: macroeconomic performance and the labour market*. Oxford: Oxford University Press.

Legge, John 1994, 'The bitter fruit of rationalism', *Australian Financial Review*, 7 January.

Lehmbruch, Gerhard 1984, 'Corporatism and the structure of corporatist networks' in John H. Goldthorpe (ed.), *Order and conflict in contemporary capitalism: studies in the political economy of western European nations*. Oxford: Clarendon Press.

Lever-Tracy, Constance 1988, 'The flexibility debate: part-time work', *Labour & Industry* 1(2): 210–41.

Levi-Faur, David 1997, 'Friedrich List and the political economy of the nation-state', *Review of International Political Economy* 4(1): 154–78.

Lindbeck, Assar 1988, 'Consequences of the advanced welfare state', *World Economy* 11: 19–38.

List, Friedrich. 1841, *The national system of political economy* (trans. Sampson S. Lloyd, 1885). London: Longmans, Green, 1909.

Macintyre, Stuart 1985, *Winners and losers: the pursuit of social justice in Australian history*. Sydney: Allen & Unwin.

Maddison, Angus 1991, *Dynamic forces in capitalist development: a long-run comparative view*. Oxford: Oxford University Press.

Mahon, Rianne 1987, 'From Fordism to ?: new technology, labour markets and unions', *Economic and Industrial Democracy* 8: 5–60.

Manne, Robert 1998, *The way we live now: the controversies of the nineties*. Melbourne: Text Publishing.

Marsh, Ian 1995, *Beyond the two-party system: political representation, economic competitiveness and Australian politics*. Melbourne: Cambridge University Press.

McCallum, J. 1986, 'Unemployment in OECD countries in the 1980s', *Economic Journal* 96: 942–60.

Meidner, Rudolf 1948, 'The dilemma of wages policy under full employment' in Erik Lundberg et al. (ed. and trans. Ralf Turvey) 1952, *Wages policy under full employment*. London: William Hodge & Co.

—— 1978, *Employee investment funds: an approach to collective capital formation* (with Anna Hedborg). London: Allen & Unwin.

—— 1980, 'Our concept of the third way: some remarks on the socio-political tenets of the Swedish labour movement', *Economic and Industrial Democracy* 1(3): 343–69.

Mitchell, Deborah 1991, 'Comparing income transfer systems: is Australia the poor relation?' in Francis Castles (ed.), *Australia compared*. Sydney: Allen & Unwin.

Musgrave, Richard A. 1985, ' A brief history of fiscal doctrine' in Alan J. Auerbach & Martin Feldstein (eds), *Handbook of public economics: volume 1*. Amsterdam: North Holland (Elsevier).

Musgrave, Richard A. & Alan T. Peacock (eds) 1958, *Classics in the theory of public finance*. London: Macmillan.

Nielsen, Klaus & Ove K. Pedersen 1988, 'The negotiated economy: ideal and history', *Scandinavian Political Studies* 11(2): 79–101.

Organization for Economic Co-operation and Development 1985a, *Indicators of Industrial Activity*. Paris: OECD.

—— 1985b, *Economic Outlook* 38 (December).

—— 1985c, *Social Expenditure 1960–1990: problems of growth and control*. Paris: OECD.

—— 1985d, *The role of the public sector: causes and consequences of the growth of government* (OECD Economic Studies no. 4). Paris: OECD.

—— 1986a, *Labour Force Statistics 1964–1984*. Paris: OECD.

—— 1986b, *Historical Statistics 1960–1984*. Paris: OECD.

—— 1988a, *The future of social protection*. Paris: OECD.

—— 1988b, *Economic Outlook* 44 (December).

—— 1989, *Economic Outlook* 45 (June).

—— 1990a, *Historical Statistics 1960–1988*. Paris: OECD

—— 1990b, *Labour market policies for the 1990s*. Paris: OECD.

—— 1990c, *OECD Economic Surveys: Sweden 1990–1991*. Paris: OECD.

—— 1991, *National Accounts Main Aggregates 1960–1990*. Paris: OECD.

—— 1992a, *Employment Outlook* (July).

—— 1992b, *Economic Outlook* 51 (June).

—— 1993a, *Economic Outlook* 54 (December).

—— 1993b, *Science and technology indicators*. Paris: OECD.
—— 1994a, *Economic Outlook* 55 (June).
—— 1994b, *Labour Force Statistics 1972–1992*. Paris: OECD.
—— 1994c, *Economic Outlook* 56 (December).
—— 1994d, *Manufacturing performance: a scoreboard of indicators*. Paris: OECD.
—— 1994e, *OECD Economic Surveys: Australia*. Paris: OECD.
—— 1995, *Labour Force Statistics 1973–1993*. Paris: OECD.
—— 1996a, *Economic Outlook* 59 (June).
—— 1996b, *Historical Statistics 1960–1994*. Paris: OECD.
—— 1996c, *Labour Force Statistics 1976–1996*. Paris: OECD.
—— 1996d, *National Accounts: main aggregates 1960–1995*. Paris: OECD.
—— 1997a, *Economic Outlook* 62 (December).
—— 1997b, *Historical Statistics 1960–1995*. Paris: OECD.
—— 1997c, *Employment Outlook* (July).
—— 1998a, *Economic Outlook* 63 (June).
—— 1998b, *OECD Economic Surveys: Australia 1998*. Paris: OECD.
Offe, Claus 1984, *Contradictions of the welfare state*. London: Hutchinson.
Ormerod, Paul 1994, *The death of economics*. London: Faber & Faber.
Paloheimo, Heikki 1990, 'Between liberalism and corporatism: the effect of trade unions and governments on economic performance in eighteen OECD countries' in Renato Brunetta & Carlo Dell'Aringa (eds), *Labour relations and economic performance: proceedings of a conference held by the International Economic Association in Venice, Italy*. London: Macmillan.
Parker, Rachel 1996, 'Industry policy: possibilities in a changing international economy', *Journal of Australian Political Economy* 37: 49–67.
—— 1997, 'Industry pipe dreams', *AQ: Journal of Contemporary Analysis* 69(4): 39–43.
Peetz, David 1992, 'Australian workplace bargaining in the international context' in David Peetz, Alison Preston & Jim Docherty (eds), *Workplace bargaining in the international context*. Canberra: Australian Government Publishing Service.
Pempel, T. John 1982, *Policy and politics in Japan: creative conservatism*. Philadelphia: Temple University Press.
Pempel, T. John & Keiichi Tsunekawa 1979, 'Corporatism without labour? The Japanese anomaly' in Philippe C. Schmitter &

Gerhard Lehmbruch (eds), *Trends towards corporatist intermediation*. London: Sage (Contemporary Political Sociology 1).

Pierson, Christopher 1991, *Beyond the welfare state?* Cambridge: Polity Press.

Polanyi, Karl 1944, *The great transformation: the political and economic origins of our time*. Boston: Beacon Press.

Pollard, Sidney 1982, *The wasting of the British economy: British economic policy 1945 to the present*. London: Croom Helm.

Pollin, Robert 1998, 'Can domestic expansionary policy succeed in a globally integrated environment? An examination of alternatives' in Dean Baker, Gerald Epstein & Robert Pollin (eds), *Globalization and progressive economic policy*. Cambridge: Cambridge University Press.

Porter, Michael E. 1990, *The competitive advantage of nations*. London: Macmillan.

Przeworski, Adam & Michael Wallerstein 1982, 'The structure of class conflict in democratic capitalist societies', *American Political Science Review* 76: 215–38.

Pusey, Michael 1992, *Economic rationalism in Canberra: a nation-building state changes its mind*. Melbourne: Cambridge University Press.

Quiggin, John 1993, 'A policy program for full employment', *Australian Economic Review* 102: 41–7.

—— 1996, *Great expectations: microeconomic reform and Australia*. Sydney: Allen & Unwin.

Raskall, Phil 1993, 'Widening income disparities in Australia' in Stuart Rees, Gordon Rodley & Frank Stilwell (eds), *Beyond the market: alternatives to economic rationalism*. Sydney: Pluto Press.

Reinert, Erik 1995, 'Competitiveness and its predecessors: a 500-year cross-national perspective', *Structural Change and Economic Dynamics* 6: 23–42.

—— 1997, 'The role of the state in economic growth', *Working Paper* 1997: 5. Centre for Development and the Environment (SUM), University of Oslo.

Reserve Bank of Australia (RBA) 1993, *Towards full employment: submission to the committee on employment opportunities*. Canberra: Ambassador Press.

Riha, Tomas 1985, *German political economy: the history of an alternative economics*, *International Journal of Social Economics* 12(3, 4, 5). Bradford: MCB University Press.

Robinson, Joan 1973, 'What has become of the Keynesian revolution?' in Joan Robinson (ed.), *After Keynes*. Oxford: Basil Blackwell.

Royal Commission on Australian Government Administration (RCAGA) 1976, *Report and appendixes*. Canberra: Australian Government Publishing Service.

Rueschemeyer, Dietrich & Peter Evans 1985, 'The state and economic transformation: toward an analysis of the conditions underlying effective intervention' in Peter B. Evans, Dietrich Rueschemeyer & Theda Skocpol (eds), *Bringing the state back in*. Cambridge: Cambridge University Press.

Saul, John Ralston 1992, *Voltaire's bastards: the dictatorship of reason in the west*. New York: Vintage.

Saunders, Peter 1985, 'Public expenditure and economic performance in OECD countries', *Journal of Public Policy* 5: 1–21.

——— 1990, *Employment growth and poverty: an analysis of Australian experience, 1983–1990*. University of New South Wales: Social Policy Research Centre (Discussion Paper no. 25).

——— 1993, *Economic adjustment and distributional change: income inequality in Australia in the eighties*. University of New South Wales: Social Policy Research Centre (Discussion Paper no. 47).

——— 1994a, *Poverty and inequality: social security in Australia in the 1990s*. University of New South Wales: Social Policy Research Centre (Discussion Paper no. 48).

——— 1994b, *Rising on the Tasman tide: income inequality in Australia and New Zealand in the 1980s*. University of New South Wales: Social Policy Research Centre (Discussion Paper no. 49).

Schmidt, Manfred G. 1982a, 'The role of parties in shaping macroeconomic policy' in Francis G. Castles (ed.), *The impact of parties: politics and policies in democratic capitalist states*. London: Sage (and the European Consortium for Political Research).

——— 1982b, 'Does corporatism really matter? Economic crisis, politics and rates of unemployment in capitalist democracies in the 1970s' in Gerhard Lehmbruch & Philippe Schmitter (eds), *Patterns of corporatist policy-making*. London: Sage.

——— 1983a, 'The welfare state and the economy in periods of economic crisis: a comparative analysis of twenty-three OECD nations', *European Journal of Political Research* 11(1): 1–26.

—— 1983b, 'The growth of the tax state: the industrial democracies, 1950–1978' in Charles L. Taylor (ed.), *Why governments grow: measuring public sector size*. London: Sage.

—— 1984, 'Labour market performance and inflation in OECD nations: a political-institutionalist view' in Knut Gerlach, Wilhelm Peters & Werner Sengenberger (eds), *Public policies to combat unemployment in a period of economic stagnation: an international comparison*. Frankfurt: Campus Verlag.

—— 1987, 'The politics of full employment in western democracies', *Annals (AAPSS)* 492: 171–81.

Schmitter, Phillipe 1974, 'Still the century of corporatism?' in Phillipe C. Schmitter & Gerhard Lehmbruch (eds), *Trends towards corporatist intermediation*. London: Sage (Contemporary Political Sociology 1).

Schott, Kerry 1984, *Policy, power and order: the persistence of economic problems in capitalist states*. New Haven: Yale University Press.

Sicklen, Derek 1994, *Industry policy briefing note*, 2. Sydney: Australian Economic Analysis.

Skocpol, Theda 1985, 'Bringing the state back in: strategies of analysis in current research' in Peter B. Evans, Dietrich Russchemeyer & Theda Skocpol (eds), *Bringing the state back in*. Cambridge: Cambridge University Press.

Smyth, Paul 1996, 'The future of Australian socialism revisited: the importance of the left's own history' in Tim Battin & Graham Maddox (eds), *Socialism in contemporary Australia*. Melbourne: Longman.

Smyth, Paul & Bettina Cass 1998, 'Introduction' to Paul Smyth & Bettina Cass (eds), *Contesting the Australian way: states, markets and civil society*. Melbourne: Cambridge University Press.

Stilwell, Frank 1996, 'Fraught with contradictions: work, wages, welfare' in John Wilson, Jane Thomson & Anthony McMahon (eds), *The Australian welfare state: key documents and themes*. Melbourne: Macmillan.

Stokes, Geoff 1992, 'Towards a national trade strategy: recovering a bilateral balance in export promotion', paper presented to the QUT, Asia/Pacific Basin Studies Unit Conference, *National strategies for Australasian countries in the age of the Asia/Pacific economy*. Surfers' Paradise, 19–21 June.

Streeck, Wolfgang 1997, 'Beneficial constraints: on the economic limits of voluntary rationalism' in J. Rogers Hollingsworth &

Robert Boyer (eds), *Contemporary capitalism: the embeddedness of institutions*. Cambridge: Cambridge University Press.

Stretton, Hugh 1980, 'Future patterns for taxation and public expenditure in Australia' in John Wilkes (ed.), *The politics of taxation*. Sydney: Hodder & Stoughton.

—— 1987, 'Tasks for social democratic intellectuals' in *Political essays*. Melbourne: Georgian House.

—— 1993, 'Who dunnit to social democracy?', *Overland* 132: 49–64.

—— 1995, 'Onwards, sideways or backwards: alternative responses to the shortcomings of social democracy', *Society* (Symposium: The future of liberal democracy) 32(6): 9–15.

Stretton, Hugh & Lionel Orchard 1994, *Public goods, public enterprise, public choice: theoretical frameworks for the contemporary attack on government*. London: Macmillan.

Stutchbury, Michael 1985, 'How EPAC was ambushed', *Australian Financial Review*, 5 August: 1, 8.

Tarantelli, Enzio 1986, 'The regulation of inflation and unemployment', *Industrial Relations* 25(1): 1–15.

Taylor, Liza (comp.) 1993, *Labor in power*. Sydney: ABC Enterprises.

Teese, Colin 1994, 'Australia after Uruguay and the crisis in international trade', *Quadrant* 38(3): 45–51.

Thelen, Kathleen 1994, 'Beyond corporatism: toward a new framework for the study of labor in advanced capitalism', *Comparative Politics* 27(1): 107–24.

Therborn, Göran 1986, *Why some peoples are more unemployed than others: the strange paradox of growth and unemployment*. London: Verso.

—— 1987, 'Does corporatism really matter? The economic crisis and issues of political theory', *Journal of Public Policy* 7(3): 259–84.

Thurow, Lester 1981, 'Equity, efficiency, social justice and redistribution' in *The welfare state in crisis*. Paris: OECD.

—— 1993, *Head to head: the coming economic battle among Japan, Europe and America*. Sydney: Allen & Unwin.

Tingle, Laura 1994, *Chasing the future: recession, recovery and the new politics in Australia*. Melbourne: William Heinemann.

Toohey, Brian 1994, *Tumbling dice: the story of modern economic policy*. Melbourne: William Heinemann.

Vernon, James et al. 1965, *Report of the Committee of Economic Enquiry*, vols 1 & 2. Canberra: Commonwealth of Australia.

Wagner, Adolf 1883, 'Three extracts on public finance' in Richard A. Musgrave & Alan T. Peacock (eds) 1958, *Classics in the theory of public finance*. London: Macmillan.

—— 1887, 'Wagner's state socialistic programme', Appendix A in William Harbutt Dawson 1973, *Bismarck and state socialism: an exposition of the social and economic legislation of Germany since 1870* (London: Swan Sonnenschein, 1890). New York: Howard Fertig.

Walter, James 1996, *Tunnel vision: the failure of political imagination*. Sydney: Allen & Unwin.

Watts, Rob 1997, 'Ten years on: Francis G. Castles and the Australian "wage-earners' welfare state"', *Australian & New Zealand Journal of Sociology* 33(1): 1–15.

Weiss, Linda 1997, 'Globalization and the myth of the powerless state', *New Left Review* 225: 3–27.

—— 1998, *The myth of the powerless state: governing the economy in a global era*. Cambridge: Polity Press.

Weiss, Linda & John Hobson 1995, *States and economic development: a comparative and historical analysis*. Cambridge: Polity Press.

Wilensky, Harold 1981, 'Democratic corporatism, consensus and social policy: reflections on changing values and the "crisis" of the welfare state' in *The welfare state in crisis*. Paris: OECD.

Wilensky, Harold, Gregory Luebbert, Susan Hahn & Adrienne Jamieson 1987, 'Comparative social policy: theories, methods, findings' in Meinolf Dierkes, Hans Weiler & Ariane Antal (eds), *Comparative policy research: learning from experience*. Aldershot: Gower.

Windschuttle, Keith 1980, *Unemployment: a social and political analysis of the economic crisis in Australia* (rev. edn). Melbourne: Penguin.

Wiseman, John 1996, 'A kinder road to hell? Labor and the politics of progressive competitiveness in Australia' in Leo Panitch (ed.), *The Socialist Register 1996: are there alternatives?* London: Merlin Press.

World Bank 1996, *World development report 1996: from plan to market*. Washington: Oxford University Press.

Young, Christabel 1989, *Balancing families and work: a demographic study of women's labour force participation* (Women's Research and Employment Initiatives Program, DEET). Canberra: Australian Government Publishing Service.

Zysman, John 1983, *Governments, markets and growth: financial systems and the politics of industrial change*. Oxford: Martin Robertson.

Index

Accord, the, 205–9
Anglo-Saxon countries, 76, 108, 122, 164, 168, 195
arbitration system, 98, 149, 162–3, 165, 202, 211
Arndt, Heinz, 7
Asia Pacific Economic Community (APEC), 84
Australia Reconstructed, 205–6, 208–9, 212, 214
Australian Chamber of Commerce and Industry, 90
Australian Council of Trade Unions (ACTU), *see* unions
Australian exceptionalism, 200
Australian Labor Party (ALP), *see* Labor Government
Australian Manufacturing Council (AMC), 90
Austria, 31, 93, 101, 121, 122, 126, 128, 132, 134, 216

'balance of payments constraint', 87–8, 169
Beilharz, Peter, 9
Belgium, 85, 93, 167
Beveridge, William, 1
Beveridge curve, 99
Brigden Report, 86
budget deficit, 88, 141–2, 221
business, *see* employers' associations

Canada, 67, 123, 126, 128

capital, 81, 99, 102, 148–9, 155–7, 159, 167, 169, 171, 174, 179, 188, 190
capital accumulation, 114, 172, 190
capital formation, *see* investment
civil society, 223, 225
class and class politics, 187
comparative advantage, 88
comparative political economy, 17–19, 46–58, 59, 195
conservative parties, 30
consumption, 103, 144
Coombs, H. C. (Nugget), 202, 210
corporatism, 157, 164, 167, 171–8, 185, 188, 193, 207–12, 223, 224
corporatism without labour, 168
cost-reduction approach, *see* productivity enhancement strategy
Crawford Report, 86
cross-subsidization, 115–16, 118, 130
current account deficit, 87, 221

debt, *see* public debt
decommodification, 123, 129, 157, 158, 193, 224
democratic principles, 75, 110, 145–6, 153–4, 158, 171–4, 186, 196, 198, 209, 222, 223
Denmark, 93, 120, 133
deregulation, 15, 35, 98, 124, 189, 194; *see also* economic liberalism
discouraged workers, 42

244

Durkheim, Émile, 160, 190

Economic Council for Canada, 28
economic growth, 30, 64–71, 80, 107, 111, 144, 175, 212
economic integration, 191
economic liberalism, 29; *see also* liberalism
Economic Planning Advisory Council (EPAC), 210–11
economic policy, 28, 220–2
economic rationalism, 33, 55, 197, 220
economics
  Keynesian, *see* Keynesianism
  neo-classical or orthodox, 53, 75, 79, 87, 95, 96, 97, 134–5, 136–8, 153, 179, 194, 222
economists, 5, 13, 80, 96, 99, 153, 213–14, 216
economy
  non-economic aspects of, 111, 190
  politicization of, 112, 152, 188, 208–9, 223–4
education, 91, 129, 191
embeddedness, 190, 191
employers' associations, 86, 151, 171, 173, 174, 176, 211–12, 214, 224
employment, 36–41, 63
  casual and part-time, 11, 12, 37, 39, 40, 41, 43, 219
  conditions of, 49, 219
  female, 37, 38, 39, 40, 42, 43
  growth, 46, 61, 66, 93–5, 221
  security, 217
enterprise bargaining, 98, 102, 214, 216, 219
European Community, 129
European Union, 85, 163
Eurosclerosis, 165
exchange rate, 88

exports, 86–7

'fight inflation first' strategy, 75
finance sector, 197
Finland, 128
fiscal policy, 53, 87
Fitzgerald Report, 143–4
flawed statism, 165
flexibility, 136, 180, 217, 218
  labour market, 40, 96, 103–4, 107, 169
foreign debt, 88
Fortress Australia, 83
France, 163, 167
free trade, 82, 88–9, 168, 189, 191
full employment, 2, 4, 8, 88, 92, 107, 108, 113, 115, 117, 142, 145–6, 149, 150, 151, 152, 163, 168, 169, 173, 185, 180, 188, 191, 195, 201, 219, 222
  resistance to, 80, 109, 110, 131, 152, 158, 159, 174, 188, 193–200, 220–1
Full Employment in Australia (1945 White Paper), 1, 201–2, 210

Galbraith, John Kenneth, 3, 78, 104, 194
General Agreement on Tariffs and Trade (GATT), 14, 84
German political economy, 117, 191
Germany, 18, 93, 100, 126, 128, 162, 163, 167, 216
globalization, 9, 213
Goldscheid, Rudolph, 119–20
Goldsworthy Report, 90
governance, forms of, *see* modes of regulation
government, growth of, 112
government capital expenditure, *see* investment, public

government interference, 120–1, 129
government revenues, see public revenues
government spending, see public expenditure
governmental activities, classification of, 114
  developmental, 114, 117, 130
  Keynesian, 114–15, 118
  social democratic, 115–16
Gray, John, 194, 197
Great Britain, see United Kingdom
growth, see economic growth

health, 91, 129
Hughes, Helen, 8
hysteresis, 79, 80, 99

imports, 87, 89
income distribution, 102–6, 188
incomes policies, 33, 73–5, 80, 81, 148, 165, 167, 172, 176–7, 188, 205–7
individualism, 145
industrial decline, 78, 91, 186, 108, 221
industrial relations, 215
Industries' Assistance Commission (IAC), see Productivity Commission
industry policy, 25, 26, 27, 28, 34, 86, 88, 90, 167, 176, 207, 213–14, 221
industry sectors, 36–8
inequality, 44, 45, 103–7, 186, 200, 216, 219
inflation, 30, 49–50, 71–82, 88, 99, 107, 111, 148–9, 151, 169, 173, 175, 176, 188
infrastructure, 27, 114, 191, 221
insecurity, 186, 190, 220

International Monetary Fund (IMF), 14
international trade, 82–90
investment, 24, 87, 135–45, 147, 179, 188, 207, 209
  private, 29, 33, 35–6, 136–40, 175, 178, 218
  public, 27, 28, 33, 35–6, 90, 91, 108, 114, 136–45, 159, 175, 178, 221
Italy, 67, 93, 128, 134, 140, 163, 167

Jackson Committee, 28
Jackson Report, 86
Japan, 11, 18, 30, 67, 77, 85, 93, 101, 112, 120, 121, 122, 123, 133, 134, 140, 142, 162, 163, 168, 186, 216

Kalecki, Michal, 103, 148, 151, 161, 190, 195
'Keating–Garnaut agenda', 83
Kelly, Paul, 5, 6
Keynes, John Maynard, 1, 6, 63, 102, 115, 144, 145, 146–7, 151, 161, 179–80, 191
Keynesianism, 6, 24, 32, 33, 63, 72, 74, 78, 108, 114–15, 118, 140, 147–8, 158, 168, 201, 202, 207
  'bastard' Keynesianism, 74, 79, 115, 161
Kriesky Commission, 2

Labor Government (ALP) 1983–96, 3, 30, 35, 53, 200, 204, 209, 213, 215, 220
labour, 81, 96, 99, 102, 104, 148–9, 157, 159, 167, 169, 171, 179, 188
labour costs, 96–106, 148
labour force, 93–5, 175

labour market, 38–45, 96–106, 131, 149, 188
labour market programmes, active, 18, 55, 56, 80, 91, 108, 128, 130–5, 150, 151, 206–8, 217, 222
'labour's mission', 157, 187
labourism, 204
Langmore, John, 7, 135
'law of expanding state activity', 117, 118
liberal failures, 168
Liberal Party of Australia, 28, 213, 220
liberal polity, Australia, 123–4, 134–5, 150–1, 162, 168, 185
liberalism, 81, 88, 96, 99, 113–15, 117, 119, 149, 152, 153–4, 156, 157–8, 164, 170, 192, 193, 200, 211, 212
liberalization, 82, 83, 93, 191, 198
List, Friedrich, 117, 189, 191
living standards, 75, 86, 88, 90, 96, 98, 100, 155, 179
long-term unemployment
Luxembourg, 101

Machiavellianism, 142
Macpherson, C. B., 161
macro-economic policy, 14, 204–7
Manne, Robert, 194
manufacturing, 16, 26, 27, 32, 34, 36, 57, 62, 86, 90–3, 102, 111, 140, 170, 178, 191, 216, 221
market mode of regulation, 9, 16, 17, 29, 60–1, 63, 86, 98, 159, 163, 185, 213–14
market sphere, 9
Marx, Karl, 151, 160
Marxian analysis, 147, 164, 186–9
Marxism, *see* Marxian analysis

micro-economic reform, 49, 107
mixed economy, 115
modes of regulation, 159, 162–70, 187, 192, 199
monetarism, 72–6, 78, 111, 148, 169, 202
Mortimer Report, 90
Multilateral Agreement on Investment (MAI), 14, 84

nation-building, 23, 27
national autonomy, 82–90, 140–1, 191
national interest, *see* public interest
neo-liberalism, 9, 33
Netherlands, 77, 85, 92, 120, 167
New Deal, 150
new political institutions, 145–51, 159, 208–9, 222, 224–5
New Zealand, 216
non-accelerating inflation rate of employment (NAIRU), 79–80
Norway, 67, 77, 100, 120, 122, 126, 132, 140

occupations and employment, 37–8
Organization for Economic Co-operation and Development (OECD), 14, 17–18, 19, 20, 29, 30, 35, 47, 59, 61, 63, 64, 72–4, 76, 77, 85, 92, 93, 94, 95, 100, 106, 112, 117, 120, 122, 125, 132, 133, 136, 138, 139, 140, 141, 150, 154, 165, 171, 172
Ormerod, Paul, 129

participation rates, 40, 41, 124, 221, 136
Phillips curve, 71, 74
Polanyi, Karl, 130 161, 173, 190
policy abstention, 25, 31, 55

policy elites, 5, 6
political capacity, *see* state, capacity
political economy, 60
political possibilities, 185, 188–9, 200, 220, 222
political will, imagination, 81, 109, 199
Porter, Michael, 89
post-Keynesianism, 10, 72–3, 75, 99, 148, 161, 186, 188, 195, 206, 207
post-liberal politics, 120, 150, 155, 157, 170–4, 186, 188, 201, 205, 206
'post-war development model', 8, 213
poverty, 44, 45, 216
prices, 81, 83
privatization, 124
production enhancement strategy, 216–18
Productivity Commission, 34, 35, 84
productivity enhancement strategy, 215–17, 219
profitability logic of action, 174; *see also* productivity enhancement strategy
'protection all round', 83
protectionism, *see* industry policy
public capital expenditure, *see* investment, public
public debt, 53, 54, 55, 142–3, 170
public expenditure, 55, 76, 112, 120–4, 141, 193
public interest, 190, 191
public revenues, 53–4
public sector, 128

Quiggin, John, 7, 135, 194

recession, 6, 7, 11, 13, 29, 59–62, 63, 64–71, 222

Rehn–Meidner model, 165
research and development, 56, 217
Reserve Bank of Australia, 15, 48, 49, 50, 51, 53, 97, 99, 100, 128, 203
Robinson, Joan, 161
Rocard, Michel, 1

Saul, John Ralston, 195–7
savings, national, 143–4
scarcity, 130
Schumpeter, Joseph, 161
services sector, 37, 90, 102
skill formation, 26, 217
social democracy, 11, 74, 96, 114, 115–16, 120, 129, 131, 149, 151, 157, 169
social democratic corporatism, 115, 166–7, 178
social welfare, 23, 51–3, 108, 114, 124–30, 221
socialization of investment, 201, 223
solidarity wages policy, 167
state, 167, 169, 171–4
    capacity, 20 53–5, 61, 108, 113, 120, 124, 193, 198, 214, 215, 222–3
    lack of capacity, 185, 186, 187, 189–92
    theory of the, 119, 187–93
state expenditure, *see* public expenditure
state responsibilities, 193, 197, 209, 222
statecraft, 110, 142, 201, 204
statism, 11, 147, 186, 190, 222
statist failures, 167–8
Stretton, Hugh, 86–7, 130, 190, 203
structural change, 64, 132, 186, 194, 199, 208, 216, 221
supply and demand, 94, 98

Sweden, 11, 19, 30, 77, 101, 112, 120, 121, 122, 126, 128, 133, 142, 163, 165, 167, 186, 207, 216
Switzerland, 67, 77, 101, 120, 122, 126, 133, 134, 140

tariffs, *see* industry policy
taxation, 25, 26, 55, 108, 118, 120–4, 141–2, 150, 200, 221
Thatcher, Margaret, 13
Therborn, Göran, 100, 171, 172
Tingle, Laura, 5–6
Toohey, Brian, 5
trade, *see* international trade
trade unions, *see* unions
training, *see* labour market programmes, active
Treasury, Australia 15, 28, 162, 202, 204, 210, 215

unemployment, 32, 43, 47–8, 59, 61–2, 67, 80, 93, 94, 95, 96–7, 99, 101, 106, 108, 120, 142, 153, 179, 186, 200, 203, 212, 221
and growth, 66, 67, 111, 178
and inflation, 30, 71–82, 111, 148, 205, 220
and investment, 135–45, 178
and labour market policies, 130–5
and labour costs, 96–106, 111
and manufacturing, 90–3
and taxation, 120–4
and the labour force, 93–5
and the welfare state, 124–30
and trade, 82–90, 178
in Australia, 11, 12, 93
model of, 174–9
of women, 42, 43
of youth, 42, 43
rates of, 29, 30, 31
social costs of, 43–5
unions, 16, 73–4, 77, 83, 91, 98, 148, 151, 155, 170–4, 176–8, 202–3, 205–6, 209, 215
United Kingdom, 30, 74, 76, 92, 123, 126, 140, 167, 204, 206, 216
United States, 30, 85, 120, 123, 126, 128, 132, 133, 216, 217
unproductive economic activity, 214

value-added production, 217
Vernon Committee, 28, 86, 202

wages and incomes policies, *see* incomes policies
wages and wage costs, 48, 49, 50, 81, 96–106, 111
real, 217, 221
Wagner, Adolph, 117–19, 120, 122, 129, 160, 189, 191
Walter, James, 4, 12
Weber, Max, 160
welfare state, *see* social welfare
White Paper on Full Employment 1945, 1, 201–2, 206, 210
1994 (*Working Nation*), 1, 3, 69, 70, 135, 202–3
Whitlam, Gough, 30
World Trade Organization (WTO), 14